Interpersonal Processes

Interpersonal Processes

Stuart Oskamp
Shirlynn Spacapan

Editors

 **The Claremont Symposium on Applied Social Psychology**

SAGE PUBLICATIONS
The Publishers of Professional Social Science
Newbury Park   Beverly Hills   London   New Delhi

For information address:

SAGE Publications, Inc.
2111 West Hillcrest Drive
Newbury Park, California 91320

SAGE Publications Inc.
275 South Beverly Drive
Beverly Hills
California 90212

SAGE Publications Ltd.
28 Banner Street
London EC1Y 8QE
England

SAGE PUBLICATIONS India Pvt. Ltd.
M-32 Market
Greater Kailash I
New Delhi 110 048 India

Printed in the United States of America

Library of Congress Cataloging-in-Publication Data

Interpersonal processes.

"Published in cooperation with the Claremont Graduate School."
Based on the papers submitted at the third Claremont Symposium on Applied Social Psychology held on Feb. 15, 1986.
Includes indexes.
1. Interpersonal relations—Congresses.
2. Social groups—Congresses. I. Oskamp, Stuart.
II. Spacapan, Shirlynn. III. Claremont Symposium on Applied Social Psychology (3rd: 1986: Claremont Graduate School) IV. Claremont Graduate School.
HM132.I555   1987   302.3′4   87-16435
ISBN 0-8039-29803
ISBN 0-8039-29811 (pbk.)

Contents

Preface

T

he chapters in this volume are based on presentations given at the Claremont Symposium on Applied Social Psychology, held on February 15, 1986. This was the third such annual conference held at the Claremont Graduate School, bringing outstanding psychologists from various sections of the country to join in discussion and analysis of important topics and issues in the field of applied social psychology. We are grateful for financial support for the past conferences from all six of the Claremont Colleges (Claremont Graduate School, Claremont McKenna College, Harvey Mudd College, Pitzer College, Pomona College, and Scripps College) as well as for a founding grant from the Haynes Foundation of Los Angeles. We also want to thank our colleagues Lois Langland, Mark Lipsey, and Allan Wicker for their help in planning the conference and preparing this volume.

In preparing the conference papers for publication, we have tried to maintain some of the informal style that made the conference talks so interesting by encouraging the authors to use a personalized, narrative tone and to include personal background information to show how they became interested in their topic. We also suggested that the authors expand and elaborate on points they did not have time to cover orally and incorporate material addressing some of the questions raised by the audience. To reflect the conference panel discussions and to provide a fuller integration of the several papers, we have included an introductory chapter tracing some of the common issues and themes in research on interpersonal processes and a concluding chapter discussing several theoretical aspects of the papers and areas of applicability of the authors' work.

We hope that this volume will be interesting and valuable to both researchers and practitioners in the area of social psychology, as well as to students and professors who want to know more about applied aspects of the field.

Stuart Oskamp
Shirlynn Spacapan
Claremont, California

1

Introduction: Studying Interpersonal Processes

SHIRLYNN SPACAPAN
STUART OSKAMP

Interpersonal processes are important to everyone. They are the stuff of our lives, the events that pervade our days — the interactions with others that make up much of our activities. They are often commonplace and expected, contributing to our sense of routine, but occasionally unexpected, arousing, or dramatic, providing the highlights that we remember. Interpersonal relationships can have a multitude of forms and characteristics, which have furnished the material for countless novelists, poets, and songwriters over many centuries.

Social scientists, too, are interested in interpersonal processes. Social psychology is sometimes defined as the study of people's real and imagined interactions with other people. And applied social psychologists in particular are concerned with understanding, predicting, and facilitating people's activities in their daily lives — in their homes, workplaces, and leisure pursuits. The chapters in this volume illustrate applications of social psychology to the study of interpersonal processes, and they show the range and variety of approaches that can be applied to understanding human behavior scientifically.

The term *interpersonal processes* itself indicates the faith that scientists (and most other people) have that regularities can be found in human behavior. The term suggests that human actions are not haphazard or incoherent but rather that they follow certain processes or principles that are potentially amenable to understanding and explanation. The chapters in this volume certainly hold to that conviction, and they focus on many of the processes that have been suggested as underlying and explaining interpersonal behavior.

What are some of these regularities and principles that can be found in human interactions? After a brief outline of the specific chapters that make up this volume, we will trace some of the themes or topics that run through social psychological research on interpersonal processes. These themes indicate many of the ways in which interpersonal processes can be analyzed and understood.

Outline of Volume

In Chapter 2, Carol Werner presents a broad overview of the transactional approach to science and illustrates it with examples from a program of research on neighborhoods. Her chapter is followed by one in which Alvin Zander draws on his extensive work in group dynamics to address two questions about group purposes that students of groups have tended to neglect. In the fourth chapter, Alison Konrad and Barbara Gutek examine effects stemming from the demographic composition of groups on the status and treatment of women and ethnic minority individuals. In Chapter 5, Harold Kelley presents a progress report on his work toward a taxonomy of interpersonal processes, illustrating his approach with research drawn from the literature on dyadic conflict. Next, the dyad of the influence professional and his or her target is the intriguing topic of Robert Cialdini's contribution. The final substantive chapter, by Sandra Scarr, presents a theory of how individual personality characteristics are formed through a combination of genetic and environmental influences.

Following these six major substantive chapters, there is a final integrative chapter discussing the key question of the applicability of the foregoing research findings, methods, and theoretical viewpoints.

Themes in Research on Interpersonal Processes

Levels of Analysis

One of the most fundamental principles in discussions of human behavior is that it can be analyzed on many different levels. At the most molecular level, behavior can be viewed as resulting from chemical reactions across synapses in the brain, and that reductionistic view can certainly be applied to some interpersonal behavior, such as emotional responses of anger or fear. At the *intra*personal psychological level, most human interaction is accompanied by a complex of thoughts, feelings, and actions—the famous Platonic triad of cognition, emotion, and conation.

Moving up the scale of complexity of analysis, away from reductionism, much psychological analysis of people's interactions is conducted at the level of dyads or triads—two or three individuals who are acting and reacting to each other in turn. In this volume, Cialdini's chapter focuses most specifically on interaction in dyads. At a more molar level, individuals' behavior can be considered as resulting from group pressures, as in families, work groups, clubs, or gangs. Several chapters in this volume incorporate this level of analysis, especially Zander's focus on processes in groups.

The next higher level of analysis is that of organizations, and systems theorists have stressed the interlocking nature of the behavior of individuals, groups, and organizations—structures where membership and the resulting influences on behavior may be both nested within larger units and also cross-cut by other affiliations (for instance, individuals' membership in neighborhood, religious, and work groups can produce cross-pressuring influences on their behavior). This systems perspective is displayed in the chapter by Konrad and Gutek on the social effects of group composition. Finally, at the most molar level, interpersonal behavior can be considered as partially shaped by large-scale societal and cultural forces (e.g., capitalistic principles and practices, national allegiances, religious precepts, cultural patterns of behavior). Among the chapters in this volume, the one by Kelley gives the most explicit attention to incorporating multiple levels of analysis.

Scope

An issue somewhat related to the level of analysis is the scope of any specific analysis of interpersonal behavior—for instance, how many levels does it consider and how broad are the substantive topics that it covers? The chapters in this book differ in their attention to issues of the level and scope of their presentations. The authors illustrate many of the different levels of analysis and degrees of scope, and we have chosen to organize the chapters roughly in order of their scope, considering a combination of both their substantive and theoretical content. As will be seen later, the broad theoretical worldview presented by Werner in the following chapter has the greatest scope, while Scarr's final substantive chapter is the narrowest in the sense that it deals primarily with the development of individual personality characteristics.

Structure, Content, and Process

Another important principle in analyzing human interaction is that not only the process but also the structure and content of the interaction need to be considered. Kelley explicitly emphasizes this point in his presentation, whereas it is implicit in the discussions of several other authors. One kind of social research that has stressed the structure of interaction situations is the work on game theory, where different cost-and-benefit structures are conceptualized as being embedded in specific situations and having quite different effects on social processes in those situations (e.g., Kelley & Thibaut, 1978). Of course, a similar point has been made by behaviorists regarding the differing effects of various reinforcement and punishment situations (e.g., Ferster & Skinner, 1957). However, it is less common for the substantive *content* of human interaction (e.g., a task-oriented discussion, a marital argument, or a decision about how to spend leisure hours) to be viewed as a dimension, separate from process and structure, that must be considered in theoretical analyses.

Complex Causation

Another important principle in analyzing interpersonal behavior is the causal assumptions that are made. This point also overlaps somewhat with the issue of levels of analysis, for most analysts agree that the causes of human behavior are complex and include several of the levels discussed above. One issue here is the form of causation that is either explicitly or implicitly considered. Werner defines this issue and devotes considerable attention to it in her chapter, pointing out the four different conceptions of cause that were described by Aristotle: efficient, material, formal, and final cause. Aristotle held that all four types of cause had to be considered in order to understand a phenomenon fully; however, the various authors in this volume give quite differing amounts of attention to these four aspects of causation.

Another aspect of complex causation, which departs from the traditional linear notion of cause and effect, is the postulate of *bidirectionality* of causation or reciprocal causation, which holds that the supposed "effect" can feed back to influence the purported "cause." An example can be seen in Zander's chapter, where individual motives are seen as important in the formation of groups, but later the group's purpose and activities help to shape its members' motives and behavior.

Theoretical Status

Related to the issue of causal assumptions are a group of other conceptual dimensions that can be used to analyze the theoretical status of any scientific presentation. As with the issues of complex causation, and of the scope and levels of analysis typical of a theory, several of these dimensions are discussed in the final chapter of this volume. One important dimension involves the formal structure of the theory—that is, how clearly its concepts and relational statements are defined and specified. Another analytical dimension is how strong and how consistent the empirical support for a theory is. Finally, the generativity of a theory in stimulating research and additional theoretical development is an important dimension to consider. See Chapter 8 for a further discussion of theoretical issues as they apply to the chapters in this volume.

Nature Versus Nurture

An issue that has been raised in psychology since its very beginnings is the nature versus nurture question; that is, the extent to which behavior is genetically versus environmentally determined. Of course, this is a continuum, and one can hold any position between the extreme poles, or theories may specify some behaviors as genetically based and others as entirely learned or environmentally caused. Most social psychologists probably lean in the environmental direction, but Scarr's chapter points out the large role played by the genetic component in the determination of interpersonal behavior.

Uniqueness Versus Universality

A theme that often arises in discussions of human behavior is the extent to which behavior follows general or universal principles, as opposed to the view that it is unique to each individual person. Most scientists are looking for principles with the greatest degree of generality possible. Examples in this volume include Cialdini's list of situational "trigger features," which can automatically induce compliance in most people in our culture, and Konrad and Gutek's discussion of how cultural expectations and stereotypes can influence the treatment of individuals. Most of the chapters here, like most of social science in general, give only implicit attention to the amount of individual uniqueness, or consider it as "error variance" to be minimized in their theories and measurements. However, Werner explicitly recognizes the uniqueness of events while still seeking to find universal principles in forming postulates about human behavior. Similarly, Scarr emphasizes the unique aspects of individuals' perception, even when they are confronted with the identical stimulus situation. This concept of unique perception is discussed further in the section on perceptual biases that may affect interpersonal processes.

Temporal Aspects of Behavior

Another theme that runs through several chapters is the importance attached to temporal aspects of behavior. Social psychologists often consider the temporal dimension of behavior only implicitly in their theories, except as they stress *change* over time as a common dependent variable in social interaction. However, several of our authors give time more direct attention as a crucial variable in behavior. Specifically, Werner's transactional viewpoint stresses the importance of temporal influences on behavior, viewing them as inseparable from the people and places involved in any phenomenon. Also Zander discusses how a group's purpose may change with the passage of time, and temporal sequences of interpersonal behavior are an intrinsic aspect of Kelley's focus on the process of conflict.

Perceptual Biases

A frequent theme in recent discussions of human interaction is the prominence of perceptual biases affecting people's cognition, emotion, and actions (e.g., Ross, 1977). In the present volume, that theme is echoed in Konrad and Gutek's analysis of biases and stereotypes that affect the status and treatment of women and minorities in groups. It also appears in Scarr's discussion of how different people glean quite different information and impressions from the same environmental stimuli, and in Cialdini's emphasis on the cognitive shortcuts that people often use to make decisions when faced with a complex environment.

Applicability

A final issue, which is especially important in this volume on applied social psychology, is the degree to which research findings have been or can be applied to real-world problems or questions. This issue will be discussed at greater length in the last chapter of this volume, after the respective authors' presentations.

Overview of Following Chapters

In this section we provide brief summaries of each chapter and note their incorporation of some of the themes concerning interpersonal processes that were discussed above.

Carol Werner

In Chapter 2, Carol Werner provides an introduction to a transactional worldview along with numerous references to the Utah program of research on neighborhoods. Either the overview of transactionalism or the review of the neighborhood research could stand alone, but she has chosen to present each in a way that supports the other. The neighborhood research illustrates the use of a transactional approach, and the description of transactional principles facilitates understanding of some of the directions the researchers took in studying neighborhoods. An especially interesting neighborhood, named "Christmas Street" for the activities of its residents during that season, served as the focus of the research.

The particular version of the transactional approach that Werner adopts is one put forth by Altman and Rogoff (in press). A first emphasis in this view is that aspects of psychological phenomena are holistically inseparable and mutually defining; these aspects include actors, physical context, social context, and time, all of which are linked through a variety of psychological processes, including interpersonal rules and relationships. Werner presents discussion and evidence concerning the idea that interpersonal processes may tie people to their social and physical environments as "person/place unities."

A second emphasis in transactionalism is that the temporal aspect is an inherent quality of the phenomena under study. In this regard, Werner notes that there are both linear and cyclical qualities in the emergence and change of person/place phenomena. A third facet of the transactional worldview is its distinctive philosophy of science. It emphasizes Aristotle's formal-cause approach to science rather than relying primarily on efficient-, material-, or final-cause explanations. Another issue that is raised first in Werner's chapter and that also emerges in later chapters involves an emphasis on studying events from multiple perspectives, from many levels of analysis.

To aid readers who are accustomed both to thinking of the aspects of a phenomenon as separate and to seeking unidirectional or bidirectional causality between these aspects, Werner provides transactional examples from a variety of areas—from sports to the city neighborhoods that she studied. To assist researchers interested in using the transactional approach, she illustrates her theoretical points with information as to how this approach has been employed in research. Finally, Werner encourages practitioners of social psychology to consider a transactional philosophy more fully, noting that many of the features of this approach are already implicit in the way we apply social psychology in the "real world."

Alvin Zander

The third chapter, by Alvin Zander, is largely theoretical. While Werner chose to consider one particular type of group (the neighborhood) in illustrating her philosophical approach, Zander discusses principles applicable to all kinds of groups. Based on his long experience in the field of group dynamics, he notes that two key questions have received little attention: "Why do people try to organize a group? What leads them to favor the purpose they choose for their group?" Zander's interest is mostly in formal organizations, enduring groups with some of the social rules and relationships mentioned as linking processes by Werner. Implicit in his discussion are a variety of interpersonal processes by which members influence one another to act in accord with the group purpose; in fact, he views the very "invention of a group's mission" as being constrained by social processes.

In Zander's view, a group purpose serves as an incentive for members and aids in the recruitment of new members. Here his ideas stand in contrast to those of others (for example, Weick, 1979) who propose that only after taking joint action does a group justify its activities and existence by naming a purpose. The idea that a group's purpose serves as an incentive for members is part of a larger framework in which Zander stresses that the formation of a group involves socially motivated behavior. Drawing upon *intra*individual motivational concepts and research findings, he proposes the existence of a group-oriented desire within individual members analogous to a person's motive for individual success. Bidirectionality is also assumed: While interaction among members determines the group purpose and the members' group-oriented desire, the purpose and desire (once formed) affect interpersonal interaction. While Zander does not describe these interpersonal processes in detail, he does provide examples of kinds and sources of group-oriented desires from which one may infer the relevance of conflict, influence, and other processes discussed by several authors in this volume. He suggests that some interpersonal processes—for example, groupthink, lack of communication, domination by powerful subgroups—may be inappropriate because they hinder a group from attaining its purpose.

This chapter provides a summary and amplification of principles discussed in Zander's most recent book (Zander, 1985). He suggests numerous properties of the group purpose that may influence members' behavior and notes several areas ripe for research. He also extends his past work by speculating on possible applications of his ideas for increasing the strength of members' desire for their group and for facilitating the wise choice of a specific group purpose. Managers and organizers of groups, who must actually apply social psychological principles, should welcome such prescriptions.

Alison Konrad and Barbara Gutek

The topic of groups is also addressed in the fourth chapter, by Alison Konrad and Barbara Gutek. Here, however, the focus is on the social categories or subgroups that are part of a larger group, organization, or society. Like Werner, these authors are concerned with presenting a framework or theory that others may find both useful as a research tool and applicable in understanding "real-world" issues. They review research on group composition, using the social categories of women and ethnic minorities as examples of their conceptualization.

Interpersonal processes play a large role in Konrad and Gutek's formulation. They hold that social distinctions arise when a particular characteristic of individuals "elicits a predictable set of reactions" from others. Often this happens because the characteristic is associated with reliable differences between social categories in their interpersonal behavior. The authors note the complex, bidirectional pattern of causality that may operate in groups. For example, the typical pattern of interpersonal behavior of one social category may set up a distinction upon which a subgroup discrimination is based and, once this social distinction is made, different interpersonal behaviors are then directed toward this new subgroup. These in turn reinforce or punish the pattern of behavior, and this may lead to even greater disparity in social behavior between various subgroups. As one example, the authors note that gender differences rarely go unreported or unnoticed in social science research, and once published, they are sometimes cited as justification for treating the sexes differently. Differential treatment may then lead to further gender differences, which receive further notice, and so on.

The bulk of this chapter explores and illustrates three ways in which groups may vary in terms of their meaningful subgroups. One way is in terms of the characteristics that are used to identify subgroups. These characteristics may range from the obvious visible, physical ones to the more insidious distinctions created by status differences and institutional practices. A second way in which groups may vary is in the pattern of interrelationships among key characteristics; for instance, status differences in a group may or may not be closely interrelated with ethnicity or with gender. The third possible group composition variable is the proportionate size of subgroups (e.g., 5% women or 50% women). Konrad and Gutek emphasize that these three variations in group composition may occur at a variety of systems levels (e.g., in work groups, in whole organizations, or nationwide), and societal-level status differences between the sexes or between ethnic groups may or may not be paralleled by status differences in organizations or smaller groups.

For researchers, this chapter nicely organizes the voluminous literature on group composition and highlights several areas needing further research. Much of the chapter is useful to practitioners as well: Group managers may gain a more sophisticated understanding of the emergence of subgroups and the potential downward-spiral effects that can serve both to reinforce group differences and to exacerbate conditions for particular subgroups. Finally, some of the research reviewed here—for example, studies on the relationships between proportion of female faculty and grades or career success of female students—clearly suggests some possible interventions.

Harold Kelley

Harold Kelley provides a thought-provoking examination of interpersonal processes in the next chapter. He believes that interaction sequences are the most basic phenomena of an interpersonal science, and his goal is to construct a taxonomy of such sequences. He illustrates this approach through the topic of conflict processes since this is the area in which the most is known about interaction. In defining conflict, Kelley includes any kind of interference by one person in the actions, thoughts, or feelings of another person. Thus behavioral, cognitive, and affective components are included in his definition of conflict.

While the content of conflict is important, Kelley mainly focuses on the *process*. He distinguishes between *intra*personal processes (psychological mechanisms within the individual that mediate between the stimulus input and reaction) and interpersonal processes. His emphasis is clearly on the latter, but at several points he discusses the intrapersonal processes that necessarily accompany and support interpersonal conflict. Kelley addresses the issue of levels of analysis of conflict process by employing five levels. The macro level of *relationships* is composed of many *episodes*, which in turn consist of *phases*; these phases may be further broken down into *sequences*, which are made up of *events* at the most micro level of analysis. A key problem in developing a taxonomy of interpersonal processes, Kelley states, is to understand the organization and patterning of the five levels.

Kelley's concern with the pattern or configuration of levels is similar to a theme expressed earlier in Werner's chapter. The inclusion of five levels in the model obviously supports the idea of multiple levels of analysis espoused by transactionalists, and the consideration of sequences of events emphasizes the importance of temporal qualities of phenomena. Like Werner, Kelley emphasizes the inseparability of personal and situational aspects: An understanding of the organization of personal interaction, he believes, must be guided by theory that includes the three dimensions of structure (persons and situations), content, and the dynamic process by which they are modified. He illustrates the bidirectional interplay of personal dispositions and situational factors by giving examples of person-situation structures and their specific, associated conflict processes.

Kelley illustrates his progress toward a taxonomy of interpersonal processes through reviewing research on a variety of topics—distressed couples, aggressive children, police arrests, and so on. He offers applicable research findings at several points, including ways to lessen ongoing conflict in unhappy couples or to prevent conflict escalation through learning not to attribute aggressive intent to another person. When it is completed, applied social psychologists will find Kelley's taxonomy of interaction sequences a useful reference, an "atlas" as he suggests, to guide them through interventions involving interpersonal processes.

Robert Cialdini

In the sixth chapter in this volume, Robert Cialdini focuses on another subset of interpersonal processes, those involving interpersonal influence toward compliance with a request. In terms of the levels of analysis mentioned by Kelley, Cialdini is examining an "episode"—the process of getting another person to do what one wishes—and the unit of analysis is a dyad composed of the target and the influencer. Cialdini suggests, as have others (e.g., Fiske & Taylor, 1984; Milgram, 1970), that in order to cope with the information overload of our complex society, we tend to take shortcuts in our decision making and to economize cognitively by focusing on only part of the available information. In the case of attempted influence from another person, Cialdini has identified several types of cues that cause us not to consider the situation fully and trigger our mindless acquiescence to the influence. A discussion of these "trigger principles" forms the bulk of his chapter.

Three compliance triggers of "reciprocity," "scarcity," and "authority" are discussed in detail in this chapter, including real-world examples of each trigger, empirical research evidence, and suggestions for the effective use of each compliance principle in organizational settings. In other sources, Cialdini has elaborated on specific conditions under which these triggers are *most* effective (e.g., Cialdini, 1985).

In this chapter, an emphasis on the ethical use of the triggers represents a new and important additional topic to consider in employing the compliance principles. Like Zander, Cialdini does not hesitate to take a prescriptive stance in his discussion. He concludes by urging applied social psychologists to be "detectives"—finding the naturally occurring triggers inherent in a situation—rather than "smugglers" who unethically import a trigger where it does not naturally exist. He believes that by so doing, organizations and individuals can reap beneficial side effects of enhanced reputations and self-esteem, in addition to influencing others.

Sandra Scarr

The theme of cognitive biases is stressed in Cialdini's consideration of how these biases can increase a person's susceptibility to being influenced. In the following chapter, Sandra Scarr attributes a similar cognitive bias to psychologists who "toss individual differences into the trashbin of error terms and fail to account for more than a trivial portion of personality variation." She sees this as the result of studying personal development and individuality only through theories of main effects. The idea that social science may reflect the biases and values of its researchers is a theme mentioned earlier by Konrad and Gutek.

In this chapter, Scarr considers one of the groups mentioned by Zander—families—but her focus is on the development of individuals within families. Concerning parent-child interpersonal interaction, Scarr mentions the prevalence of bidirectional causality—that is, while we generally think of the parent creating most of the child's social environment, the child also creates an important part of the environment for the parent. Also, similar to Werner's emphasis on the importance of subjective impressions of the environment, Scarr stresses that people experience the same environments in different ways, and that children from the same family perceive different parental treatment.

Scarr proposes a genetically based theory that can account for such findings as the remarkable similarity of monozygotic twins reared apart and the relative lack of similarity in personality of adopted siblings who have been reared under the same family influences. Scarr notes that these findings indicate how small an effect the environment has on personality development, and she emphasizes the role of individuals' genetic makeup in determining their personality and interpersonal behavior. More specifically, her theory holds that genetic makeup determines an individual's responsiveness to the environment, and she delineates three separate effects by which one's genotype can influence one's environment. A second postulate of her theory is that the relative importance of these effects varies over time; this too can be attributed to one's genotype, since genetic makeup also largely controls maturation. Third, she posits decreasing environmental influence from one's family (and thus increasing genetic influence) over the course of childhood and adolescence as individuals begin to select their own environments more actively.

Thus, in Scarr's conceptualization, an individual's interpersonal processes with the social environment (even within-family processes) are largely a function of that individual's genotype. To take one example, attractive children, compared to unattractive children, are more popular among their peers, are judged by their teachers to be more intelligent and to have greater potential, and are given the benefit of the doubt regarding discipline for unruliness (e.g., Clifford & Walster, 1973; Dion, 1972; Dion & Berscheid, 1974). Thus physical attractiveness may evoke in one's social environment all manner of positive reactions, from liking and friendship to increased instructional attention in the classroom to decreased probability of punishment. In short, a genetically determined characteristic may result in a higher probability of one's engaging in specific interpersonal interactions rather than others.

One might ask what place a theory of the development of individual differences—that is, a personality theory—has in a volume on applying social psychology. One answer is that the theory bears directly on the topic of this volume, the individual's interpersonal processes. Also, as Scarr notes, it is in applied settings where individual cases really matter. The applied fields of school psychology, clinical psychology, and organizational psychology have all been concerned with the individual through such topics as recruitment, selection, placement, assessment, and treatment.

Theory and Application

The concluding chapter in this volume discusses major theoretical aspects of the preceding six chapters and emphasizes possible applications of each author's work. Building on Kurt Lewin's (1944/1951, p. 169) statement that "there is nothing so practical as a good theory," the authors assert that practitioners and consumers will benefit most from applied work that is carried out with careful consideration of the theoretical foundations underlying the current applied problem. Thus Chapter 8 begins with a brief analysis of the chapters of this volume on relevant theoretical dimensions such as breadth, causal assumptions, and formal structure. From there, the discussion turns to a consideration of the applicability of the theory and research contributions of each of the preceding substantive chapters. While the possible areas of application are numerous, five areas are explored in some detail: management of groups, counseling, influence and persuasion, regulatory activity, and other public policy concerns.

In summary, this volume offers a variety of approaches to the topic of interpersonal processes—a topic that is important to all applied social scientists. It offers insights into human interaction that are useful in dealing with organizations, small groups, dyads, and even in analyzing intrapersonal dynamics.

References

Altman, I., & Rogoff, B. (in press). World views in psychology: Trait, interactionist, organismic, and transactionalist approaches. In D. Stokols and I. Altman (Eds.), *Handbook of environmental psychology.* New York: John Wiley.

Cialdini, R. B. (1985). *Influence: Science and practice.* Glenview, IL: Scott, Foresman.

Clifford, M. M., & Walster, E. H. (1973). The effect of physical attractiveness on teacher expectation. *Sociology of Education, 46,* 248-258.

Dion, K. K. (1972). Physical attractiveness and evaluations of children's transgressions. *Journal of Personality and Social Psychology, 24,* 207-213.

Dion, K. K., & Berscheid, E. (1974). Physical attractiveness and peer perception among children. *Sociometry, 37,* 1-12.

Ferster, C. B., & Skinner, B. F. (1957). *Schedules of reinforcement.* New York: Appleton-Century-Crofts.

Fiske, S. T., & Taylor, S. E. (1984). *Social cognition.* Reading, MA: Addison-Wesley.

Kelley, H. H., & Thibaut, J. W. (1978). *Interpersonal relations: A theory of interdependence.* New York: John Wiley.

Lewin, K. (1951). *Field theory in social science* (D. Cartwright, Ed.). New York: Harper. (Original work published 1944)

Milgram, S. (1970). The experience of living in cities. *Science, 167,* 1461-1468.

Ross, L. (1977). The intuitive psychologist and his shortcomings: Distortions in the attribution process. In L. Berkowitz (Ed.), *Advances in experimental social psychology* (vol. 10, pp. 173-220). New York: Academic Press.

Weick, K. (1979). *The social psychology of organizing.* Reading, MA: Addison-Wesley.

Zander, A. (1985). *The purposes of groups and organizations.* San Francisco: Jossey-Bass.

2

A Transactional
Approach to
Neighborhood Social
Relationships

CAROL M. WERNER

I
t may seem odd in a volume on
applied social psychology to discuss
something as esoteric as the transac-
tional worldview. In fact, it makes perfectly good sense because the
transactional worldview has features that are already being used
implicitly, and other features that could be used to good advantage in
both basic and applied social psychology. A transactional perspective
attempts to understand a phenomenon as a total entity, rather than
studying its elements as separate parts. In addition, it emphasizes
change and other dynamic temporal qualities rather than conceiving of
phenomena as fixed and unchanging. In the same way, social psychologists who work in organizations or on social problems must attempt to
understand the organization or problem as a total entity, rather than
studying isolated parts of it. And they must understand the change and
evolution of phenomena rather than assuming that features and
relationships remain the same.

My goal in this chapter is to describe the transactional worldview in
some detail, using as illustrations some of the work my colleagues and I
have been doing at the University of Utah on neighborhood social

relationships (Brown & Werner, 1985; Oxley, Haggard, Werner, & Altman, 1986; Werner, Altman, Oxley, & Haggard, 1986; Werner, Brown, & Peterson-Lewis, 1984; Werner, Peterson-Lewis, & Brown, 1985). I will begin with a brief overview of the research and the neighborhoods that were sampled, move to a description of the transactional worldview and how we attempted to fulfill its goals in the research, and finish with some implications for other research topics.

It is important to stress at the outset that, although in many ways the transactional approach is distinctive and novel, in other features it is not a completely new approach within social psychology. There are two key advantages of the transactional view. First, it provides in a systematic form many of the principles that social psychologists have been using at an intuitive level; by putting them into an orderly framework, I hope to encourage a more conscious appreciation of these principles. Second, it directs researchers to look at new kinds of phenomena, as well as looking at familiar phenomena in new ways. This latter feature is nicely illustrated in its (1) emphasis on temporal qualities, and (2) insistence that the physical, as well as social, environment be incorporated into our thinking about phenomena. Also, (3) a particularly intriguing aspect of the transactional worldview is the idea of inseparability of elements and the consequent focus on formal rather than efficient cause (i.e., patterns of relationships rather than antecedent-consequent relationships). These ideas will be discussed in more detail later in the chapter, but first let me turn to a description of the two neighborhoods where we conducted our research.

Two Neighborhoods

As implied above, the transactional worldview leads to research in which the social, physical, and temporal qualities of phenomena are studied simultaneously. Neighborhood social relations lend themselves well to such an analysis because, by definition, they contain people and places, they have a history and a future, and they can have other temporal qualities (e.g., daily and seasonal rhythms). Therefore, in our research we were interested in linking social relationships to their physical context, and understanding the temporal qualities of these person/place unities.

One street that we selected for study provided such a unique opportunity that we treated it as a case study, using in-depth interviews, lengthy questionnaires, and observational methods in our analysis.[1] The street is known as "Christmas Street" in the larger community because of its four-decade history of extensive decorations and festivities at Christmas time. During the year, with its tree-lined sidewalks and evidence of children, the cul-de-sac strikes the passerby as an ordinary, tidy, residential area. However, at Christmas, it is transformed by extensive brightly colored lights and decorative Christmas objects. A large red and green neon sign declaring this as "Christmas Street" arches over the entrance to the street; a large, decorated Christmas tree stands in the middle of the circle at the opposite end; and every year, most or all of the 31 homes have individual decorations (lights on the house and in the yard, decorative objects, door decorations, etc.).

In addition to the decorations, there is a variety of coordinated activities during the Christmas season, such as blockwide meetings, a party for the children, a Santa Claus in residence, coordinated dates for mounting and removing decorations, and a daily schedule for turning lights on and off. Thus the social and physical environments are interrelated with temporal qualities, and it appeared to us that this would be an ideal setting within which to apply a transactional approach.

The other, comparison neighborhood in which we have been working covers a much larger area, and has no history of communal activities—in fact, during our observations only about 65% of the 139 residents whom we interviewed decorated their houses for Christmas. Our sampling procedure was quite different from our work on Christmas street in that we drew only one resident from each block.[2] We chose this strategy in part so that we could draw a larger and more diverse group of people as our sample, but the kind of data collected and the basic issues were quite similar. We wanted to understand both neighborhoods as multifaceted and complex entities.

Transactional Perspective

The transactional worldview is an approach to science first explored most fully by Dewey and Bentley (1949) and Pepper (1942, 1967), and more recently advocated by a variety of psychologists (Altman &

Rogoff, 1987; Coyne & Lazarus, 1980; Fisher, 1982; Lazarus & Folkman, 1984; and Spiegel, 1971). Different authors developed somewhat different versions of transactionalism; therefore, for clarity, when I refer to the transactional worldview, I use that version developed by Altman and Rogoff. They highlighted a number of defining characteristics of this worldview, and much of the following is drawn from their analysis (see also Werner, Altman, Oxley, & Haggard, in press).

Phenomena Are Made Up of Inseparable and Mutually Defining Aspects

The essence of transactionalism is that psychological phenomena should be studied as holistic unities composed of inseparable and mutually defining psychological processes, physical and social environments, and temporal qualities. There are no separate parts to an event; people are not separate from their actions; the actions of each person are understood in relation to the actions of other people and the physical, social/situational and temporal circumstances in which the total event unfolds. Similarly, the different aspects of an event are mutually defining; that is, they lend meaning to one another, and are so interconnected that one aspect cannot be understood without the others. Indeed, in order to stress inseparability and mutual definition, Altman and Rogoff use the term *aspects* (as opposed to elements or entities) to refer to actors, social context, physical context, and time. As described below, these aspects do not "cause" one another, but are unified through actions, perceptual processes, rules, patterns and sequences, and other psychological processes.

Because psychologists are so accustomed to thinking in terms of separate elements and uni- and bidirectional causality, it may be worthwhile to expand on the ideas of inseparability and mutual definition. Good illustrations can be found in most sports activities in which the apparatus and playing field define and are defined by the activities of the players, and in which the activities of each player are defined by and define those of other players. Consider, for example, the differences between tennis and squash (two racquet sports with different environments, apparatus, rules, and skilled actions). Consider also the difference between a team that has been playing together for some time and a team that has not; the former knows routine plays and anticipates and responds quickly to spontaneous moves of team members; in general, the players fit together as a unity, and a newcomer who can't "fit in" is not likely to be retained.

As a more specific example, consider the sport of tennis. The physical layout of the court and viewing stands is interdependent with the activities that they contain. Furthermore, the behaviors of the players and fans can only be understood in the context of this environment, the equipment, the rules and purpose of the game, the point in time, and each player's actions. To see one person hit a small ball to another is meaningless without a context, but to comprehend that "John won the match on an ace" is exciting indeed. Certainly it is possible to define the physical features of the tennis court, as it is possible to isolate a player and highlight that person's performance; and these are legitimate forms of inquiry. However, in the transactional view, the elements cannot be understood independently. Understanding why the court is so constructed and painted, why the people are there, and what is taking place requires knowing the social, physical, and temporal context.

Similarly, a full understanding of a neighborhood requires that we consider all its aspects holistically. Figure 2.1 represents the neighborhood as a transactional unity. Inseparability and mutual definition are indicated in a number of ways. First, the aspects are embedded within a whole circle, the neighborhood. Although the aspects are separated by lines, the lines are dashed to indicate that the aspects are inseparable and mutually defining. Thus in this worldview neighbors and their interpersonal relationships cannot be understood outside of their physical and social milieu and their inherent temporal qualities. Note that in the Figure people and psychological processes are treated together in order to stress that the psychological processes (actions, feelings, cognitions, relationships, etc.) are of particular interest in a transactional analysis.

A second way that mutual definition and inseparability are represented is in the many practices and activities that reflect the unity of people, place, and time. Around the outer edge of this figure are a number of activities through which neighbors are bonded over time to one another and to their physical environment. These activities are not in any particular location on the circle but simply represent some concrete examples of people/environment/temporal unities. The use of arbitrary positions is deliberate, in order to emphasize that each activity contains all three aspects simultaneously, and that it should not be conceived of only as an environmental, or a temporal, or a people/process phenomenon.[3]

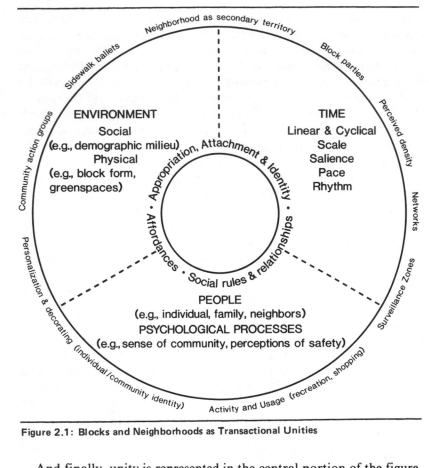

Figure 2.1: Blocks and Neighborhoods as Transactional Unities

And finally, unity is represented in the central portion of the figure with three general kinds of processes that link residents with their neighborhood: appropriation, attachment, and identity; social rules and relationships; and affordances. Each of these linking processes will be discussed in turn.

Appropriation and identity. Appropriation is a broad term that generally refers to processes by which individuals invest their environment with meaning, and through which they themselves are changed. Similarly, such concepts as social imageability, place attachment, territoriality, and personal identity represent psychological processes through which people can engage and become part of their environment (Koresec-Serfaty, 1976; Stokols, 1981; Werner, Altman, & Oxley,

1985). Decorating, displaying identity, remodeling, cleaning, gardening, enjoying, and using are all ways of appropriating the environment, establishing territory, and expressing personal and/or communal identity. When a neighborhood like Christmas Street decorates in a collective way, the residents as a social group are appropriating their environment and investing it with their own particular identity. According to a transactional view, they simultaneously change themselves in that during the collective decorating and appropriation they become bonded as a social group.

There is considerable evidence that individuals do become attached to both their neighbors and their physical environment, and that the term *neighborhood attachment* refers simultaneously to person and place bonds (Erikson, 1976; Fried, 1963; Fried & Gleicher, 1961; Fried & Levin, 1968; Rowles, 1983). Recent observations and research also suggest that group identity in neighborhoods is reflected in such things as choice of decor (Pratt, 1981) and decoration and upkeep of the front yard (Greenbaum & Greenbaum, 1981).

Similarly, in our work on neighborhoods, we conceived of residents and their environment as being linked or mutually defined through processes of appropriation and identity, and therefore we collected measures of people and place that reflected a sense of community identity. In both study areas, we measured attitudes that expressed a sense of psychological attachment to neighbors and neighborhood, and complemented these with questions that linked social relations to the physical environment (e.g., whether a neighbor had access to the respondent's backyard, whether the respondents spent time in their front yard, and so forth). In addition, we collected information about the physical appearance of the yards and homes, measuring environmental upkeep and decorating on dimensions such as unique/common and attractive/unattractive *relative to neighbors' homes and yards*. Thus we measured people and place on similar dimensions so as to study these aspects at their interface.

In the case study of Christmas Street, we collected information about psychological attachment to the block and the Christmas tradition by measuring our 25 respondents' social interaction and attitudes during the holiday season. Social interaction was indexed through two scales, one indicating general socializing (e.g., people "you spoke to casually" and people "you had inside your home for a social visit"), and the other indicating Christmas-oriented activities (e.g., "gave you a gift or treat," and "gave you a Christmas card"). Attitudes toward Christmas were tapped with two scales, one indicating the degree of enthusiasm for Christmas activities (e.g., "proud of being a resident of Christmas Street" and "enjoyed Christmas Street events"), and the other indicating their social visibility during the holiday season (e.g., "took a walk to look at other homes," and "spent time out on street interacting with neighbors"). In addition, we photographed the decorations and developed a coding system for measuring them on a variety of attributes (e.g., overall uniqueness, total volume of Christmas lights, presence of objects, and so forth), which were summed into a single score indicating the extensiveness and uniqueness of the Christmas decorations. The social interaction and attitude variables all correlated significantly with our ratings of the Christmas decorations (socializing, $r = .46$; Christmas exchange, $r = .66$; enthusiasm, $r = .45$; social visibility, $r = .37$; df = 23, all p's $< .04$). Thus, as expected, the aspects fit together holistically such that the most psychologically attached individuals had the most extensive and unique Christmas decorations.

In the other comparison sample area, we obtained similar evidence that the aspects were interconnected; however in this group, the most consistent relationships were obtained at Halloween (results for Christmas are reported at a later point in this chapter). In addition to collecting measures indicating respondents' strength of social ties to neighbors (total number and intimacy of contacts on the block) and their psychological attachment to the block (satisfaction with block; identification with block; security/sense of community), we collected data at Halloween indicating (a) whether the respondent's home was decorated and (b) what proportion of the neighbors' homes was decorated for the holiday. Correlations[4] among the social, attitudinal, and decorating variables indicated that decorating was a block-level phenomenon (i.e., if one home was decorated, so were others, $r (135) = .20$, $p < .01$); that it was related to the respondent's friendships with neighbors ($r (135) = .19$, $p < .05$); and, to some extent, that decorating was reflective of their attachment to the block (identification with block correlated with the presence of decorations, $r (135) = .14$, $p < .10$). Thus, even in this neighborhood, where Halloween decorating was not such a strong tradition, the most psychologically attached individuals were most likely to have put up holiday decorations.

Another perspective on decorations is that they can also express one's individuality and distinctiveness from neighbors. Thus, in a second analysis of the larger neighborhood sample, we examined the extent to which residents' psychological attachment to the house as a primary territory was related to their decorations. That is, we looked for another holistic relationship involving psychological attachment and environmental decor. Three scales were used to tap psychological attachment to the house (pride in appearance, private appearance, and enjoyment of decorating). None of these measures was related to the presence of decorating at either Halloween or Christmas, so we next examined whether the *quality* of decorations might be related to psychological attachment. At Christmas (but, unfortunately, not at Halloween), we were able to obtain photographs of the decorations on a subset of the homes. These photographs were carefully examined, and coding systems were developed to quantify the degree of uniqueness and the subjective attractiveness. Neither uniqueness nor attractiveness was related to the resident's expressed attachment to the house. In other words, a holistic pattern that obtained at the level of attachment to the group did not obtain with respect to attachment to the house.

This failure to find relationships between personal attachment and decorating stands in contrast to an earlier finding in this same neighborhood sample, using the same attitude measures. In her dissertation, Brown (1983), using environmental factors obtained in a previous study (Brown, 1980), found that psychological attachment to the house was related to environmental upkeep and decorating. In particular, expressed pride in the appearance of the home and enjoyment of decorating it were both correlated with the use of identity markers (e.g., name plates, address numerals), suggesting that residents did use some aspects of their decorating to reflect a unity with their home. Thus personal attachment may fit holistically with a different set of variables.

Social rules and relationships. Situations in which social rules and social relationships link people with their physical and social environments have been discussed rather extensively (Pervin, 1968; Price & Bouffard, 1974; Wicker, 1979). In most societies, there are clear rules defining what behaviors are appropriate in different settings, who has access to various settings and under what circumstances, and so on (Altman & Chemers, 1980; Altman & Gauvain, 1981). In American neighborhoods, we do not walk on neighbors' lawns or through their flower beds, nor do we enter their backyards without permission.

A way in which this idea was reflected in our work on Christmas Street was in rules about access to primary territories (Altman, 1975). That is, we learned what kinds of relationships neighbors had with one another, ranging from superficial acquaintanceships (e.g., would recognize by sight; have spoken to casually), to more interdependency (e.g., have borrowed from), to more intimate contact and personalized support (would ask for help in an emergency; consider to be intimate friends). Based on Altman's ideas about limited accessibility of primary territories (Altman, 1975; Altman & Chemers, 1980), we hypothesized that there would be a congruence between the degree of intimacy in their relationship and the extent to which neighbors were admitted into the home. Thus we conceived of superficial relationships between neighbors as involving less access to the home than would be the case with more intimate ties, and we asked questions about which neighbors were entertained inside the home and which neighbors took care of their house when the resident was out of town. As expected, factor analysis revealed that items suggesting a more personalized relationship with neighbors clustered with items indicating these neighbors had access to the primary territory (for example, "consider to be an intimate friend" was in the factor with "watches home while you're away"; in another factor were "you have had inside your home socially" and "you would like to know better").

Affordances and other cognitive-perceptual processes. Another kind of psychological process that serves to link individuals with their environments is cognitive-perceptual and cognitive-perceptual-behavioral processes. We did not address these processes in our research, so I will not describe the ideas in much detail. The first type, called "affordances," refers to particular kinds of perceptual processes that unite people with their physical environment (Gibson, 1979; Stokols, 1981; Werner, Altman, & Oxley, 1985). According to Gibson, we see not the physical qualities of objects, but their uses and functions. For example, a chair is not something with a particular shape and dimensions but rather is a place to sit. To extend this idea to the neighborhood, when a resident looks at a cul-de-sac like Christmas Street, he or she perceives the kinds of activities it can support rather than particular physical qualities. According to this view, neighbors perceive the opportunities for their children to play safely in the street, the difficulty of driving on this relatively narrow street, and so on. Thus affordances are a kind of glue that unify people and their physical environment through perceptual/behavioral processes.

Another kind of cognitive-perceptual process that has received attention recently comes from the literature on person-situation interactions, and refers to the idea that people cognitively construct their social and physical environments. People choose to enter certain settings and to avoid others, and once in these settings, they interpret and respond to, and in other ways impose a cognitive structure on, the physical/social qualities and events. These subjective evaluations link people with their context in that neither person nor place can be understood outside of this perceptual process (Cantor & Kihlstrom, 1981; Pervin, 1968; Smith & Rhodewalt, 1986). A similar perspective is advocated by Lazarus and his colleagues (Lazarus, 1966; Coyne & Lazarus, 1980; Lazarus & Launier, 1978; Lazarus & Folkman, 1984), who use the term *appraisal* to describe person-environment unities. As Lazarus and Folkman (1984) said,

> In a transactional model separate person and environment elements join together to form new meanings via appraisal; threat, for example, does not refer to separate person and environment factors, but to the integration of both in a given transaction. (p. 326)

These ideas reflect the belief that persons' subjective impressions of their environment are often more important than the objective environment; put more strongly, they indicate that there is no environment outside of the person's impression of it, and no person outside of this environment. We did not actively seek examples of this concept in our research, but anecdotes from residents suggest that their perceptions of the Christmas Street tradition were often flavored by their personal perspective. Some commented that decorating had grown too competitive, others noted that competition was not a problem and was actively discouraged; some felt that the tradition no longer served their needs, and others were fully enthusiastic about it; a few felt that the activities were too dominated by a single religious group, and others felt that the activities were sufficiently egalitarian. Thus each person constructed an impression of the tradition based on his or her own experiences, biases, and other personal qualities.

This view is quite different from more traditional views of person-environment interactions, in which persons and their physical or social environment were thought of as distinct entities, separate from one another, and in which some feature of the environment engaged or triggered some aspect of the personality (see, for example, research on the authoritarian personality syndrome by Mitchell & Byrne, 1973; Werner, Kagehiro, & Strube, 1982; White, Alter, & Rardin, 1965). It is also different from a more current approach to conceptualizing person-situation interactions, often called "person-environment transactions"

(Pervin, 1968) or "dynamic models of interactions" (Endler & Edwards, 1978). These latter approaches posit reciprocal cause-and-effect relationships between people and their environments: "*Reciprocal Causation* means that not only do events affect the behavior of organisms but the organism is also an active agent influencing environmental events" (Endler & Magnusson, 1976, p. 969). Although the latter approaches are in some respects transactional, both they and earlier interactional approaches conceive of persons and environments as separate entities, and tend not to examine explicitly persons and environments as aspects of one another (Endler, 1981).

Appropriation, social rules, and affordances/cognitive-perceptual processes are three very broad and general kinds of processes by which persons and environments are united. Considerable work remains to be done on developing and refining this typology (the categories overlap to some extent, and can also be further subdivided), as well as on understanding each process separately. Still, they do provide a useful heuristic for thinking about person/place unities.

Temporal Qualities Are Inherent Aspects of Phenomena

This principle emphasizes the temporal aspects of person/place unities. A transactional worldview considers temporal qualities to be an intrinsic part of the definition and character of phenomena, and transactional research is concerned with the flow, the unfolding, and other dynamic aspects of events. Elsewhere, my coauthors and I have described *linear* and *cyclical* temporal qualities and suggested ways in which they inhere in environmental/interpersonal phenomena (Werner, Altman, & Oxley, 1985; Werner & Haggard, 1985; Werner, Haggard, Altman, & Oxley, in press). *Linear* qualities refer to the ideas that transactional unities emerge and unfold through time; that they contain past, present, and future aspects; and that both continuity and change are inherent in these unities. *Cyclical* temporal aspects also reflect the inherent flow of events, but refer to recurrent processes and activities that link people with place, such as rituals and habits involving particular settings and people, time after time. Neighborhood social relationships can reflect linear qualities both of continuity and change, in that old friendships have a long, stable history, but also continue to evolve and change. In addition, neighborhoods can contain cyclical qualities in that seasonal activity patterns bring neighbors into more or less contact, or bring different subsets of neighbors together at different times.

To a great extent, linear and cyclical qualities are not completely distinct, and one can often find elements of both in phenomena. [Indeed, J. E. McGrath (personal communication, 1986) feels that they should not be separated at all.] For example, in the early stages of an event becoming a tradition, there is considerable blurring between linear and cyclical qualities. Furthermore, events rarely occur identically from one time to another, so even recurrent events have a linear changing quality to them (in previous work we used the term *spiraling* instead of *cyclical* to emphasize this point). In general, if the events are continuous (e.g., length of residence) or primarily one-time-only occurrences (e.g., rites of passage), we have considered them to have a primarily linear quality, whereas if they are recurrent events, we have considered them to have a primarily cyclical quality.

Subordinate temporal qualities. These two overarching temporal qualities can be further subdivided into the five subordinate dimensions of temporal *salience, scale, pace, rhythm,* and *sequencing* (Werner, Altman, & Oxley, 1985; Werner & Haggard, 1985; Werner, Haggard, Altman, & Oxley, in press). *Temporal salience* or orientation (see Rakowski, 1979) refers to the extent to which past, present, or future aspects of person/environment unities are present in memory. Temporal salience can vary, sometimes being past-salient, such as when residents reminisce about previous events, and at other times being present- or future-salient. Or a linear or cyclical event can contain all three foci at once, such as when a community action group is —in the present— attempting to preserve something from the past for future generations. *Temporal scale* refers to the scope or length of a person/environment transaction, such as the length of time two neighbors have known one another (linear scale), how long a social action group has been functioning (linear scale), how long an annual neighborhood party tradition continues (cyclical scale), and so on. *Temporal pace* refers to how rapidly events unfold, such as a family moving quickly into their new home (linear), or children rushing to the neighborhood school in the morning but returning home at a more leisurely pace in the afternoon (cyclical). Temporal *sequencing* refers to the order of events (linear), or to a recurrent (cyclical) order of events and activities, such as a person's regular daily routine around the neighborhood, a shop owner's typical pattern of activities, and so forth. Temporal *rhythm* refers to patterns and recurrent patterns of activities (more fully described by Werner, Altman, & Oxley, 1985). Like rhythm in music (Ammer, 1972), these patterns can include pace, scale, and sequences, as well as the emphasis or accent on particular events. That is, rhythm includes how rapidly events occur, how much time is spent on separate events, in what order events occur, and how important they are. For example, Petonnet (1973) described daily rhythms among neighbors in a housing development, noting that the combination of varying pace, duration, sequence (especially regular time of day), and importance of activities lent a rhythm to each day, and that these rhythms varied depending on day of the week and time of year.

In one analysis (Werner, Haggard, Altman, & Oxley, in press), we were able to describe the Christmas Street tradition in terms of these concepts. For example, the Christmas Street tradition has both linear and cyclical qualities, as well as a number of the subordinate dimensions. It contains linear qualities in that both continuity and change are apparent in its 40-year history: There has always been a tree in the center of the circle, and the "Christmas Street" sign has been put up for many years, but other aspects of the decorating have changed (e.g., lights connecting all of the homes are no longer as evident as they once were). It contains cyclical qualities in that it is an annually recurring event with distinct scale (e.g., specific starting and ending dates; particular times for illuminating the decorations each day) and sequences of events (e.g., an annual children's party always has a particular series of activities). During the Christmas Season, there are daily rhythms involving light traffic and slow activity during the days—but heavy traffic and brisk activity in the evenings— and residents have to adapt or synchronize to this rhythm (e.g., coming home early in order to avoid the traffic).

Temporal qualities are integral to phenomena. An important aspect of the transactional view is that events are described in terms of natural temporal units. That is, unlike other worldviews in which time is treated as a separate dimension that marks or locates the state of a phenomenon, a transactional worldview holds that temporal qualities are inherent in phenomena and should be permitted to emerge from events rather than being imposed on them. Psychological qualities—not measures of time external to the events themselves—determine beginnings and endings, rhythms, recurrences, and so on. For example, in behavior setting observations, behaviors are grouped according to natural breaks in behavior rather than according to the experimenter's schedule (Barker, 1968; Wicker, 1987). Similarly, when researchers study friendship formation on college campuses, they often take into account the academic calendar, relating interpersonal and behavioral phenomena to the calendar as an aspect of the students' lives rather than using an arbitrarily determined period of weeks or months (Hays & Oxley, 1986; Hill, Rubin, & Peplau, 1976).

In our work on Christmas Street, we deliberately chose summer and Christmas because they represented two times of year when we could study the interrelationships among the social, psychological, and environmental aspects. That is, Christmas was *the* event of the year for this block, suggesting that social, psychological, and environmental factors might be linked. Furthermore, it provided an opportunity to study temporally specific environmental decorating. Similarly, summer was a time when residents could be outside, enjoying the temperate weather, and having more opportunities to engage in casual interaction with neighbors. In addition, it was a time when environmental upkeep was at its most demanding and the yards were most spectacular (watering the yard in the desert climate entails considerable effort, as does trimming, pruning, and so on; flowers were in full bloom when we took the summer photographs). Thus in the summer, as well as at Christmas, the environmental component was seasonally specific, and represented special effort on the part of the residents. In sum, these two times of year were chosen because they were integral to life on the block, not because they represented a particular, externally imposed temporal interval.

In our larger comparison sample, we similarly tried to select observation periods that would be integral to neighborhood relationships. We collected data on the presence, location, and quality of holiday decorations at Halloween and at Christmas on the grounds that those were two holidays when visitors were expected in the home, and when residents might use holiday decorations as signs of welcome. They were also times when the current resident was fully responsible for the decorations, as opposed to permanent environmental features that could have been placed by a previous resident.

This quick look at the temporal qualities of Christmas Street only suggests the scope and possibilities of such an analysis. In future work, we hope to examine more systematically a number of issues involving these temporal qualities, such as how residents experience and adapt to the daily rhythms, how each family synchronizes its holiday activities, and whether there is a relationship between commitment to a holiday and its salience during other times of year.

The Transactional Worldview Has
a Distinctive Philosophy of Science

(1) Emphasis on formal cause. A primary feature of this philosophy is that it adopts Aristotle's *formal cause* approach to science, *focusing on description of the pattern and form of an event,* and giving less attention to efficient cause (i.e., antecedent-consequent relationships), material cause (i.e., personality traits), or final cause (i.e., teleological goals) (Rychlak, 1977).

In the transactional worldview, elements are not seen as pushing or causing one another, but rather as working together or fitting together as total unities.

> [One tries] . . . to identify relationships among component parts and processes — but none of the components is "caused" by the prior occurrence of another component; and even more important, none of the components "causes" the action or act of which they are components. (Ginsburg, 1980, p. 307)

To return to the tennis analogy, the elements fit together in a particular pattern but none of the elements "causes" the other to happen. The rectangular court does not "cause" the server to stand in the center of one end and hit the ball into the service area. Nor does the service "cause" the receiver to return the ball. The setting and activities fit together coherently in order to achieve the overriding goals of playing and winning the match. Thus the actions fit together according to the rules of the game, and one goal of a transactional analysis is to identify these relationships and the rules that hold them together.

Rules and goals are relatively easy to see in athletic events, but they can also be identified in neighborhoods, and in fact are implicit in the kinds of issues researchers have chosen to study. Studies of neighborhood social networks often presume that neighbors provide support and services that other friends cannot provide, and that social cohesiveness in neighborhoods is a desirable outcome. Research then focuses on the correlates of these outcomes, such as perceptions of safety, and health and well-being (see Unger & Wandersman, 1985, for a review). Similarly, studies of neighborhood action groups focus on the goal(s) of the action group, studying effectiveness at achieving the goal(s), the number of goals, the longevity of the group, and so on as desirable outcomes; research in this domain then focuses on the correlates of these outcomes (see, for example, Pretsby & Wandersman, 1985; Steiner & Mark, 1985; Unger & Wandersman, 1983; Wandersman, Florin, Chavis, Rich, & Pretsby, 1985). Similarly, in a transactional approach, specifying the goals is a first step toward identifying the properties of events and analyzing how they fit together—not as antecedents and consequences, but rather as aspects of a unity.

The focus on patterns and configurations does not preclude hypothesis testing, but it does guide the choice of hypotheses. As Fisher (1982) noted:

> The problems of specifying hypotheses are exacerbated in transactional research because of the necessity of articulating a theory that by definition does not have independent elements. (pp. 314-315)

In applying a transactional approach to families, Fisher (1982) proposed

> the necessity of specifying transactional hypotheses as sequences of actions or configurations of behaviors within a specified setting. . . . A transactional hypothesis might call for the increased occurrence of certain *patterns* of family behaviors in certain kinds of families rather than in others. . . . Or, alternatively, a transactional hypothesis might call for a given sequence of family behavior under certain conditions. (pp. 317-318)

Thus transactional approaches can involve hypotheses about patterns as well as hypotheses about differences. It would be well within the domain of a transactional worldview to hypothesize that the pace and rhythm with which behaviors unfold might differ from one group or situation to another, or that the sequence of actions would differ for different transactions. Or one might hypothesize that the psychological processes binding people and place might differ in different neighborhoods or at different times in the same neighborhood, or that the configurations or patterns by which aspects fit together would shift and change with neighborhood and time (Werner, Altman, Oxley, & Haggard, in press).

In our work on Christmas Street, we adopted this last hypothesis and examined the relationships among residents' interpersonal relationships, their psychological attachment to the neighborhood, and their use of the environment. We did not have any hypotheses about how the aspects would fit together during the summer, but because of the integral role of decorating in the celebration of Christmas, we expected to see clear interrelationships during the Christmas season.

In fact, that is exactly what we found. As noted earlier, social relationships, attitudes expressing cohesiveness with neighbors, and the extensiveness and uniqueness of decorations were intercorrelated during the Christmas season. In contrast, during the summer, intercorrelations among similar variables revealed a different pattern. At that time, social relationships did correlate with attitudes expressing cohesiveness with neighbors; however, a single index of environmental upkeep and decorating was unrelated to the social and attitudinal variables. Instead, the environmental variable was related to a number of demographic variables, suggesting that care and attention to the home's exterior were associated with a combination of practical and psychological factors rather than being a reflection of social cohesion. People who were retired, who owned their homes, who were long-term residents, and who had few children living at home had the most well-kept and attractive homes and yards (respectively, $r(27) = .41, .41, .62,$ and $.33,$ all p's $< .04$). Thus care and decorating were linked to factors that might be construed as time availability (i.e., being retired, not having young children to care for), financial ability (not having young children to support), and psychological commitment to the home (owning the home, and being a long-term resident). In sum, the patterns of relationships among the aspects were different at two times of year, the aspects being most closely interrelated during the communal Christmas season.

A similar pattern emerged in the other, larger neighborhood sample in that psychological attachment, contacts with neighbors, and environmental decorations were related differently at Halloween and at Christmas. As noted earlier, in that sample the aspects fit together holistically at Halloween, with the strongest evidence found between decorating and neighboring relations (i.e., if the respondent decorated, many of the neighbors also decorated, and respondents who had broad and intimate ties with neighbors were most likely to decorate), and a weaker relationship between decorating and psychological attachment to the home.

However, at Christmas, the linkages in this sample were somewhat different. Although decorating was still a block-related phenomenon [i.e., if one resident decorated, neighbors were more likely to do so, $r(134) = .23 \, p < .05$], friendships with neighbors were not associated with the presence of decorations on the respondent's home [$r(135) = .11, p > .10$]. In addition, correlations between attitudes expressing attachment to the block and the presence of decorations were only marginally significant [satisfaction with block as place to live, $r(135) = .14, p < .10$; feelings of security on block, $r(135) = .16, p < .10$]. So friendship and cohesiveness were somewhat, though not strongly, related to whether a respondent would decorate at Christmas.

In this larger neighborhood sample, the different patterns at Halloween and Christmas may reflect differences in communal orientation at each holiday. At Halloween, most residents had children who went trick-or-treating in their immediate neighborhood, and decorating may have been used to symbolize welcome and enthusiasm for the event. In contrast, it may be that Christmas was a time when other factors *outside* of neighborhood cohesion determined decorating (e.g., religious values, church pressure), obscuring the relationship between cohesion and decorating.

The idea of studying patterns rather than antecedent-consequent relationships differs dramatically from traditional research approaches, in which prediction and control of phenomena are the goals— here description and understanding are also important. The formal cause approach also differs from strict "trait" models of behavior (i.e., Aristotle's "material cause," Rychlak, 1977), in which something about the organism is believed to determine behavior, and the organism is expected to behave fairly consistently from one setting to another. Finally, this view of causality differs from "final cause," in which phenomena are drawn toward teleological goals or ideal end-states (Rychlak, 1977). In the transactional worldview, it is assumed that psychological events unfold in a purposeful and goal-directed fashion, but goals can be both short- and long-term, and can change with time and circumstances.

(2) Interest in both unique events and universal principles. A second feature of the transactional philosophy of science is that both unique events and universal principles are of interest. In this regard, transactional approaches are similar to dialectic analyses in that a dynamic interplay between opposites is expected (Altman, Vinsel, & Brown, 1981). Both poles of such dialectic dimensions as continuity/change, unique/universal, and individual/community are all expected to be relevant. So, for example, continuity and change are present simultane-

ously in all phenomena; sometimes continuity is more evident, sometimes change is more evident, and this dynamic ebb and flow is a natural aspect of phenomena. Similarly, sometimes unique and sometimes universal principles apply; the individual's identity is sometimes and in some places distinct and identifiable, and at other times and places it is immersed in a larger group identity.

One implication of this view is that both sides of the dialectic should be expected and measured, and their relative importance should be expected to change with time and circumstances (this process is noted subsequently in an analysis of the meaning of holiday decorations). Another implication is that change is continuous, and therefore special measures may be needed for research projects in different settings and times. This does not mean that one cannot use standardized measures, but rather that one should be alert to the possibility that special measures may be needed as idiosyncratic indicators of a phenomenon. This is not a particularly novel idea—good researchers always try to make sure that the measures they collect will be appropriate for their particular population and setting. I do think, however, that it is useful to reiterate it here, to make it an explicit research goal.

For example, in developing our rating scales for the environmental decorations on Christmas Street, we needed to develop one set for summertime and one set for Christmas. At first we simply looked at slides taken of the street in the two seasons, trying to get a sense of the kinds of dimensions that we might tap. Simultaneously, however, we knew that we were interested in variables that would reflect the owner's personal identity and uniqueness, as well as variables that would reflect group identity and attachment to the block. So for many of the items that we measured, we simply coded how unique something was relative to the others on the block. We also rated attractiveness and items indicative of effort, on the grounds that they represented appropriation of the environment. Thus our philosophical and theoretical orientations guided our selection of dimensions for these ratings.

In our larger, more diverse neighborhood sample we also attempted to develop rating scales that were appropriate for that sample. As noted earlier, there was relatively weak evidence that having Christmas decorations was related to psychological attachment to the block. Additional analyses explored the possibility that cohesion with neighbors was related to *where* decorations were placed rather than to *whether* decorations were placed. A number of authors have noted that entryways are zones of transition between the exterior and interior of the home, places where friends can be greeted and welcomed into the home and strangers excluded (Altman & Chemers, 1980; Korosec-Serfaty, 1978, 1985; Lawrence, 1982). Consequently we hypothesized that placing decorations on the door would symbolize welcome, whereas placing them elsewhere would be less inviting.

Decorations were observed at five locations on respondents' homes (doors, windows, yard, house facade, roof). Zero-order correlations indicated that social contacts and attachment were related only to placing decorations on the door (correlations among the variables ranged from .13 to .21, df = 137, p's < .06), supporting the view that cohesion would be related to this specific spatial index of environmental decorating.

We collected similar data among the Christmas Street sample, and found no relationship between the location of decorations and residents' psychological attachment to the block and its activities (i.e., Christmas spirit) or to their reported contact with neighbors. However, as noted earlier, other aspects of the decorating did relate to these indices of social cohesion. Thus the relationships that obtained in one neighborhood were not replicated in the other. This is consistent with the idea that different neighborhoods have different ways of expressing their psychological attachment and openness to neighbors. Such differences would be especially likely when the comparison involves a neighborhood with a 40-year tradition such as Christmas Street's.

The emphasis on formal causation and focus on specific events does not rule out the use of general theoretical principles. We did use the themes of appropriation and identity (individual and group) in developing both sets of rating scales. Furthermore, as noted above, the general phenomenon of Christmas decorating (whether measured as location or total amount) was associated in both samples with psychological attachment to the block and the neighbors.

(3) Use of multiple perspectives. A final feature of this worldview is that events can be seen from multiple perspectives, each of which contributes to an understanding of the total event; it is important to study events from as many perspectives as possible. For example, unlike other worldviews, which assume that phenomena can be studied by objective and detached observers, transactional approaches assume that phenomena are partly defined by the observer and the observation process. Similarly, understanding a psychological event requires an appreciation of the meaning of the event to its participants. Events may be construed in different ways by different participants, none of which is

the single correct interpretation; and the researcher should "home in" on an event from all of these perspectives. Finally, events can be viewed at many levels of scale, from micro to macro levels of analysis. No single level is the only possible one or the only correct one, and using multiple levels provides a more holistic view of a phenomenon.

In our analysis of Christmas Street, we attempted to achieve this goal of multiple perspectives in a rather simple way, by varying the unit of analysis. Heretofore I have been speaking of social contacts, psychological attachment, and environmental decorating at the level of the block, examining interrelationships among the individuals' contacts, attachment, and decorating. In addition, we identified social networks on this block (i.e., subgroups of residents with similar interaction patterns) and examined how membership in these networks was related to psychological attachment to the block and to the quality of environmental upkeep and decorating.

These two levels of analysis revealed different aspects of the block, and they also supported and clarified one another. For example, the analysis of individual respondents suggested that in the summer there were various kinds of people on the block: Some knew many others, depended upon them for personal support, and reported being psychologically attached to the block; others were not involved socially or psychologically on the block, but spent considerable time decorating and keeping up their yard and house exterior. The analysis of networks supported and also clarified this picture, showing that there were complex social interaction and attitudinal relationships, such as two kinds of friendship-based networks and two kinds of low-contact networks. One of the two friendship-based networks had extensive and intimate ties within the group, and the other was neither so intimate nor exclusive. Of the low-contact networks, one was more casually involved with other members and other residents on the street, and the other had very few ties to the block at all. As might be expected, both of the friendship-based groups expressed more psychological attachment to the block and neighbors than did the other networks. Relative to the two low-contact networks (with minor exceptions), members in the friendship-based groups expressed a stronger sense of community [$F(3, 23)$ = 5.42, $p < .05$]; a greater desire for similarity with neighbors [$F(3, 23)$ = 4.23, $p < .05$]; and a greater concern about the appearance of their homes [$F(3, 23)$ = 3.34, $p < .05$]. The network analysis also confirmed that there was no relationship between feeling bonded to the neighborhood and having an attractive, well-kept house and yard in summer [analysis of variance showed no relationship between networks and environmental upkeep and decorating; three $Fs(3, 23)$ close to $1, p > .20$. In the block-level analyses, the three measures were combined into a single scale].

Thus the two levels of analysis revealed similar information but also showed subtle differences. If we had only used the block-level analysis, we would have failed to realize that different subgroups exhibited distinctly different patterns of social interaction. Conversely, if we had used only the network analysis, we would not have seen a number of subtle relationships among the different kinds of social contacts, attitudes, and environmental upkeep and decorating in the summertime. Also, the analyses supported each other, such as when both revealed a similar pattern of relationships among the aspects at Christmas time.

In the neighborhood where we drew our larger sample, we approached the idea of obtaining multiple perspectives somewhat differently. In that sample we were interested in how residents became integrated into the social fabric of their neighborhoods, and we measured their self-reported sociability as well as naive raters' estimates of their openness and sociability. To obtain naive raters' estimates, we selected 16 homes in which the residents were either extremely sociable or extremely unsociable with their neighbors, half of the homes being decorated and half not decorated for Christmas. We showed photographs of those homes to college undergraduates, and asked them to indicate how sociable the resident appeared to be (based only on the information in the photo), how much they wanted to get to know the resident of the house, and what cues they had used in arriving at their impression.

The naive observers were quite accurate at identifying, and actually wanted to meet, the more sociable residents—as long as the house was not decorated for the holiday season [apparently, seeing decorations led them to infer that the resident was sociable, sociability by decoration interaction $F(3, 53) = 12.61$, $p < .001$]. On undecorated homes, three general kinds of cues were used by raters in forming their impressions: (1) "fixed features" (i.e., architecture, context), such as the presence of adjacent homes, the closeness of the front door to the street, and many windows facing forward; (2) "modifiable features" (i.e., decorative aspects), such as vivid colors, light-colored door, evidence of curtains, and interesting landscaping; and (3) "apparent usage" (i.e., upkeep and a "lived-in" look), such as walks and driveway cleared of snow (an almost universally mentioned clue), neatly trimmed shrubbery, no clutter on porch, opened curtains, personalizing objects, and footprints in the snow. Thus naive observers could identify residents with low social contacts, and they used a variety of cues to guide their inferences. These ratings of outsiders provided another perspective on the residents, one that complemented and enhanced the residents' own self-descriptions.

Summary of Findings

In using these research projects to illustrate various aspects of a transactional orientation, the methods and findings have been presented in a rather scattered way. The present section contains a brief, but more coherent description. Two large-scale studies were conducted to address the general issue of the interconnectedness among neighborhood social contacts, psychological attachment to the neighborhood, and environmental decorating and upkeep. Consistent with a transactional orientation, it was expected that psychological cohesion among neighbors would be reflected in group-related decorating, and that the degree of interrelationship would vary with time and circumstance.

In the case study of Christmas Street, a block with a 40-year history of communal Christmas decorating, we conducted intensive interviews with almost all of the residents to learn their social contacts with neighbors and their psychological attachment to the block. Data were collected in the summer and again just after Christmas to permit comparison of the patterns of interconnectedness at a noncommunal and a communal time of year. We also photographed their house facades and yards at both times, and coded them for the attractiveness, uniqueness, and effort involved in maintaining or decorating these areas (naturally, the coding systems were different for the two times of year). We found different patterns of relationships in summer and at Christmas. In summer, decorating was not integral to social cohesiveness; however at Christmas, the three aspects fit together holistically: Close social ties with neighbors, feelings of bonding to the block, and attractive and extensive decorations were all intercorrelated. These time-specific patterns generally obtained whether the block was studied from a social network or an individualistic perspective.

We conducted similar research in a larger neighborhood in which we sampled 139 respondents from 139 different blocks. In this neighborhood, we examined the interconnections among the aspects at Halloween and at Christmas but not in the summer. The results were complex, but in general, they supported the ideas that social ties, psychological attachment, and environmental decorating fit together holistically to indicate group cohesion. In this example, the relationships were strongest and most consistent at Halloween.

Aside from illustrating a transactional approach to research, these two projects have also helped us to understand the meaning of holiday decorations. One conclusion that seems quite clear from both of these data sets is that holiday decorations are much more an index of cohesion with neighbors than a statement of personal identity. We found consistent correlations between social contacts and decorating, moderate to strong correlations between psychological attachment to the neighborhood and decorating, and—in the large sample—correlations among contacts, block attachment, and placing decorations at the entryway (as though decorations were used to symbolize welcome). Finally, naive raters inferred that people who had holiday decorations were more sociable than people who did not. In contrast, we found no evidence that the presence or quality of holiday decorations was associated with psychological attachment to the home (although other kinds of decorations were associated with bonds to the home). Naturally, additional research is needed to be certain, but for now it appears that holiday decorations reflect, not individual identity, but the group side of an identity dialectic.

Review of the Transactional Worldview

In this brief overview of transactional worldviews, I have stressed that (1) events are composed of inseparable and mutually defining aspects; (2) the temporal aspect is an inherent part of events; (3) these worldviews are based on a distinctive philosophy of science that advocates the use of formal cause rather than other causal orientations, use of multiple perspectives and levels of analysis, and an emphasis on uniqueness of events as well as general principles, as reflected in dialectic polarities of unique/general and continuity/change.

Although there are dramatic differences between transactionalism and other worldviews, I am not advocating that this perspective is better than others. Instead, I believe that this worldview is an alternate approach to identifying psychological processes, and that it has been unduly neglected in psychology, especially in regard to the study of social relationships. Nor do I present our research projects as ideal types within the transactional perspective; they are initial steps, even somewhat exploratory, but they do represent an effort to change our ways of thinking about how to study phenomena.

I am particularly intrigued by this worldview because of a theme that runs through both Pepper's (1942) and Dewey and Bentley's (1949) writings. They provided examples of how physics and biology could adequately account for many phenomena without embracing a transactional perspective. However, they also noted that great strides had been made in some areas only after a more dynamic, holistic approach was adopted. More recently, Keller (1985) reviewed the literature in biology and showed that major advances in DNA research occurred only when researchers began to study complex rather than single-cell organisms, and when they abandoned the idea that DNA was a separate "master" and adopted the view that it was integral to the organism and its environment.

Dewey and Bentley stressed that different worldviews are adequate for particular kinds of problems and levels of analysis. Keller noted that the "master" model of DNA complemented the more holistic one. Similarly, psychological phenomena can be fruitfully studied from nontransactional perspectives, but it is exciting to consider the kinds of advances that might be made within such a framework.

Implications for Applied Social Psychology

At the beginning of this chapter, I suggested that the transactional worldview would be relevant to applied social psychology because its holistic approach fits the applied researcher's need to address problems and organizations as total and complex entities. Throughout the chapter, I have attempted to provide a structure for such holistic analyses.

First, it is essential to consider the total situation—the people, psychological processes, social and physical environment, and temporal qualities. In Altman and Rogoff's transactional worldview, these aspects are considered to be mutually defining, and they should be measured and studied with this point in mind. Therefore we should study aspects at their "interface," that is, selecting features of people and place that fit together, and focusing on the relations among aspects rather than thinking of the aspects as separate entities.

The idea of "mutual definition" can be difficult to grasp, especially since we are so accustomed to thinking in terms of simple causality, or at our most complex, mutual causality. So let me propose, as a close approximation, the form of transactionalism that guided Lazarus and Folkman (1984). In their view, people and their social environment are separate aspects; however, these aspects are mutually influencing and *become something new* in the process of a transaction.

> Another distinguishing feature of transactional thought, the one that gives the term *transaction* a quality missing in the concept of interaction, is that transaction implies a newly created level of abstraction in which the separate person and environment elements are joined together to form a new relational meaning. In interaction, particularly in statistical analyses that fractionate the variances of a cause-and-effect sequence . . . , the interacting variables retain their separate identities. From a transactional perspective, the characteristics of the separate variables are subsumed. (p. 294)

This view is subtly different from the idea of mutual definition, but is a useful way to become accustomed to thinking more transactionally.

A second opportunity to relate the transactional worldview to applied social psychology is to pay more attention to temporal qualities as significant aspects of psychological phenomena. At a minimum, this means being more explicit about the timing of interventions and data collection, so that they are intrinsic to ongoing events, rather than being imposed at the researcher's or organization's convenience. In addition, this means paying more attention to the various temporal qualities outlined here and elaborated elsewhere (Werner, Altman, & Oxley, 1985; Werner & Haggard, 1985).

An implication of the temporal qualities that was not addressed by us in our work on neighborhood cohesiveness is that we ought to be studying how events unfold over time, rather than studying snapshots or single instances of behavior. This is a challenging task, but there are a number of ways of approaching it. For example, M. M. Chemers (personal communication) is able to study group interaction processes by planting certain information with different group members and observing the extent to which that information shows up in the group's final solution. Lazarus and Folkman (1984) reported research in which data were collected on three different occasions in order to tap the varying psychological experiences of a difficult and anxiety-provoking exam. They found distinct differences in reported emotions at each stage, corresponding to "changes in the *meaning* of the person-environment relationship as that relationship shifted throughout the examination process" (p. 295).

Fisher's (1982) suggestion that we measure patterns of activity over time also shows promise as a way of measuring emerging processes. In my own work (Werner, Brown, & Damron, 1981), I have observed sequences of behavior, or the patterns of verbal and nonverbal behaviors, used by interlopers when effecting an intrusion in a game arcade. We had trained confederates to look possessive or unpossessive of a video game, and we found some evidence that verbal and nonverbal behaviors were more likely to be complementary (i.e., to communicate the same information) when the machine appeared to be in use by another person than when the other's control of the machine was more ambiguous. Thus the intruder's patterns of behavior shifted according to the needs of the situation.

None of these illustrations fully captures the idea of dynamic changing processes because each simply takes snapshots at different points in the process. We await the development of moving picture technology for a fuller examination of changing and evolving processes.

A final way in which applied social psychology can utilize this worldview is to begin to scrutinize its philosophy of science. As noted above, the philosophy that guides the transactional worldview has three primary features: formal cause rather than material, efficient, or final forms of determinism; an appreciation for both unique events and general principles; and a desire to understand phenomena from many perspectives. I think that applied social psychologists can especially resonate to the idea that every situation is unique. People with whom they work in the community need to understand their setting in its uniqueness, and understand whether relationships among variables observed in other settings are at all relevant to their particular circumstances. Similarly, applied social psychologists can appreciate the need to see their setting from multiple perspectives; the leader has a different perspective than the follower; individuals at different levels in the administrative hierarchy have different information, different pressures, different constituencies, and so forth; and all of these perspectives should be considered in an analysis of the organization. This may seem excessively complex; however, if one understands the setting as a complex holistic phenomenon, one will be in a better position to know how it functions, what prior research is and is not relevant to this particular place, and how innovations will affect individuals at all levels—that is, one will be a better psychologist.

Notes

1. For greater detail about this study see Oxley et al. (1986) and Werner, Altman, Oxley, and Haggard (in press). Altman deserves credit as the originator and driving force behind the study of Christmas Street.

2. Research in this neighborhood began as an analysis of the association between neighboring relationships and defense of territory, and the sample was drawn to permit comparison of burglarized and nonburglarized homes on cul-de-sacs or through streets. That sampling procedure involved matching nonburglarized with burglarized homes, and can be reviewed in more detail in Brown (1983). For additional information, see Brown and Werner (1985); Werner et al. (1984); and Werner, Peterson-Lewis, and Brown (1985).

3. For additional information, see the following references: community action groups (Pretsby & Wandersman, 1985; Steiner & Mark, 1985; Unger & Wandersman, 1983; Wandersman et al., 1985); sidewalk ballets (Jacobs, 1961; Seamon, 1979); secondary territory (Altman, 1975; Brown, 1980, 1983); surveillance zones (Rowles, 1980, 1981).

4. For this sample, unless otherwise noted, correlations are partial correlations, controlling for number of children in the respondent's home and number of homes on the block.

References

Altman, I. (1975). *The environment and social behavior: Privacy, personal space, territory, and crowding.* Monterey, CA: Brooks/Cole.

Altman, I., & Chemers, M. (1980). *Culture and environment.* Monterey, CA: Brooks/-Cole.

Altman, I., & Gauvain, M. (1981). A cross-cultural and dialectic analysis of homes. In L. Liben, A. Patterson, & N. Newcombe (Eds.), *Spatial representation and behavior across the life span* (pp. 283-319). New York: Academic Press.

Altman, I., & Rogoff, B. (1987). World views in psychology: Trait, interactionist, organismic, and transactionalist approaches. In D. Stokols & I. Altman (Eds.), *Handbook of environmental psychology* (Vol. 1: pp. 7-40). New York: John Wiley.

Altman, I., Vinsel, A., & Brown, B. B. (1981). Dialectic conceptions in social psychology: An application to social penetration and privacy regulation. In L. Berkowitz (Ed.), *Advances in experimental social psychology* (Vol. 14, pp. 108-160). New York: Academic Press.

Ammer, C. (1972). *Harper's dictionary of music.* New York: Barnes & Noble.

Barker, R. G. (1968). *Ecological psychology: Concepts and methods for studying the environment of human behavior.* Palo Alto, CA: Stanford University Press.

Brown, B. B. (1980). *Territoriality, defensible space, and residential burglary: An environmental analysis.* Unpublished master's thesis, University of Utah.

Brown, B. B. (1983). *Territoriality, street form, and residential burglary: Social and environmental analyses.* Unpublished doctoral dissertation, University of Utah.

Brown, B. B., & Werner, C. M. (1985). Social cohesiveness, territoriality, and holiday decorations: The influence of cul-de-sacs. *Environment & Behavior, 17*, 539-565.

Cantor, N., & Kihlstrom, J. F. (Eds.). (1981). *Personality, cognition and social interaction.* Hillsdale, NJ: Lawrence Erlbaum.

Coyne, J. C., & Lazarus, R. S. (1980). Cognitive style, stress perception, and coping. In I. Kutash, L. B. Schlesinger, & Associates (Eds.), *Handbook on stress and anxiety: Contemporary knowledge, theory, and treatment.* San Francisco: Jossey-Bass.

Dewey, J., & Bentley, A. F. (1949). *Knowing and the known.* Boston: Beacon.

Endler, N. S. (1981). Situational aspects of interactional psychology. In D. Magnusson (Ed.). *Toward a psychology of situations: An interactional perspective* (pp. 361-373). Hillsdale, NJ: Lawrence Erlbaum.

Endler, N. S., & Edwards, J. (1978). Person by treatment interactions in personality research. In L. A. Pervin & M. Lewis (Eds.), *Perspectives in interactional psychology* (pp. 141-169). New York: Plenum.

Endler, N. S., & Magnusson, D. (1976). Toward an interactional psychology of personality. *Psychological Bulletin, 83*, 956-974.

Erikson, K. T. (1976). *Everything in its path.* New York: Simon & Schuster.

Fisher, L. (1982). Transactional theories but individual assessment: A frequent discrepancy in family research. *Family Process, 21*, 313-320.

Fried, M. (1963). Grieving for a lost home. In L. J. Duhl (Ed.), *The urban condition.* New York: Basic Books.

Fried, M., & Gleicher, P. (1961). Some sources of residential satisfaction in an urban slum. *Journal of the American Institute of Planners, 27*, 305-315.

Fried, M., & Levin, J. (1968). Some social functions of the urban slum. In B. J. Frieden & R. Morris (Eds.), *Urban planning and social policy* (pp. 60-83). New York: Basic Books.

Gibson, J. J. (1979). *An ecological approach to visual perception.* Boston: Houghton-Mifflin.

Ginsburg, G. P. (1980). Situated action: An emerging paradigm. In L. Wheeler (Ed.), *Review of personality and social psychology* (Vol. 1, pp. 295-325). Newbury Park, CA: Sage.

Greenbaum, P. E., & Greenbaum, S. D. (1981). Territorial personalization: Group identity and social interaction in a Slavic-American neighborhood. *Environment & Behavior, 13*, 574-589.

Hays, R. B., & Oxley, D. (1986). Social network development and functioning during a life transition. *Journal of Personality and Social Psychology, 50,* 305-313.

Hill, C. T., Rubin, Z., & Peplau, L. A. (1976). Breakups before marriage: The end of 103 affairs. *Journal of Social Issues, 32,* (1), 147-168.

Jacobs, J. (1961). *The death and life of great American cities.* New York: Vintage Books.

Keller, E. F. (1985). *Reflections on gender and science.* New Haven, CT: Yale University Press.

Korosec-Serfaty, P. (Ed.). (1976). *Appropriation of space.* Proceedings of the Third International Architectural Psychology Conference, Louis Pasteur University, Strasbourg, France.

Korosec-Serfaty, P. (1978, September). Formes de l'accueil et du reject dans l'habitat: Fonctions et statut de l'entree d'immeuble. *Neuf Revue Europeenne d'Architecture, 76,* 25-32.

Korosec-Serfaty, P. (1985). Experience and use of the dwelling. In I. Altman & C. Werner (Eds.), *Home environments: Human behavior and the environment* (Vol. 8, pp. 65-86). New York: Plenum.

Lawrence, R. (1982). A psychological-spatial approach for architectural design and research. *Journal of Environmental Psychology, 2,* 37-51.

Lazarus, R. S. (1966). *Psychological stress and the coping process.* New York: McGraw-Hill.

Lazarus, R. S., & Folkman, S. (1984). *Stress, appraisal, and coping.* New York: Springer.

Lazarus, R. S., & Launier, R. (1978). Stress-related transactions between person and environment. In L. A. Pervin & M. Lewis (Eds.), *Perspectives in interactional psychology* (pp. 287-327). New York: Plenum.

Mitchell, H. E., & Byrne, D. (1973). The defendant's dilemma: Effects of jurors' attitudes and authoritarianism on judicial decisions. *Journal of Personality and Social Psychology, 25,* 123-129.

Oxley, D., Haggard, L. M., Werner, C. M., & Altman, I. (1986). Transactional qualities of neighborhood social networks: A case study of "Christmas Street." *Environment & Behavior, 18*: 640-677.

Pepper, S. C. (1942). *World hypotheses: A study in evidence.* Berkeley: University of California Press.

Pepper, S. C. (1967). *Concept and quality: A world hypothesis.* LaSalle, IL: Open Court.

Petonnet, C. (1973). *Those people: The subculture of a housing project.* Westport, CT: Greenwood.

Pervin, L. A. (1968). Performance and satisfaction as a function of individual-environment fit. *Psychological Bulletin, 69,* 56-68.

Pratt, G. (1981). The house as an expression of social worlds. In J. S. Duncan (Ed.), *Housing and identity: Cross-cultural perspectives* (pp. 135-180). London: Croon Helm.

Pretsby, J., & Wandersman, A. (1985). An empirical exploration of a framework of organizational viability: Maintaining block organizations. *Journal of Applied Behavioral Science, 21,* 287-305.

Price, R. H., & Bouffard, D. L. (1974). Behavioral appropriateness and situational constraints as dimensions of social behavior. *Journal of Personality and Social Psychology, 30,* 579-586.

Rakowski, W. (1979). Future time perspective in later adulthood: Review and research directions. *Experimental Aging Research, 5,* 43-88.

Rowles, G. D. (1980). Growing old "inside": Aging and attachment to place in an Appalachian community. In D. Datan & N. Lohmann (Eds.), *Transitions of aging* (pp. 153-170). New York: Academic Press.

Rowles, G. D. (1981). The surveillance zone as meaningful space for the aged. *Gerontologist, 21*, 304-311.

Rowles, G. D. (1983). Place and personal identity in old age: Observations from Appalachia. *Journal of Environmental Psychology, 3*, 299-313.

Rychlak, J. F. (1977). *The psychology of rigorous humanism.* New York: John Wiley.

Seamon, D. (1979). *A geography of the lifeworld: Movement, rest, and encounter.* New York: St. Martin's Press.

Smith, T. F., & Rhodewalt, F. (1986). On states, traits and processes: A transactional alternative to the individual difference assumptions in Type A behavior and physiological reactivity. *Journal of Research in Personality, 20*: 229-251.

Spiegel, J. (1971). *Transactions: The interplay between individual, family, and society* (J. Papajohn, Ed.). New York: Science House.

Steiner, D. D., & Mark, M. M. (1985). The impact of a community action group: An illustration of the potential of time series analysis for the study of community groups. *American Journal of Community Psychology, 13*, 13-30.

Stokols, D. (1981). Group X place transactions: Some neglected issues in psychological research on settings. In D., Magnusson (Ed.), *Toward a psychology of situations: An interactional perspective.* Hillsdale, NJ: Lawrence Erlbaum.

Unger, D. G., & Wandersman, A. (1983). Neighboring and its role in block organizations: An exploratory report. *American Journal of Community Psychology, 11*, 291-300.

Unger, D. G., & Wandersman, A. (1985). The importance of neighbors: The social, cognitive, and affective components of neighboring. *American Journal of Community Psychology, 13*, 139-169.

Wandersman, A., Florin, P., Chavis, D., Rich, R., & Pretsby, J. (1985, November). Getting together and getting things done. Psychology Today, 19, pp. 64 ff.

Werner, C. M. Altman, I., & Oxley, D. (1985). Temporal aspects of homes: A transactional perspective. In I. Altman & C. M. Werner (Eds.), *Home environments: Human behavior and the environment* (Vol. 8, pp. 1-32). New York: Plenum.

Werner, C. M., Altman, I., Oxley, D., & Haggard, L. M. (in press). People, place and time: A transactional analysis of neighborhood social networks. In W. Jones & D. Perlman (Eds.), *Advances in interpersonal relationships.* Greenwich, CT: JAI Press.

Werner, C. M., Brown, B. B., & Damron, G. (1981). Territorial marking in a game arcade. *Journal of Personality and Social Psychology, 41*, 1094-1104.

Werner, C. M., Brown, B. B., & Peterson-Lewis, S. (1984, June). *The individuality/communality and accessibility/inaccessibility dialectics in Christmas decorations.* Paper presented at meeting of Environmental Design Research Association, San Luis Obispo, CA.

Werner, C. M., & Haggard, L. (1985). Temporal qualities of interpersonal relationships. In M. L. Knapp & G. R. Miller (Eds.), *Handbook of interpersonal communication* (pp. 59-99). Newbury Park, CA: Sage.

Werner, C. M., Haggard, L. M., Altman, I., & Oxley, D. (in press). Temporal qualities of traditions: A comparison of Christmas Street and the Zuni Shalako. In J. E. McGrath (Ed.), *Research toward a social psychology of time.* Newbury Park, CA: Sage.

Werner, C. M., Kagehiro, D. K., & Strube, M. J. (1982). Conviction proneness and the authoritarian juror: Inability to disregard information or attitudinal bias? *Journal of Applied Psychology, 67*, 629-636.

Werner, C. M., Peterson-Lewis, S., & Brown, B. B. (1985, June). *Perceived "friendliness" of home exteriors.* Paper presented at meeting of Environmental Design Research Association, New York.

White, B. J., Alter, R., & Rardin, M. (1965). Authoritarianism, dogmatism, and usage of conceptual categories. *Journal of Personality and Social Psychology, 2*, 293-295.

Wicker, A. W. (1979). *An introduction to ecological psychology.* Monterey, CA: Brooks/Cole.

Wicker, A. W. (1987). An expanded conceptual framework for analyzing behavior settings. In D. Stokols & I. Altman (Eds.), *Handbook of environmental psychology* (Vol. 1, pp. 613-654). New York: John Wiley.

3

Forming Groups for
the Good of All

ALVIN ZANDER

Many phenomena in interpersonal behavior have not received the attention they deserve because, as we sometimes say, they are "not researchable." To be not researchable means that it is inconvenient to get reliable measures or even elementary facts about the matter at hand. Two of my favorite examples of studiously ignored questions are these starkly simple-minded ones: Why do people try to organize a group? What leads them to favor the purpose they choose for their group? Although these issues have been largely neglected by researchers and practical-minded persons, they are not trivial topics because answers to them would help us better understand many things members do in, and in behalf of, their organizations. I shall try to shed some light on these questions in this chapter.

A group cannot be without a reason for being. This simple fact colors a group's nature because its purpose determines how group members function as a body and persist as an ensemble. Thus there is an ubiquitous connection between a group's characteristics and its purposes.

I became interested in the purposes of groups while conducting a program of investigations into the origins and consequences of group goals on tasks that required physical activity and overt coordination among members. In those studies, my attention was fixed on quantifiable goals ranging from easy to hard. I examined how members modify the goals they prefer for their group and how these objectives affect members' performances in behalf of their unit. That series of field studies and laboratory experiments is described and interpreted in my book, *Motives and Goals in Groups* (1971). The results reported there demonstrate that a member's motivation to have his or her group succeed closely resembles (in its dynamics) people's individual motivation to succeed on their own. These findings should interest students of the need for achievement because they broaden the basis for understanding a person's hope for success. People who are members of a group do not always work for themselves alone; their group's success is important to them as well.

The ends that members work toward in many organizations, however, are more loosely defined, broader in scope, and more humanistic than the goals relating to the hard or easy tasks that we asked subjects to work on while studying their goal-oriented behavior. Such general purposes are valuable to society as a whole because they involve politics, religion, culture, education, welfare—many different aspects of organizations and of society. These larger purposes are affected by members' values, motives, or emotions, and by qualities of the organization itself. My earlier research offered little help in understanding such abstract purposes in groups, so I set out to learn more about them.

The ideas presented here are taken from my recent book, *The Purposes of Groups and Organizations* (1985), which draws more on my experience in life than on the results of empirical research. I approach our two questions (Why do people create a group? Why do they choose a particular purpose for their group?) through the eyes of an organizer, manager, or consultant of a group, and I try to see whether a more fully developed social psychology of group purposes could enlighten practitioners and scholars on these two issues, and if so, in what ways.

The kind of group I have in mind is a formal organization, an enduring body with established characteristics, such as requirements for membership, a name, a charter, a program, and officers, rather than a temporary association of people without these qualities, such as a picnic, citizens' discussion meeting, working party, or busload of tourists. I am mainly interested in units of a size that will allow some interaction and interdependency among members. By a group's *purpose*, I mean a desirable state of affairs that members intend to bring about through their joint efforts. It is desirable because members foresee, preferably in a uniform way, the satisfaction they can derive from moving toward that end and achieving it. Usually, but not always, it is a plan that organizers put into place prior to taking steps in, or for, the group. The impact of a group's purpose on participants depends at the very least on whether persons in the group know and understand this aim. If the objective is publicly accepted by most members (which at once grants it a degree of validity), and if it describes a course that is understood similarly by members, this shared view has the weight of a vow about how they will guide their collaborative behavior in the group. Ideally, each member expects other members to adhere to requirements that this pledge places on all. The chances are good thereafter that they will press one another to think and behave in accord with the group's purpose.

I assume for our present discussion that a group's purpose, aim, objective, mission, rationale, or goal are conceptually similar. In technical parlance, however, some of these terms are given a special meaning. A purpose of a group, for instance, is usually considered to be a relatively loosely defined, abstract, and value-laden end. In contrast, a goal ordinarily refers to a sought-for level of achievement that is precisely defined. I will consider purposes of both kinds, vague and clear, as well as ones that differ in other characteristics. In accord with the common convention, I will use the term *group purpose* when the unit's end point is less measurable or is inaccessible, use the term *goal* when the hoped-for level of achievement for the group is quite exactly delineated, and use other terms noted above when this distinction concerning clarity is not important.

Functions Served by Groups

Because a group is created for a purpose, it would be helpful to identify and classify some of the most basic or inclusive among all such purposes. One way to seek these primary purposes is to look into the programs and plans of social entities in ancient times. What impulses led people to organize then? Were group objectives different long ago from ones in groups today? Reliable records allow us to go back as far as 300 B.C. I will start there and selectively illustrate a few of the group purposes that developed (some for the first time) during the following

1500 years. These remarks are based on my notes from reading history books while watching for occasional comments about groups, so the sources of these notes are too widely scattered to cite. Perhaps a proper historian will some day prepare a history of the ways that people have created and used groups.

In the very first societies, families banded together to create tribes if the male or female parent was a descendant of a common ancestor, or if they worshipped the same deity, followed a particular chieftain, or needed one another for help, protection, or procreation. People in tribes jointly built walls, dug ditches, ambushed animals, dragged fish nets, cut wood, stole from neighbors, worshipped gods, or created shelters. For their mutual protection, tribes collaborated to form a clan, and a wider community then was created to control relations between clans. People clung to the family in peace, to the clan in a crisis. In places where many persons had to cooperate throughout a large geographical area (for example, to control floods in Egypt and China), workers from widely separated villages were coopted by powerful strangers to build dams and ditches for irrigation beneficial to all. These construction companies constituted an early form of bureaucracy. By 300 B.C., laborers in villages of China formed workers' guilds that defined strict standards of behavior toward distant superiors and village elders; these bodies survive today with many of the same beliefs.

In Athens, at about the same time, membership in the Senate was restricted to wealthier men. There were no political parties, but clubs were formed by the "haves" to work against granting the vote to members of the middle and lower classes. The latter in turn formed clubs to influence the views of the senators.

By 50 A.D., the slaves in Rome, who were one-fourth of the population, sought to relieve their unpleasant days through collectives called *collegia*. These were unions for each of many types of labor. They provided mutual help, emergency funds, and social events for members. They turned into political organizations when they sold their votes to demagogues. Later, they helped Christianity to pervade Rome after members heard leaders of this new faith promise a heavenly quality of life following death—a new religious idea at that time and place, though already a familiar notion elsewhere.

Christianity popularized a process of worship in groups where participants took active parts in religious meetings. Saint Paul traveled around the Mediterranean Sea area organizing congregations and subsequently sent advice to these bodies on how to maintain their assemblies. He also instructed them that members were to obey managers at work and leaders in government, regardless of the behavior shown by these superiors. A central church administration arose in Rome for controlling the local groups, and this headquarters eventually fostered many other groups designed to legitimize preferred beliefs, punish people who disagreed with the accepted creed, build temples for religious activities, and provide sanctuary for persons who wished to withdraw from secular life. In subsequent years, church bodies were developed to run the state as well as the church, including armies, schools, hospitals, police, and financial institutions. Other religions formed groups for many of the same purposes. The Brethren of Purity, a philosophical society, was created in Baghdad to study and compare Greek philosophy, Christian ethics, Sufi thought, mysticism, Shia politics, and Moslem law. The Brethren issued 51 tracts, presenting the world's first unitary system of science, religion, and philosophy.

Greed and aggression fostered the formation of many groups in those days. The tightly organized armies of Rome and the fighting units in other lands inspired by the arrival of Roman troops are well-known examples. Gangs of mobile thieves raided mile-long caravans of camels in Arabia and took the traders as slaves, while the Scandinavian countries provided Viking pillagers who stole from homes and churches throughout Europe and Asia. Several kingdoms financed crusades to take "holy" lands from non-Christians or sent out pirate bands to rob merchant ships on the high seas.

International traders among countries of northern Europe formed a corporation to defend their ships against piracy. This Hanseatic League, as it came to be called, wrote and enforced rules to regulate and protect the commercial interaction among merchants from each nation. Gradually, the League's priorities shifted and it became an oppressive organization engaging in questionable trading practices, forcing cities to join the League against their will, creating selfish monopolies, and controlling commerce to the advantage of the traders. As is often true in today's large firms, these actions and their managers were beyond the reach of law (Stone, 1975).

In sourthern Europe, by the year 1400, guilds of workers and merchants in varied businesses were strong enough to outweigh the local government in influencing the behavior of residents. Guilds required members to follow its rules, not those of the city, and to settle disputes in the guild's courts rather than the city courts. Student guilds were extraordinarily powerful. They paid the salaries of the faculty, boycotted poor teachers, required professors to swear obedience to the student union, regulated hours of classroom appearances, fined instructors for not covering what they had agreed to teach, evaluated the skill of each lecturer, and reported deficiencies to the student union. Modern youth have much to learn from those of 500 years ago!

Perhaps the first advisory council for evaluating a research proposal was appointed by King John II of Portugal. This committee was asked to judge an exploratory investigation proposed by an Italian named Columbus, in which he planned to reach eastern Asia by sailing west across the Atlantic Ocean. The council advised the king not to provide the funds sought by Columbus because his estimate of the distance across the Atlantic was too low and a trial trip would be a waste of taxpayers' money. As you know, the queen favored this research and gave Columbus a grant on her own.

The first printed books stimulated new kinds of groups. Few ordinary people could make out printed words, so groups of men would pool their money and hire a skilled person to read to them in taverns, on the job, or on the streets. These readings and the subsequent discussions among listeners stirred the beginnings of the Protestant Reformation (Boorstin, 1983).

What observations can we make about this odd sample of organizations? We see, first of all, that humans centuries ago established entities for many reasons. These purposes included responding to fear, danger, or hostility; making sure people were fair to one another; providing food, leisure, fun, and social welfare for members; completing tasks too big for one person; helping clarify philosophical notions; worshiping a god; making laws for family, tribe, clan, community, assembly, senate, corporation, guild, or church; changing the beliefs of others in the society; and arbitrating disputes between individuals and groups. Many bodies changed their purposes from time to time, while others persisted in their set course for centuries.

Nowadays, similar group purposes still abound, and the interests of organizers are often like those of earlier years. We can list more aims of groups today, but not dramatically different ones, though more purposes exist in all kinds of bodies than we will ever know. Perhaps a greater proportion of group purposes in very early times took care of physiological needs and of desires for physical security than is true today, and currently we surely have more technically sophisticated groups for manufacturing products, storing information, filling leisure time, and murdering one another than people did earlier. All in all, however, most of the reasons people have for forming groups in current times existed in some of humanity's first groups.

Several conclusions are notable. Individuals create a group when they develop a purpose that collaboration with colleagues will help them meet. Although groups are organized for different functions, all units are alike in one respect: They are intended to be useful to members, nonmembers, or both. When desires change among those who have a stake in a group, some of the purposes of that body shift unless conditions exist that are intended to prevent any reshaping of the group's ends, as in an army or a church.

Conditions Fostering the Formation of Groups

I take it for granted that people form a group if they believe a specific situation should be modified and if they also believe that actions by a solo person cannot create this change. At least four facilitating conditions (discussed in detail below) must exist if organizers are to progress toward developing a new unit. The first of these has already been implied.

(1) Conditions in the environment, or in the behavior of influential persons, are unsatisfactory or suggest an opportunity for desirable change. Examples of discomfort over unfavorable situations, often called grievances, are students' complaints about the relevance of college teaching, or about their school's investments in companies doing business in South Africa; citizens' dislike of air pollution; customers' dismay over downtown traffic; mothers' anger over drunken drivers; people's resistance to high taxes; citizens' fear of immigrant groups who have unfamiliar ways of life; or workers' dread of losing employment. Examples of opportunities than can inspire new groups include chances to help one another learn, convalesce, or create; make and offer a new product for sale; outwit old rivals; develop new knowledge; or provide assistance for people who have limitations or disabilities.

Either a grievance or an opportunity is a necessary but not sufficient condition for forming a unit, for people do not always organize when there is an adequate stimulus to do so. Take terrorist gangs as an instance. Such bodies usually have a grievance they want to publicize widely. Action by these groups, according to Laquer (1977), occurs more often in democratic societies, where grievances are undoubtedly less common than in dictatorships. Yet terrorist gangs seldom develop in the democratic Scandinavian countries, although no one knows why not. Laquer states that the only thing one can confidently say about terrorist groups is that their members are always young—in some places and times that may be a sufficient source of discomfort.

(2) A different and satisfactory state of affairs is conceived of by organizers. A potential developer of a group must have new ideas about what could be done differently and how these innovations might improve things. The invention of a group's mission is an intellectual procedure in which some or many members take part, and it occurs in accordance with social processes of thought, preference, decision, and motivation. Surprisingly often, a group's creation is initially inspired by just one person who assembles sympathetic colleagues, garners needed resources, and gives this set of individuals faith in itself. A prophet converts listeners to join a cult. An executive creates a committee within a larger organization. A coach develops a basketball team. Or, a concerned person starts an action group, union, club, community coordinating council, association for civil rights, or militant cell.

Remarkably little objective evidence exists about the ways in which recruits are gathered and taught their parts in a group's proceedings. It seems sensible to assume as a basic postulate that bystanders will not be interested in joining a body unless it has a reason for its existence and they understand the reason. Otherwise, neophyte members would not know what benefits the group offers and why colleagues behave as they do. Neophytes would also ask themselves questions such as: Are their individual efforts appropriate for the organization? Will their performances be fairly evaluated by fellow members? Is the group doing what it is supposed to do?

I emphasize such questions because some scholars hold that most groups never develop a purpose. Other students of groups (e.g., Karl Weick, 1979) propose that responsible members name a purpose for the group only after members have taken joint actions and then need an objective to justify or explain these steps. Such a purpose, Weick points out, is not an inducing agent for participants; it is a rationalization for, or an interpretation of, their behavior.

Although Weick's ideas fit many groups, we must keep in mind that members—even ones who act first and later decide why they did so—initially came together in the group for some reason, and the group can be said to exist for that specific reason (or purpose). Because members are part of the unit, they probably are aware of and accepting of the unit's aim. This initial purpose describes what they *expect* to happen. Since at first they have no past experience with the group, the purpose cannot be the product of what occurs there. People thus require, ahead of time, that the group have an objective before they will take part in it. Perhaps a good proportion of the groups that Weick describes as creating a group purpose after members act are in the process of changing these purposes, modifying them, or creating new ones. Or perhaps they are merely making them more measurable, or evaluating their group's progress.

(3) Members believe they will achieve a more satisfying state of affairs through activities by the assembled set of persons. In order for new joiners to become committed belongers, organizers and managers must give recruits confidence that their unit can accomplish its declared aims. Writers like Barnard (1938), Cohen and March (1974), Likert (1961), and Peters and Waterman (1982) urge leaders of established units to behave in ways that help members believe their organization will reach its long-term purposes. In recruiting for business firms, however, as Wanous (1980) makes clear in an extensive study, a "head-hunter" often sells a prospect on joining the organization by painting an excessively rosy picture of the gains the job will provide, while playing down any demands the organization will make of the worker. As a result, the new employee often works for private goals rather than those of the firm. However, I suspect, a recruiter is less likely to make enticing promises about a neophyte's personal gains under conditions where the firm is not in need of many employees, the candidate is not a good prospect, good-quality members are easy to find, or the organization is built on the belief that the group's achievements are more important than the rewards to individual employees. I also anticipate that groups outside the world of business are more likely to emphasize the value of the group's goals for the group as a whole or for society at large rather than for the benefit of an individual belonger. Such speculations are researchable and worthy of study.

(4) Conditions in the community encourage persons to establish a unit and to take part in its activities. Some people inherently dislike being in a group or working for one—any group—and would rather take on a solo task. In several studies of students and of female workers in a factory, about two-thirds reported that they preferred to work for their personal benefit instead of having a part in working for a group goal (Zander, 1971; Zander & Armstrong, 1972). The possibility that

there is a learned and lasting disposition either to approach group membership or to avoid it has never been studied well. However, these research findings are fascinating when one recalls that 9 out of 10 wage earners in the United States are employed as members of some organization (Funk, 1982).

Persons are more likely to create a group if the surrounding situation supports such a move or, at the least, offers little resistance to it. Some of the possible supporting circumstances are frequent contacts among potential members, similarity among potential members, benefits available to members, laws that require the creation of a given kind of body, or presence of a way of life in a given place that enhances such activity. We know, for instance, that individuals more often jointly create or join a group if they live in the same neighborhood and share the same sidewalk, entrance door, or mailbox area (Festinger, Schachter, & Back, 1950). People from the same workplace, courtyard, church, or pub are more commonly found in any given other organization than ones who seldom see each other. And much evidence indicates that persons who are similar in interests, values, or problems come together more readily (Berscheid & Walster, 1978; Kanter, 1972; Zander, 1977). Finally, in order for persons to perform certain legally constrained activities, laws require them to form designated kinds of organizations such as school boards, company director's committees, corporations, churches, banks, unions, cooperatives, or partnerships in business (Funk, 1982).

Other facilitators to group formation exist in society. According to Scott (1982), these include conditions where a high proportion of the relevant population can read print, many of the people live in cities, some political unrest exists, citizens compete with one another for resources, and complex roles are available for people to perform. Traditions also influence the way groups are formed and employed. Japan and the United States, to illustrate, have constrasting missions for their social entities. Japanese put greater weight on the good of the group while Americans cede most importance to the good of the member. The reasons for groups, and the parts played by them, differ from culture to culture in ways that are worthy of closer psychological research.

Matters that must be attended to if a group or behavior setting is to be activated have been described by Wicker (in press), who holds that five types of resources must be used. He defines a *resource* as a state, person, or object that can contribute to a planned situation. The first resource is people, ones who know what is expected of them in that circumstance.

Next, relevant tools, supplies, or equipment are necessary. Third, appropriate space must be available for the activities to be carried out. Fourth, there is a need for specific or general knowledge that bears on the group's operations. Finally, reserves of money, supplies, plans, or persons should be ready for use as needed. In order for a group to be developed, says Wicker, the required resources must be located, assembled, and given a place in a planned program. This process of finding, organizing, and gathering resources demands that people who are developing a group devote their time, energy, and money toward fulfilling what they have in mind for that body.

All in all, the formation of a group requires an evaluation of current circumstances, an appraisal of what can be accomplished through joint effort, an arousal of shared confidence in such activity, and a plan both to use resources as well as to overcome barriers to group action. Clearly, these steps all involve socially motivated behavior, a topic we will consider a little later.

Properties of Group Purposes

A group's objective has certain qualities that can influence members' behavior. Each of these properties may vary in strength across different purposes and different groups. It is important to note that more or less of a given characteristic is not necessarily good or bad.

The most familiar among these properties are the clarity of the purpose and the clarity of the path to its fulfillment. I call these *measurability* and *accessibility* of the purpose, respectively. The *measurability* of a group's objective denotes the degree of precision possible when one is determining whether a group has lived up to its intentions. A measurable objective describes exactly what change should be observed if one is to say that the purpose of the body has been met. Examples of precisely measurable objectives are numbers of dollars taken in, packages delivered, points made, students graduated, skills learned, friendships developed, articles written, or crises calmed. An unmeasurable purpose is more vaguely described, and therefore one cannot reliably tell whether or when the group has accomplished its mission. Instances of less exactly measurable ends are to advance international understanding, to be a high-quality organization, to improve the culture of a community, or to reduce the impact of human activity on the environment.

It is easy to think of organizations that prefer or require measurable objectives if the bodies are to function at all; I will note examples later on. Other groups, however, often state an objective in unmeasurable terms for good reasons. The objective may deliberately be made obscure because its authors cannot put its basic, usually abstract, ideas precisely, and they find that poetry does it better than prose. A purpose may also be worded loosely for strategic reasons. A vague statement, for instance, may serve as an acceptable front for a more exact but less acceptable aim (Etzioni, 1975). As actual illustrations, a local group claimed to be raising funds to help feed hungry citizens but really used its income for the personal pleasure of the founders; a mental hospital's stated public purposes that were not like the ones pursued by workers on the wards; a gang of bank robbers said they were a civil rights organization; and a camping supply house pretended to be a character-building organiza- tion. Another situation where a vague purpose may be helpful (for instance, a purpose like "community improvement") is when the purpose must cover all the varying interests of separate members; in this case the vagueness helps the groups avoid interpersonal conflict among persons who differ in their preferences. A nebulous objective also can be useful because it does not constrain the behavior of participants in organizations where members intentionally are given freedom to behave as they wish, so that they can heal themselves or learn or create in their own way. In groups where members are required to do work interdepen- dently, on the other hand, there is evidence that lack of a clear objective causes confusion and awkward relations among members (Hackman, 1985; Raven & Rietsema, 1957; Van de Ven, 1980). Accordingly, it seems reasonable that managers and members will prefer more measur- able objectives in bodies where accomplishment of a group task is important.

The *accessibility* of a group's purpose refers to the clarity of the path to accomplish it—that is, whether given activities in the group serve to move it toward attainment of its purpose. An accessible aim can be reached in known ways. An inaccessible one has no defined or definable path toward its attainment. Thus the accessibility of a purpose is the perceived probability that the paths being pursued in the group will take it to its objective. After a bit of practice, a T-maze for a rat has perfect accessibility because there is a known procedure that takes the rat to the goal box. A clinic's use of a new therapeutic method has unknown accessibility at the outset, but perhaps more later on. Reasonable accessibility undoubtedly requires adequate measurability. An inaccessi- ble objective causes consequences much like those noted for an unmeasurable one, and thus is usually avoided if the group must accomplish specific tasks.

Another property of a purpose is the degree to which it inspires *cooperativeness* versus competitiveness among members. Cooperativeness denotes readiness to help one another toward an outcome that is beneficial to the group as a whole. If each person's personal gain is a fair share of the group's total production, each member will usually work readily in behalf of the group's good. A *competitive* purpose, in contrast, allows each member to work directly for his or her own benefit, not for the gain of colleagues or of the group as a whole. The sharp differences in interpersonal relations among groups with cooperative versus competitive aims have been discussed in many places (e.g., Deutsch, 1973).

Other properties of group purposes can also generate notable effects. These include the purpose's *power* to change the behavior of members (or to weaken the impact of other purposes), susceptibility to alteration (called *flexibility*), substantive similarity to other purposes (called *consonance*), and the effort and resources required to attain it (called *difficulty*).

It seems, generally speaking, that group decision makers prefer properties for the group's purposes that will help the group to be most satisfying to members. In many groups, as an example, they would favor a purpose that is powerful rather than weak, measurable rather than unmeasurable, accessible rather than inaccessible, flexible rather than inflexible, a challenge rather than easy, and consonant rather than dissonant with other objectives of that group. But one can think of conditions that might cause members to prefer the latter characteristic in the pairs just cited—that is, to see value in a weak, unmeasurable, inaccessible, inflexible, or easy purpose. It would be desirable to learn more about the properties of group purposes, but I know of no research on such matters.

What Leads People to Favor a Particular Group Purpose?

The substantive content of a group's purpose is influenced by many things, including the problems that people wish to attack, the procedures they use in selecting an objective, the size of the group, the inclination of organizers regarding whether to seek help from supernatural sources, how members judge the goodness or badness of behaviors to be sponsored by the group, and the individual motives of members. I cannot take up all of these influences here, so I shall concentrate on the one most interesting to me: how their personal dispositions cause members to prefer particular purposes for their group. Other determinants of a group's objectives are discussed more fully in Zander (1985).

When individuals select a purpose for a newly assembled body, they not only seek to modify certain conditions through their joint efforts, they also want to satisfy individual desires aroused in them while they are in the group situation. These wishes affect the nature of the objectives they choose for their unit. Such motives of participants may be composed of either *self-oriented motives, group-oriented desires,* or both. Self-oriented motives cause people to seek *personal* pride, fun, help, purity, excitement, knowledge, or the relief of a worry. Group-oriented desires lead participants to seek certain states *for the group as a whole*—for instance, in respect to its productivity, success, influence, harmony among members, or nurturance of members.

A personal motive (ignoring group membership for the time being) is defined as a capacity to find satisfaction in the attainment of a particular incentive and a disposition to seek that satisfaction for oneself. An individual's *incentive* is a state or outcome that, when attained, promises to provide satisfaction for a relevant motive. For example, an individual with a motive to succeed has a tendency to be satisfied upon achieving a success, whereas a person with a motive to influence other people will derive satisfaction from inducing changes in others' behavior. Incentives vary in their incentive *value*; that is, they differ in the amount of satisfaction they promise to provide a person. The amount of value one assigns to a given incentive is not fixed; it can change as a result of one's reaction to attainment of the incentive or as a result of knowing others' reactions to that achievement. The *perceived probability* of an incentive is the likelihood, as one sees the matter, that the outcome that will generate satisfaction is attainable. In accord with a widely accepted approach to explaining individual behavior (Atkinson & Feather, 1966), I assume that strong motives or valued incentives will more surely affect a person's behavior if the perceived probability of attaining satisfaction is high.

Many groups are formed mainly to help an organizer fulfill his or her *self-oriented* motives. A merchant hires a staff to work for his financial profit, a politician recruits a campaign crew to help win an election, or a popular singer assembles a band of musicians to accompany her. A group also may come together to help one another fulfill personal motives that all share—for instance, artists who wish to exhibit their paintings, purchasers who seek to save money through creating a consumers' cooperative, or workers who are dissatisfied and want to improve their own working conditions. A group may define and develop one common personal motive for all: to lose weight, improve investments, or support sobriety. Or, members may decide to encourage a variety of dissimilar motives, each member on his or her own, with the group trying to assist all belongers in satisfying these personal motives. Art studios, research centers, and convalescent homes are units of this latter kind. In some groups, in contrast, people mainly meet to compete as rivals: individual-sport clubs, stock trading pits, college classrooms, and conferences of professors who read prepared papers to each other.

In groups that are formed to aid individuals in meeting their personal motives, I expect that participants will more often be concerned about achieving personal satisfactions than about what happens to the state, outcome, or effectiveness of the unit as a whole. This is not unusual or unacceptable in many quarters. Indeed, it is the basic assumption that most students of business firms make about profit-earning organizations. In some groups, however, even commercial ones, matters are reversed, and a primary interest of members is in what happens to the group as an entity, or in the effects members generate while acting jointly. Examples are citizen-action committees, manufacturing companies, or governmental fact-finding commissions. Here, the efforts of participants are devoted more to the good of the whole group than to the gains of each member.

In thinking about these latter, group-centered units, it is useful to employ group-level concepts framed to parallel those noted above for the individual. I have already used the term *group-oriented desire* to denote a member's wish for the group to attain a given state. I use the term *desire,* rather than *motive,* because this group interest of members is not an enduring disposition (like a motive) but a product of interpersonal interaction here-and-now within this particular organization; it does not apply to other social entities. The desire for the group, I assume, acts like a person's motive does, but the focus of the member's concern is the group's fate, not the individual's. A *group incentive* is a state or outcome of the group that, when attained, provides satisfaction for a member who has a given group-oriented desire.

A *group's purpose* is another name for a group incentive, but a group's purpose is not simply a member's private notion about what the group's purpose should be. Instead it is a shared public belief, because it is the product of a decision among some or all responsible members and is seen by many participants to be an attractive state of affairs for that body. Examples of such group incentives (purposes) are to win a contest, increase membership, achieve media coverage of the group's actions, improve a crew's efficiency, perform a surgical operation, or present a concert. The *strength of a group's incentive* (or purpose) is the amount of satisfaction its attainment is perceived to provide for members. The *perceived probability of the group's incentive* (or purpose) is the likelihood, as members see the matter, of attaining the group's objective. The member's tendency to act in accord with their desire for the group, I assume, is a resultant of the strength of the desire, times the strength of the group purpose, times the perceived probability of the group's purpose. These group-oriented aspects of purposeful group behavior are made stronger or weaker, and are largely determined, during the interaction among members. As a result, I believe that members' tendencies to act in behalf of a group's purpose are often more compelling than their tendency to act toward their own personal goals.

Kinds of Group-Oriented Desires

The desires members have for their group's condition may be of many different kinds. A familiar one is the desire for the group to succeed in a task. The purpose in this case is to complete movement toward the objective. One can speak about the strength of the desire for group success with respect to a particular purpose, and the probability of this achievement. A group may also have a desire to avoid group failure or to evade the consequences of failure. We can then talk of the strength of that desire, the probability of avoiding failure, and the negative value of achieving various goals (Zander, 1971, 1977).

A third kind of group-oriented desire is one for group-supported fun, and it will have accompanying purposes, each with their own value for members and their own probability of being attained. In a contrasting vein, members may desire that their group have influence to change the views or behavior of targeted persons in the community, such as bosses, members of the city council, young voters, or local businesspersons. In such a case, the desire for the group would be that it be influential; the purpose of the group would describe whom they wish to change, how, and perhaps by how much; and the members would see a particular degree of probability of achieving this purpose of their body.

Sources of Group-Oriented Desires

Where do group-oriented desires come from? In some cases, no doubt, they may stem from personal motives—individuals who have similar or conflicting personal motives may bargain or maneuver in order to ensure that the group's purpose will support their private motives. Cyert and March (1963) and Olson (1971) make such an assumption about organizations in the world of business, but this belief has never been closely studied. In situations where, at the outset, members put greater weight on personal satisfaction than on satisfaction with the group, the group-oriented desire may end up as a compromise that has little attraction for members.

The origin of participants' desire for their group is easier to understand when the unit is created to achieve some outcomes for the body as a whole, regardless of its relevance to self-oriented motives. As an example, consider the development of the desire for group success. We may assume that the unit's task is one it will repeat periodically (e.g., planning a new program of speakers, running an annual financial campaign, conducting a regular cycle of manufacturing, or completing a summer's harvest) and that, at the end of each time period, the group has a numerical result such as dollars received, products sold, or patients cured. Members will recognize that some scores are easy to reach and others are more difficult, but they cannot confidently estimate what score their group will earn until after they have had experience on the task, or know what the group's best achievement could be, or what other groups make in this activity, or otherwise judge what would be an easy or infeasibly hard outcome for this group. They will realize that, in the abstract, getting a higher group score is more satisfying than getting a lower one, and that the array of all possible outcomes from easy to hard provides a scale of excellence.

After some experience in working as a group, members begin to assess with assurance what level of accomplishment is too difficult for their unit and what is too easy for it—that is, they develop a perceived probability of success for each possible outcome. When such estimates of probability become available, participants react to any later evidence about the group's attainment in ways that are no longer simply cognitive. Their anticipation of the group's subsequent performance generate affect-laden responses to the score the group actually attains; members are pleased if the group as a whole does better than they had expected and are disappointed if it does not do as well. The satisfaction causes members to value attainment of the goal that members set, to value group success; and the dissatisfaction causes them to disvalue the failure to reach the goal, to avoid group failure. Thereafter, any given outcome earned by the group serves as a score of either more satisfaction or dissatisfaction as it is evaluated in comparison to the anticipated level of attainment. Members thus have developed a desire in themselves for a success by the group and/or for avoiding group failure.

As a second example, we can speculate about the source of the desire for joking and fun in an organization. In this case it seems likely that those who organize or join such a body previously enjoyed repartee and horseplay and were good at it. Perhaps several such individuals were together on some occasion and recognized that they were having more good humor as a group than they would if they were only two or three. They liked the kind of spirit among them (which is the potential group-oriented desire), and they believed that individuals would be willing to assemble and to create this condition at regular meetings (which is an indicator of their perceived probability of satisfaction). They doubtless recognized as well that their banter could create hurt or disapproval, but were confident that they would be able to limit such interpersonal harm.

As a third example, individuals' desire for influence as a group is likely to be aroused when they recognize that they need to increase their social power over particular others in order to make changes they desire, and that joint efforts through a planned group may help them fulfill this need. Examples are a labor union, political party, conservationist group, or religious sect.

Increasing the Strength of
Members' Desire for the Group

If we accept the idea that members may have any of a number of desires for their group and that the strength of these desires can vary from time to time, it becomes useful to think about how an organizer or manager of a group may encourage members to increase the strength of their group-oriented desire. The following suggestions ought to be tested to learn whether they do, in fact, augment the strength of members' desire for their group.

(1) Be sure that members understand the differences between a group-oriented desire, the purpose of the group, the value of the purpose, and the probability of attaining that purpose.

(2) Define the group's purpose, programs, work plans, and resources so that members can surely attain satisfaction with their group. Satisfaction arouses the taste for more.

(3) Emphasize the sources of satisfaction with their group—what causes satisfaction to develop among members and what consequences that has for the group.

(4) Help the organization establish a clear purpose. Members develop a stronger group-oriented desire, and a better means to satisfy that desire, if the group's purpose is measurable and attainable.

(5) Indicate to members how membership in this group can satisfy their personal motives.

(6) Make it clear to each member how they help the body attain its purpose.

(7) Emphasize the importance of unity in the group and of its output as a joint product, because then members are collaborating toward satisfaction with the outcome for the group as a whole.

(8) Be ready to change purposes that are not being attained.

(9) Observe what obstacles prevent fulfillment of the group's purposes and help members overcome these obstacles.

(10) Encourage members to feel responsible for the group's condition.

Desires for the Group
and the Purposes of the Group

How do group-oriented desires affect members' choice of a group objective? This is easiest to illustrate when the group has a specific task to perform. In this situation, I assume that members desire their group to be successful in its task. The strength of this desire for success depends upon what motives members bring to the group and what experiences they expect, or have, in the group. The perceived probability of satisfaction for members is the likelihood, as they see it, that their group can succeed in its work. Consequently, the objective they choose is normally one that will provide a good probability of success (that is, be quite attainable) but not be so easy that its accomplishment provides little satisfaction. For reasons explained more fully elsewhere (Zander, 1971), as members' desire for group success increases, they more often choose, and work harder to attain, a particular group goal (a precisely stated purpose) that is a bit more difficult than any they have achieved previously. This kind of goal is described as a challenging one. And, as members' desire to avoid group failure increases (so that it outweighs the strength of their desire for group success), members prefer, but work less hard to attain, group goals that are too difficult for the body to achieve. In such cases, instead of trying to succeed, they strive to avoid embarrassment caused by the group's failure, by abolishing goals, making excuses, or avoiding the task entirely (Zander, 1977). Clearly, group-oriented desires can affect the goals members choose. This effect will become stronger as experience in the group's work shows them how well the group can perform and increases their desire to succeed, or to avoid failure.

Consider a different kind of body, the "Du Nuthin Club," a weekly gathering of macho males who formed their organization because they wanted more fun in their lives. They meet to eat, tell jokes, and kid one another—nothing serious is allowed. They could conceivably do these things without creating a formal organization, but they have chosen to develop a structured body with officers, dues, and rules. Their group's purpose then is determined by their joint desire. This objective, to generate satisfying group fun, will be met only if their horseplay succeeds in precluding unpleasing pain for one another. If it should happen that the group's purpose cannot meet members' desires, members' desires may be modified, the purpose of the group may be changed, its program revised, or the group may even be disbanded.

In another kind of group, where members' desires are to be influential, these desires may also help them to select a purpose for their group. Their chosen target and method—whom they will try to change, how, and how much—will depend on the incentive value of each alternative purpose, and on the subjective probability that a given purpose is likely to provide a satisfying degree of influence. All in all, I would suggest that as members have a stronger desire for a given state in their group, they are more likely to prefer purposes that will provide that satisfaction and that are more certain to be achieved (Zander, 1985).

It may be helpful to speculate about how purposes can be most wisely chosen for a group in a natural setting, and how responsible members can best encourage such efforts. The following suggestions appear plausible:

(1) Define desires that members hold for the group, in order to evaluate various potential group purposes as to their ability to provide satisfaction for members.

(2) State each of the alternative purposes for the group as precisely as possible.

(3) Demonstrate to members how much, and why, their group's purpose will generate satisfaction for them.

(4) Show members how their group-oriented desires can influence their appraisal of several group purposes.

(5) Encourage members to participate in evaluating how much each group purpose can generate satisfaction for them.

(6) Obtain accurate measures of the group's performance on its task or, if that is not possible because the purpose of the group is too obscure, develop a sound description of the state of affairs within the body over a period of time. This information, whether quantitative or qualitative, should be given to decisionmakers in the group. Such feedback about events in a group is necessary if responsible members are to have a basis for selecting sensible purposes.

(7) Help members define measurable and accessible subgoals if the group's purposes are too vague to provide guidance or satisfaction for members.

(8) Encourage members to move on to different purposes when current ones are not reachable to a reasonable degree.

The Origin of Subgoals in a Group

If members have in mind a rather vague desire for their group (such as wielding power, or preserving the environment), they still express this group-oriented wish in one or more purposes for their group. Usually a purpose based on such desires is not a numerical quantity, such as a score or a dollar income, and is not located along a scale of excellence, as the goals for a group's work task may be. Instead, it is likely to be an obscure and value-laden aim that is low in measurability, accessibility, or both.

A vaguely stated purpose, I contend, is not always an inducer of action by members because they are not sure what efforts are most likely to meet that kind of objective. In place of an obscure purpose, decision makers tend to substitute a more exactly defined aim or subgoal (more measurable and accessible), since this clarity allows members more effectively to steer, stimulate, and assess their joint behavior. The tendency is to turn to clearer, and narrower, objectives.

An example of this process can be seen in a group in which mutual acceptance of all comers, regardless of race, creed, or behavior, is the central mission and people of all kinds are to be made comfortable. It is not easy to move toward this kind of general intention, in part because the valued activity (approaching and interacting with strangers) is often hard for participants. Practice can make this interaction somewhat less stressful, so those in charge of the body may want to know whether its programs and procedures relax members, provide proper practice, and move them toward their joint objective. The leaders can best evaluate these matters using methods that yield precise and reliable measurements of the behavior of participants. They might, for example, count the number of new members and record the variety among them in race, religion, age, and the like. Tallies can also be made of the number of persons who approach one another during a meeting, the kinds of members who talk most freely, or the nature of accepting and rejecting actions among them. In addition, data may be obtained by asking participants about their attitudes or feelings of acceptance and inhibition. If measures like these are used in making an audit of members' behavior, the scores tend to be used thereafter when naming goals for the group, and better scores on these simple measures become the group's prime objectives. Participants will usually want their group's sessions to be a bit more satisfying at each measurement period. Consequently, the group will later on be run in ways that are likely to achieve such measurable substitute goals, even if they have doubtful relevance to the obscure purposes originally stated for the body.

Suppose, as another illustration, that a group is formed to convince the city council that something ought to be done about excessive traffic on local streets. Their aim, they soon realize, needs to be defined more sharply so that their members can know where to apply their energy and can determine whether their efforts are creating desirable changes in actions of the council and in the flow of auto traffic. This need for more precise goals may also be fostered by the fear among city council-members that they will meet difficulties when they attempt to introduce new patterns in movement of traffic. Obstacles may arise from the council's lack of basic information, dislike of methods used by the pressure group, or the resistance of merchants who prefer to have more cars (not fewer) drive near their shops. Responsible persons in the pressure group then may try to determine what would please most citizens, what barriers restrict the decision freedom of council members, and how strong these barriers are. The advocates of change will then press for actions that seem doable, that will not arouse much resistance, and will show the council that there are potent incentives for efforts to thin crowded traffic lanes. Note that these various considerations give the influencing body more measurable and accessible subgoals than it had at the outset.

We might, in a similar manner, examine members' goals in groups formed for any other purpose, from bird watching to worshipping. Motives of individuals, whether these are to satisfy self, to aid in the satisfaction of other members, or to generate satisfaction with the outcomes for the unit as a whole, can lead to specificity of a group's purpose. It seems, then, that members of groups develop preferences for precisely stated ends, even if these are not close relatives of the group's initial purpose. These preferences, I believe, originate in the desires of participants to know how to attain their group's objectives (accessibility) and to know whether they have in fact done so (measurability). Without information on such matters, members' satisfaction with their group is not probable, and without such satisfaction the organization cannot long endure. However, at the present time, these conclusions must remain tentative, for I know of no research findings on the frequency or origins of measurable and accessible subgoals.

Activities in Groups

A group's programs and procedures, called its *activities,* can be viewed as paths to the group's objective because they help members move through physical or psychological space to reach a designated end. An activity is created when participants plan the things that must be done in that body, how they will make these things happen, who will do what, the actions they must take against barriers along the way, and why they need to attain completion of the group's objective. I call a group's activities *appropriate* when they more efficiently lead toward attainment of the group's objectives; that is, they provide greater probability of attainment of these objectives at less expenditure of resources because they are more direct, less costly, and/or faster ways for achieving the group's aims than are other possible activities. Appropriate activities are most often used by members when the group's objective is more measurable and accessible because, in that case, it is easier to be certain about what will work in efforts toward the group's purpose.

It is not uncommon, nevertheless, for a group to engage in inappropriate activities and for these not to be recognized as such even though they provide inefficient progress toward the purpose of the body. An inappropriate activity, compared to an appropriate one, demands more effort of members, more resources, or more time to reach the end point, and is characterized by a poor fit, redundancy, and/or conflict with other activities in the group. Familiar examples of inappropriate activities (in contrast to appropriate ones) include marking folded paper ballots instead of punching buttons on electric voting machines, procedural planning done solely by managers and foremen instead of revising work programs in quality-control circles, soldiers shooting from trenches instead of following tactics of rapid movement toward the enemy, use of straight jackets in a mental hospital instead of psychotherapy and calming medicines, and religious services broadcast by radio instead of via television.

Speaking in general terms, members who are concerned about the satisfactoriness of their group will probably favor appropriate activities over inappropriate ones. But they may not do so for several reasons, such as the following:

—the purpose is not stated precisely enough to aid in making a decision about the group's activities;
— members prefer activities that will satisfy their personal interests regardless of those supported by other persons in the unit;
—negotiations among members to arrive at an acceptable goal does not succeed;
— members engage in an uncreative problem-solving process called *group-think* (Janis, 1982);
— the views of a powerful subgroup dominate and stultify the choosing of activities for the group;
— urgency leads to errors among members;
— values are given more weight than facts when a rational choice is badly needed;
— members focus on overcoming embarrassment over the work of their group; and
— decision makers become defensive when discussing plans for the organizations.

Clearly, an appropriate activity is not always employed even when it is eagerly desired.

Summary

In efforts to understand the nature of group behavior, two basic questions have received less attention than they deserve: Why do people try to organize a group? What leads them to favor the purpose they choose for their group? Some studies of group behavior have been concerned with the sources and consequences of specific goals in a task-oriented group. The determinants of looser, broader, and more humane group purposes, however, await investigation.

A group's *purpose* or objective means a desirable state of affairs that members intend to bring about through their joint efforts, and the attainment of which will bring them satisfaction. A group's objective has particular properties that themselves can influence members' actions. The *measurability* of a group's objective denotes the degree of precision with which its attainment can be determined. The *accessibility* of a group's purpose means the clarity of the path to accomplish it. The *cooperativeness* of a purpose indicates how much it stimulates members to help one another toward an outcome that is beneficial to most members alike. Other noteworthy properties of group purposes are *power, flexibility, consonance,* and *difficulty*.

The substantive content of a group's purpose is influenced by many matters. One of the most interesting among these influences is the motivation of members, whether it be self-oriented (for personal satisfaction) or group oriented (for satisfaction with the group's state of affairs). Many groups are formed primarily to facilitate satisfaction of personal motives. However, other groups are based upon *group-oriented desires* that are held in common by members. These lead members to seek certain outcomes for the group as a whole: for example, success, support of fun, influence, or nurturance.

A member's group-oriented desire is an analog of a personal motive—a desire for the group to attain a given condition. A group's purpose is a group-oriented incentive, a state or outcome in the group that, when attained, provides satisfaction for members. It is a shared public belief that most members agree with. The *strength* of a group purpose is the amount of satisfaction its attainment promises to provide for members. The *perceived probability* of the group's purpose is the estimate that members make about the likelihood of attaining the objective. Members' tendency to act in accord with their desire for the group is the resultant of the strength of this desire, times the strength of the group's purpose, times the perceived probability of this purpose.

In principle, the strength of members' desires for their group is amenable to change, and organizers, leaders, or consultants of groups can use several methods to develop stronger desires. Members' desires for their group affect their choice of a purpose for that entity. Thus it follows that persons who have enough power to influence a group can help its responsible members choose a sensible purpose for the organization, by ways discussed in this chapter.

A vaguely stated group purpose is often not an inducer of action by members because persons in the group cannot be sure what steps to take toward it or whether they have actually reached it. In place of an obscure objective, members usually prefer to have a more precisely defined aim (i.e., a subgoal) that will allow them to steer, stimulate, and evaluate their joint behavior reliably. Because they provide satisfaction, these subgoals often may be valued even though they have little relevance to the initial, broadly stated purposes of the group.

A group's programs and procedures, called its *activities,* can be conceived as paths to the group's objective. Appropriate activities efficiently lead a group toward this objective; inappropriate ones do not. Yet, many characteristics of a group and its processes serve to foster inappropriate activities.

References

Atkinson, J. W., & Feather, N. (1966). *A theory of achievement motivation.* New York: John Wiley.

Barnard, C. (1938). *The functions of the executive.* Cambridge, MA: Harvard University Press.

Berscheid, E., & Walster, E. (1978). *Interpersonal attraction.* Reading, MA: Addison-Wesley.

Boorstin, D. (1983). *The discoverers.* New York: Random House.

Cohen, M., & March, J. (1974). *Leadership and ambiguity.* New York: McGraw-Hill.

Cyert, R., & March, J. (1963). *A behavioral theory of the firm.* Englewood Cliffs, NJ: Prentice-Hall.

Deutsch, M. (1973). *The resolution of conflict.* New Haven, CT: Yale University Press.

Etzioni, A. (1975). *A comparative analysis of complex organizations.* New York: Free Press.

Festinger, L., Schachter, S., & Back, K. (1950). *Social pressures in informal groups.* New York: Harper & Row.

Funk, D. (1982). *Group dynamic law: Integrating constitutive contract institutions.* New York: Philosophical Library.

Hackman, J. (1985). A normative model of work team effectiveness. In J. Lorsch (Ed.), *Handbook of organizational behavior*. Englewood Cliffs, NJ: Prentice-Hall.

Janis, I. L. (1982). *Groupthink: Psychological studies of policy decisions and fiascoes* (rev. ed.). Boston: Houghton Mifflin.

Kanter, R. (1972). *Commitment and community*. Cambridge, MA: Harvard University Press.

Laquer, W. (1977). *Terrorism*. Boston: Little, Brown.

Likert, R. (1961). *New patterns of management*. New York: McGraw-Hill.

Olson, M. (1971). *The logic of collective action*. Cambridge, MA: Harvard University Press.

Peters, T., & Waterman, R. (1982). *In search of excellence*. New York: Harper & Row.

Raven, B., & Rietsema, J. (1957). The effects of varied clarity of group goals and group path upon the individual and his relation to his group. *Human Relations, 10,* 29-44.

Scott, W. (1982). *Organizations: Rational, natural, and open systems*. Englewood Cliffs, NJ: Prentice-Hall.

Stone, C. (1975). *Where the law ends*. New York: Harper & Row.

Van de Ven, A. (1980). Early planning, implementation, and performance of organizations. In J. Kimberly, R. Miles, & Associations (Eds.), *The organizational life cycle: Issues in the creation, transformation, and decline of organizations*. San Francisco: Jossey Bass.

Wanous, J. (1980). *Organizational entry: Recruitment, selection, and socialization of newcomers*. Reading, MA: Addison-Wesley.

Weick, K. (1979). *The social psychology of organizing*. Reading, MA: Addison-Wesley.

Wicker, A. (in press). Behavior settings reconsidered: Temporal stages, resources, internal dynamics, context. In D. Stokols & I. Altman (Eds.), *Handbook of environmental psychology*. New York: John Wiley.

Zander, A. (1971). *Motives and goals in groups*. Orlando, FL: Academic Press.

Zander, A. (1977). *Groups at work: Unresolved issues in the study of organizations*. San Francisco: Jossey-Bass.

Zander, A. (1985). *The purposes of groups and organizations*. San Francisco: Jossey-Bass.

Zander, A., & Armstrong, W. (1972). Working for group pride in a slipper factory. *Journal of Applied Social Psychology, 2,* 193-207.

4

Theory and Research on Group Composition: Applications to the Status of Women and Ethnic Minorities

ALISON M. KONRAD
BARBARA A. GUTEK

Much theory and research has been devoted to the study of groups and, more recently, to the study of group composition. The study of group composition may be defined as the examination of groups in terms of the subgroups that compose them. Pfeffer's (1981) studies of organizational demography and Taylor's work (e.g., Taylor, Fiske, Etcoff, & Ruderman, 1978) on contextual bases of stereotyping are examples of work in this area. In this chapter, we organize and review empirical work examining the impact of group composition, with special emphasis on the status and treatment of women and ethnic minorities.

Our interest in the area of group composition developed as an offshoot of the field of women and work. There are two very striking characteristics of women's work outside the home. First, women's work is poorly compensated (Treiman & Roos, 1983), and second, women's work is separated or segregated from men's work (Bielby & Baron, 1986). Many researchers have connected these two features of women's work, suggesting that occupational sex segregation is primarily responsible for working women's relatively low earnings (England, 1984). Fascinated with the hypothesis that the sex composition of occupations could affect an individual woman's earnings, we became interested in developing a comprehensive theory that could explain how the composition of groups could affect the outcomes of individuals. The individual outcomes we are most concerned with are status outcomes, such as earnings, education, performance evaluation, dominance, influence, or prestige. We feel that status variables are important because they are among the most potent factors affecting the individual's quality of life.

To begin work on this topic, we collected all of the studies we could find that examined group composition as an independent variable. In doing so, we quickly became aware of the inconsistencies that plague the field. For example, while Latane and Wolf (1981) theorized that the influence of individuals in the numerical minority *increases* as the size of the minority increases, Taylor et al. (1978) theorized that the influence of numerical minority individuals *declines* as the size of the minority increases. Similarly, while Kanter (1977) suggested that individuals will experience the most prejudicial behavior when they constitute a *small* minority of the group, Blalock (1957) suggested the contradictory hypothesis that individuals will experience more prejudicial behavior when they constitute a *large* minority of the group. (For a detailed discussion of the contradictions between the theories of Kanter and Blalock, see South, Bonjean, Markham, & Corder, 1982, 1983.) Some studies have shown that individuals have more *positive* outcomes in groups when they are in the minority (South et al., 1982, 1983; Taylor et al., 1978), while other studies have shown that individuals have more *negative* outcomes when they are in the minority (Braddock, 1981; Burnim, 1980; Fleming, 1985; Holahan, 1979; Tidball, 1980).

This literature presented us with such an inconsistent set of theories and research findings that we initially despaired of developing a comprehensive statement about group composition as an area worthy of study in its own right. Yet, by stepping back to the more fundamental question of what defines a category of people as a socially distinct group, we feel that we have been able to conceptualize group composition in a way that can resolve some of the inconsistencies present in the existing literature.

In this chapter we first define group composition and describe how group distinctions occur. From that basis, we then outline and discuss three major ways in which group composition can vary. Throughout the discussion, we focus on group composition regarding women and ethnic minorities since these are strong social distinctions and have been the subjects of extensive research. The general framework presented in the chapter should apply, however, to other social distinctions besides gender and ethnicity, such as religion, occupation, or language.

Defining Group Composition: When Does a Mere Characteristic Become a Social Distinction?

To undertake the tasks of organizing the group composition literature and, we hope, resolving some of its inconsistencies, we begin by developing the construct of group composition. If group composition refers to a group's makeup in terms of subgroups, the first question one might ask would be how to distinguish subgroups within a group. Researchers have studied subgroups distinguished on the basis of race (e.g., Fleming, 1985), sex (e.g., Kanter, 1977), personal opinion (e.g., Latane & Wolf, 1981), and organizational position (e.g., Konrad, 1986b); but they have neglected the study of subgroups distinguished on the basis of eye color or blood type. Why do some personal characteristics seem to be appropriate for study while others seem inappropriate or even foolish? An obvious answer to this question is that some distinctions have social meaning, while others do not. Social scientists have not studied subgroups distinguished on the basis of hair color or blood type because these characteristics have little or no social meaning. In most settings, it does not matter if one is the only "A negative" among a group of "O positives."

To say that a characteristic must have social meaning in order to distinguish a subgroup is not particularly helpful, however. The question, "When does a mere characteristic become a social distinction?" may be answered with more precision when stated in behavioral terms. In terms of behavior, a social distinction may be defined as a characteristic of individuals that, when known and salient, elicits a predictable set of reactions from other people.[1] As such, social distinctions may range from physical characteristics of the individual, such as skin color or sex, to labels attached to the individual by institutions, such as a job title, to behaviors performed by the individual, such as typing or commanding, since all of these social distinctions elicit a relatively predictable set of responses from others. For the field of group composition, a subgroup may be defined as all individuals within a group sharing a particular social distinction.

Defining social distinctions as characteristics eliciting predictable reactions from others is preferable to the more subjective definitions offered by previous authors. For example, Tajfel (1982), labeling the concept *group identification,* defined it as a known categorization of the individual that is linked to value connotations and an emotional investment. There are two reasons a definition based upon objective criteria is superior to a subjective definition. First, subjective criteria are difficult to measure. For example, different observers may not agree on whether or not a given individual has an emotional investment in a social distinction. It is much easier for observers to agree on whether or not one individual has been treated differently than another individual in a given situation. The second reason why a behavioral definition of a social distinction is superior to a subjective definition is its greater substantive impact. The research literature has shown that subjective attitudes may often be poor predictors of behavior (Wicker, 1969). How important are social distinctions defined by subjective attitudes if those attitudes may not lead to differences in the treatment of the individual? But if social distinctions are as defined as characteristics that elicit systematic reactions from others, the distinctions that are studied will be those that are more likely to have a significant impact on the individual.

Social distinctions may be most simply operationalized as dichotomous variables indicating whether or not a given individual belongs to a given social category, for example, blacks versus nonblacks, secretaries versus nonsecretaries. Conceptually, it may be helpful to think of group composition as a multidimensional space defined by a set of operative social distinctions that serve as axes (Blau, 1977). Each individual in any given group has a position on each axis and thus may hold more than one social distinction. For example, an individual may be black, a secretary, and a woman, thus holding three social distinctions. The entire constellation of salient distinctions held by the individual should be considered when predictions are being made about the impact of group composition. For example, when examining behavior toward blacks in a group, one should note whether blacks tend to be janitors, secretaries, or managers in the group.

How Group Composition May Vary

Group composition can be seen as varying in at least three ways, each of which may affect the outcomes of individuals. First, groups may vary as to which characteristics serve as social distinctions identifying subgroups. For example, in one society, people of different skin colors may be treated in systematically different ways. In such a society, subgroups identified on the basis of skin color would be socially meaningful. In another society, skin color may be totally unrelated to the treatment of the individual. There, defining subgroups on the basis of skin color would make no social sense, and research on the characteristic of skin color would show no significant differences in treatment.

The second way that group composition may vary is in the interrelationships between the social distinctions defining subgroups. For example, in one organization, the two social distinctions of sex and hierarchical status may be strongly intercorrelated (e.g., women may be concentrated among low-status positions), while in another organization no such relationship may exist (both women and men may be proportionately distributed among the organizational hierarchy).

The third way that groups may vary is in the distributions of their members among their subgroups. For instance, women may make up 5% of one organization and 75% of another.

Each of the following three major sections of this chapter discusses in detail one of the three types of variations in group composition. Occasionally in the chapter, we will use the term *group* to refer to socially meaningful categories of people (not just to sets of people who actually interact), for we will consider the composition of groups at a variety of system levels, such as work groups and organizations, classrooms and student bodies of colleges. Often, instead of using the generic term *subgroup* to identify the smaller groups making up a particular group of interest, we will specify the relevant social category (e.g., women, men, blacks, whites, etc.).

Types of Social Distinctions

The first way that group composition may vary is in which human characteristics function as social distinctions. Thoughtful consideration of how social distinctions arise should help to direct inquiry in this area. As defined earlier, human characteristics become social distinctions when people treat individuals having one characteristic differently than ones having another characteristic. The conditions leading to the creation of a given social distinction should affect the way individuals who share that distinction are treated. Five types of conditions seem most likely to lead to the creation of social distinctions between groups or social categories, though other conditions may foster social distinctions as well. These five conditions (which are discussed in detail below) are:

(1) Categories of individuals behave in systematically different ways (Berger & Luckmann, 1966).
(2) Conflict exists between groups (Sherif, Harvey, White, Hood, & Sherif, 1961; Tajfel, 1982).
(3) Status differences exist between groups or categories (Henley, 1977; Tajfel, 1982).
(4) Institutional practices exist that distinguish groups or categories (Becker, 1963; Katz & Kahn, 1978).
(5) Groups or categories are easy to distinguish visually.

Social Distinctions Based on Reliable Behavioral Differences

Differences between groups in social behavior vary in strength and reliability. As groups or categories become increasingly different in their typical social behavior, the likelihood that social distinctions between the groups will be made increases. For example, teenagers typically behave in reliably different ways from senior citizens, and they are treated differently in many situations. In contrast, differences between the behavior of engineers and accountants may be smaller and subtler, and these two groups may be treated quite similarly.

The processes of social reward and punishment may explain why reliable behavioral differences between social categories lead to the creation of social distinctions. An individual's failure to anticipate reliable differences in social behavior between social categories may lead to inappropriate behavior in the presence of category members. Social behavior eliciting a positive response from members of one category may yield no response or even a negative response from members of another category. For example, in India it is quite common for men who are friends to hold hands while walking together. In the United States this behavior is uncommon and is often stereotyped as homosexuality. Thus if an Indian man took the hand of an American man (a gesture usually eliciting a positive response from his male friends in India), he might be quite surprised at the negative reaction elicited from the American and would learn not to behave in this way toward American men. When such reliable differences in social behavior exist, individuals may learn to alter their social behavior in the presence of members of a particular category in order to facilitate accurate communication and successful social interaction (Berger & Luckmann, 1966). As many individuals begin altering their social behavior in the presence of members of the other category of people, social distinctions, as we have defined them, evolve. As one result, "good manners," such as opening a door for a woman and holding her chair at a dinner table, help both to create and to perpetuate people's perception of the socially distinctive categories of male and female.

Social Distinctions Based on Conflict Between Groups

Sociologists such as Dahrendorf have suggested that the existence of conflict between groups should increase the likelihood that social distinctions between the groups will be made (Turner, 1982). Research evidence indicating that members of groups in conflict engage in in-group favoritism and out-group deprecation supports this hypothesis. A well-known study by Sherif et al. (1961) of the behavior of boys at summer camp is a good demonstration of the social boundaries that form between groups in conflict. When two groups of campers were placed in situations of conflict of interest, in-group favoritism and out-group deprecation occurred. When the same groups of boys were later placed in situations that required cooperation, these behaviors vanished. Diab (1970), in a study similar to that of Sherif et al. (1961), reported the same findings in a Lebanese setting. Other evidence of increased out-group deprecation under conditions of conflict includes studies showing that attitudes toward national groups become significantly more negative with the onset of a war between the individual's own country and the country of the out-group (Dudycha, 1942; Seago, 1947; Sinha & Upadhyaya, 1960).

Social Distinctions Based on Status Differences

Status and power differences between groups should encourage the development of social distinctions between the groups (Tajfel, 1982). Research evidence indicating that people systematically alter their social behavior depending upon the status of the individual with whom they are interacting (Henley, 1977) supports this hypothesis. Even where the others' behavior is identical, systematic differences have been found between reactions to the behavior of low- and high-status individuals (Moore & Johnson, 1983; Perry, 1980). As one example, Stevens (1980, 1981) found that adults were more likely to label a child as behaviorally disordered if that child were indicated (fictitiously) as being of low socioeconomic status (SES).

Social Distinctions Based on Institutional Practices

When individuals are categorized for different treatments by an institution on the basis of a particular characteristic, individuals sharing that characteristic become a distinct social group within the institution. Turner, Sachdev, and Hogg (1983) found that simply by randomly assigning school children one of two types of personal code numbers and categorizing them into two groups, they were able to induce in-group favoritism. When numbers were assigned without categorizing the children into groups, no in-group bias occurred. Tajfel (1982) found over 30 similar studies of diverse populations using a variety of dependent measures, all of which showed that in-group bias could be elicited by assigning individuals to categories on the basis of very minimal criteria (for examples, see Howard & Rothbart, 1980; Locksley, Ortiz, & Hepburn, 1980; Tajfel, Billig, Bundy, & Flament, 1971). These findings indicate that categories assigned by institutions may easily become social distinctions.

When many institutions use the same characteristic to classify individuals, a social group on a societal level may evolve, especially when the treatment given individuals sharing the same characteristic is similar across institutions. For example, physicians in any institution are treated rather similarly and differentiated from other subgroups (e.g., by being called "doctor"). Many workers in different organizations are in job classifications that require very similar skills and duties, and these classifications come to be known as "occupations" at a societal level. For example, the positions of secretary, janitor, or accountant are very similar in most work organizations, and an individual with experience in these jobs in one organization can transfer their skills to another organization. These jobs also usually command similar earnings, treatment, and prestige across work organizations.

The labels attached to individuals within institutions may directly affect how others respond to the behavior of individuals both inside and outside of the institutions (Becker, 1963). Organizational titles, labels attached by institutions of justice (Rovner-Pieczenik, 1976), and diagnoses of mental illness (Rosenhan, 1973) are examples of institutionally attached labels that affect how others respond to individuals in many situations inside and outside of the institution. Sociologists, such as Goffman (1969), have noted that once individuals are labeled as mentally ill, and especially when they are diagnosed as having a type of mental illness that is thought to be incurable, the label influences how others interpret and respond to their every action, regardless of the action's appropriateness or inappropriateness.

A dramatic demonstration of the effect of labeling on the treatment of individuals may be found in Rosenhan's (1973) well-known study of pseudopatients admitted to mental hospitals. Eight normal subjects entered mental institutions saying that they had been hearing voices, and they were labeled as schizophrenics. Once admitted, subjects behaved normally, but none of the subjects was identified as sane by hospital staff, and they remained hospitalized an average of 19 days. As recorded by the pseudopatients, the modal response of hospital staff to self-initiated contacts by the pseudopatients was to ignore them, moving on with head averted: 71% of attempted contacts with psychiatrists and 88% of contacts with nurses and attendants were received in this way. In contrast, the same subjects (without the labels of mental illness), sent to initiate contacts with faculty at Stanford University and physicians at the University Medical Center, were never treated in this fashion.

Social Distinctions Based on Visible Characteristics

Social distinctions between groups do not necessarily develop *merely* because the groups differ in appearance. Yet it is difficult to name a distinctive visible trait of individuals that does not evoke a social reaction from others. Even the relatively nominal trait of hair color evokes stereotypes such as the "dumb blonde" or the "hot-tempered redhead." But some visible traits of individuals elicit stronger social reactions than others. Visible characteristics seem most likely to elicit strong social reactions when they are associated with other conditions fostering the development of group distinctions, such as when conflicts occur between visibly different groups or when behavioral, status, or institutional distinctions between such groups develop. Since one theoretical function of group distinctions is the guidance of social behavior (Berger & Luckmann, 1966; Katz & Kahn, 1978), visible characteristics may be especially apt to become social distinctions. For a human characteristic to function well as a guide to social behavior, it must be easily observable to others.

Bidirectional Causation of Social Distinctions

The five conditions that foster social distinctions listed above are not mutually exclusive categories. As noted above, visible differences between individuals are not in themselves sufficient for creating strong social distinctions. Generally, more than one condition is present when strong social distinctions occur. This is the case for race and gender categories. Other weaker, singly based distinctions—for example, between engineers and accountants—may exist within certain settings, but they are at best subtle distinctions to most people.

The direction of causality between the five conditions that foster social distinctions and the social distinctions themselves is probably reciprocal. For example, differences between groups in social behavior may be seen as outcomes as well as antecedents of a social distinction. Once social distinctions are made and members of one group are treated differently from members of another group, the members of each group learn that they must behave differently in order to obtain social rewards and avoid social punishments. For example, when behavior that is rewarded when displayed by a man, such as aggressiveness, is punished when displayed by a woman, it should not be surprising that men show higher levels of aggression than women. By altering the contingencies for social reward and punishment faced by individuals, social distinctions increase group differences in social behavior.

The tendency of individuals to justify their actions to themselves also leads to bidirectional causality between the bases for social distinctions and the distinctions themselves. Once social distinctions are made, observers look for reasons they treat members of different social groups differently. Thus they look for reliable differences in status or social behavior or institutional practices that differentiate the groups. For example, people may justify paying men more than women who work in the same organization by noting that men and women are performing different jobs (an institutional distinction), or that men are in the more important or valuable jobs (a status distinction), or that men are more competitive and aggressive than women in their efforts to "get ahead"(a behavioral distinction). Differences in behavior or institutional practices rarely go unnoticed because they provide bases for continuing the social distinction.

Social scientists, too, are influenced by this dynamic, even in their research activities. One can interpret the extensive literature on gender differences, for example, as a justification for maintaining gender as an important social distinction. Few studies involving both male and female research subjects fail to look for gender differences. Thus gender differences, no matter how small, rarely go unnoticed and unreported, and the same can be said for race differences. In fact, it seems likely to us that the literature may reflect greater differences between men and women than actually exist. Gender differences found in the social science literature also receive a significant amount of attention from journalists. Many lay people are aware of gender differences in aggressiveness and mathematical performance found in the social science literature. Individuals cite these gender differences as reasons to treat men and women differently. Thus the same conditions that lead to social distinctions are used to justify the maintenance of those distinctions.

Interrelationships Among Some Major Social Distinctions

The second important aspect of the field of group composition comprises interrelationships among social distinctions. Social distinctions become interrelated when individuals sharing one social distinction (e.g., Hispanic ethnicity) become disproportionately represented among those sharing another social distinction (e.g., low SES) within a group. As social distinctions become closely interrelated, the social behaviors associated with those social distinctions should become increasingly similar. For example, in an organization having Hispanic women concentrated among low-status positions, individuals will seldom see Hispanic women in high-status positions and may come to think of Hispanic women as a low-status group. Conversely, in an organization having Hispanic women concentrated among high-status positions, individuals will often see Hispanic women in high-status positions and may come to think of Hispanic women as a high-status group. In this way, the stereotyping, evaluation, and behavior of individuals may be systematically affected by interrelationships between social distinctions.

Research evidence supports the hypothesis that, as social distinctions become interrelated, the social behaviors associated with those distinctions will become increasingly similar. In particular, unequal distribution of higher visible groups along *status dimensions* has been found to have significant effects on behavior, influence, dominance, stereotyping, and evaluations of performance. The following sections summarize research on the interrelationships between status distinctions and the highly visible social distinctions of ethnicity and sex. Then, the implications of introducing a perspective emphasizing the interrelationships among social distinctions are discussed and pertinent research is reviewed.

Status and Ethnicity

The fact that for many years in the United States black and Hispanic ethnicity has correlated with low socioeconomic status (SES)—usually defined as a combination of earnings and education—suggests that evaluations and treatment favoring whites over blacks and Hispanics will be common. Because people in this country often see low-SES black and Hispanic persons and seldom see high-SES black and Hispanic persons, they may generally think of blacks and Hispanics as low-status groups and treat them accordingly. Thus it might be hypothesized that black and Hispanic individuals are disadvantaged compared to white individuals and are treated more negatively in many situations. Indeed, this hypothesis is implied by supporters of affirmative action policies. What we are adding to existing thought on the subjects of prejudice and discrimination is the argument that these two processes stem from the group composition of U.S. society. We argue that because ethnic minority groups are disproportionately concentrated among low-status positions in society, perceptions, judgments, and stereotypes about these groups may be expected to show a negative bias. And because many ethnic groups are highly visible, the stereotypes associated with these groups can be especially strong and difficult to overcome.

A diversity of research findings support the hypothesis that black and Hispanic groups in the United States are disadvantaged compared to whites in many situations. Research in the area of status attainment has shown that whites attain higher earnings and occupational status than blacks even when education and work experience are equated (Corcoran & Duncan, 1978; Hoffman, 1981; Kaufman, 1983; Kerckhoff, 1984; McDougall-Young, 1979; Porter, 1974). It is quite likely that pro-white evaluation bias is partially responsible for the relatively low earnings of blacks in the United States. While the studies cited above cannot refute the argument that the lower earnings of blacks may be due to other factors, it is clear that blacks experience pro-white evaluation bias in many situations. Both black and white boys have been found to rate the aggressive behavior of blacks as being more violent than the identical behavior of whites (Sagar & Schofield, 1980). Similarly, Perry's (1980) study of 1626 marines convicted of violent crimes resulted in the finding that black marines were much more likely than white marines to be imprisoned upon conviction, regardless of severity of crime, military rank, or educational attainment.

In another study, black and Hispanic children were disproportionately likely to be labeled as behaviorally disordered by teachers and school psychologists (Stevens, 1981). Moore and Johnson (1983), using data from a large probability sample, found that ethnicity affected elementary school teachers' occupational aspirations for their students. Black and Hispanic students were less likely than white children with identical school performance to be expected to be in the professional category, and more likely to be assigned to the unskilled laborer category. Teachers' occupational stereotyping was found to exaggerate actual differences in occupational attainment between ethnic groups.

Studies of children's preferences for social groups have also demonstrated the effects of the status of social groups on evaluations of those social groups. Children from high-status social groups generally show strong preferences for members of their own groups (Tajfel, 1982). However, low-status children have often been found to prefer high-status groups to their own social groups (Tajfel, 1982). In the United

States, black children have been found to prefer whites over blacks in a number of studies (for reviews of this literature, see Katz, 1976; Milner, 1975, 1981; Pushkin & Veness, 1973). The preference of children from low-SES social groups for high-SES groups has also been documented in a number of different nations (Tajfel, 1982).

Status and Gender

The advantage men have over women in earnings and education, which has long existed in the United States, suggests the hypothesis that other status distinctions favoring men over women will be made. Since women are more often in positions of low status, they may come to be seen as a low-status group. A great deal of diverse research evidence supports the hypothesis that women will behave and be treated as low-status individuals while men will behave and be treated as high-status individuals. We see the behavior, treatment, influence, and evaluation of women as reflecting the concentration of women among low-status social positions in the United States.

In the research literature women have been consistently found more likely than men to exhibit behavior indicative of low status in a variety of situations (Frances, 1979; Frieze & Ramsey, 1976; Hacker, 1981; Henley, 1977; Instone, Major, & Bunker, 1983; Kipnis, 1984; Leffler, Gillespie, & Conaty, 1982). For example, Kipnis (1984) found that among dating and married couples, men reported using strong influence tactics (tactics used by individuals with power and resources) far more frequently than women. It is interesting, however, that when women and men holding organizational positions of similar power and prestige were compared, no sex differences in use of strong influence tactics were found (Kipnis, 1984). Henley (1977) and Frieze and Ramsey (1976) found that women use nonverbal signals of dominance much less often than men in a variety of situations. Frances (1979) reported that men were more likely than women to show dominating verbal and nonverbal behaviors in conversations with strangers.

Researchers have also found that men are treated more favorably than women who behave or are described in the same way. Bradley (1980) reported an experimental study of verbal behavior toward male and female opinion deviates in predominantly male groups of college students. Confederates of the researcher were instructed to show either low or high competence on a group decision-making task. Then, in a subsequent group decision, the confederates chose an opinion deviating from the rest of the group. Incompetent female deviates received more dominating and hostile behaviors and also had much less influence on the attitudes of the group than did incompetent male deviates. However, in this study, competent male and female deviates were treated similarly and had similar influence on the group. Juni and Brannon (1981) conducted a field experiment studying helping behavior toward a male and a female confederate posing as blind persons. Subjects were 165 individuals approached in college buildings. Results showed that subjects touched the female confederate more often than the male confederate, indicating greater respect for the personal space of the male.

Other research on social influence has shown that women are less influential than men even when they are of equal status (Pugh & Wahrman, 1983). For example, Hurwitz-Inwald and Bryant (1981) studied interaction patterns among 240 public high school teachers. Teachers were placed in ad hoc groups composed of two women and two men to work on a task. Results indicated that men's suggestions were accepted more often by the groups than were women's suggestions, even though women made just as many suggestions as men did. Lockheed (1985) conducted a meta-analysis of studies of sex differences in influence and concluded that men were generally more influential than women. Among the 64 data sets included in the analysis, men were more influential than women 45 times, women were more influential 8 times, and men and women were equally influential 11 times.

Researchers in the area of evaluation have found that women are evaluated less positively than men having equal qualifications (Kaschak, 1981; Nieva & Gutek, 1980; Piacente, Penner, Hawkins, & Cohen, 1974; Stake, Walker, & Speno, 1981). For example, in their review of the research literature, Nieva and Gutek (1980) concluded that women experience discrimination as job applicants. They found that employers did not rate men and women having poor job qualifications differently, but men with strong qualifications were rated significantly more highly than women with equally strong qualifications. Discrimination against women was found to increase as the hierarchical level of the job being applied for increased.

Finally, in actual job settings, full-time working women have been found to receive less pay and on-the-job training than full-time working men having the same work experience, and educational and occupational attainment. This result has held for data bases compiled from 1960 through 1983 (Brown, 1976; 1978; Corcoran & Duncan, 1978; Hoffman, 1981; Kerckhoff, 1984; Konrad, 1986a; McDougall-Young, 1977; Persell, 1983; Rytina, 1982; 1983; Sieling, 1984; Suter & Miller, 1972; Treiman & Roos, 1983). While these studies cannot refute the argument that women's low earnings stem from other factors, it is quite likely that the documented pro-male evaluation bias plays an important part in the determination of women's low earnings.

Relationships of Social Distinctions
at Different System Levels

When distinctions that are important at the societal level are also intercorrelated with status within a group at a lower system level (for example, within a work organization), the behavioral effects should be exacerbated. As we have argued previously, in a society where blacks are disproportionately likely to be of low SES, blacks will be devalued. As a logical extension to this argument, we suggest here that the relative devaluation of blacks may be affected by the group composition of an organization. In an organization where blacks are concentrated among low-status positions, people in the organization should be *more* likely than people outside it to devalue blacks. In an organization where blacks are equally likely to be found at any hierarchical level, people in the organization should be *less* likely than people outside it to devalue blacks.

Few studies testing these hypotheses were found in the literature. The only three studies focusing upon the effects of the extent of white-male domination of high-status positions within groups showed the same pattern of results: Increased white-male domination of high-status positions appears to be detrimental to the outcomes of females and ethnic minorities. For example, Petersik and Schneir (1980) found a strong positive relationship ($r = .77$) between the grades obtained by female students and the percentage of female faculty in the students' departments. Tidball (1980) found an even stronger positive relationship ($r = .94$) between the female-faculty-to-female-student ratio of a college and the likelihood that a female graduate from that college would be listed in registries such as the *Who's Who* series.

A study by Ramirez and Soriano (1982) is of interest because of the researchers' recognition of the effects of status in the organizational hierarchy. In a small survey of Hispanic undergraduates in Chicano studies courses, students were asked what percentage of the students, teachers, and administrators at their high schools were Hispanic. Students from high schools having a very low percentage of Hispanic teachers and administrators were found to have significantly more negative school experiences than students from schools having a very high percentage of Hispanic teachers and administrators. For example, among students at high schools with few Hispanics in authority positions, 16% stated that their counselors had advised them to go to college, while 17% stated that their counselors had never mentioned college and 67% stated they had been advised *against* going to college. In contrast, among students attending high schools with many Hispanics in authority positions, 92% stated that their school counselors had advised them to go to college.

Proportionate Size of Subgroups

The effects of distributions of social categories within groups is a third important area regarding group composition. Groups may vary in degree of homogeneity along any given dimension of social distinction (Blau, 1977). For example, a group or an occupation may be 5% female or 50% female. As noted in the previous section, when groups become homogeneous on a given social distinction, they tend to become stereotyped (Eagly & Steffen, 1984; Gutek & Morasch, 1982; Krefting, Berger, & Wallace, 1978; Lavine, 1982; Moore & Johnson, 1983; Taylor et al., 1978). At a certain critical point, the group becomes perceived as, for example, a man's or a woman's group (Kanter, 1977), though this critical point may vary for individual perceivers of the group. As one example, sex stereotyping of occupations has been found to be strongly linearly related to the percentage of women in the occupation (Krefting et al., 1978). Often, people within the group stereotype the group just as people outside it do. Those in the numerical majority of an unbalanced group may come to think of it as "their" group, or a group for persons of their social type. For example, whites may speak of blacks "invading" their neighborhoods, or men may refer to women "taking" their jobs. Homogeneous or unbalanced groups that have existed for long periods of time, such as years or decades, are quite likely to be stereotyped.

Studies of distributions of social categories within groups have focused primarily upon two outcome variables: evaluation and social integration/isolation. This section first discusses studies on the impact of subgroup proportions on evaluation, and it makes a distinction between evaluations of groups as a whole and of individuals within groups. As will be seen, we feel that this distinction is of theoretical importance and helps to explain some of the inconsistent findings reported in the literature. Next, studies on the impact of subgroup proportions on social integration are discussed. Here, the concept of group heterogeneity is emphasized, since it has been a particularly important concept to researchers examining social integration. Finally, the implications of considering subgroup proportions at different system levels are discussed and relevant studies are briefly reviewed. We focus here on gender distinctions, since almost all of the research literature in this area has dealt with gender.

Subgroup Proportions and Evaluation of Groups

When a group or occupation becomes stereotyped as belonging to a low-status social category, such as women or ethnic minorities, it may become devalued in the minds of observers. Conversely, when a group becomes stereotyped as belonging to a high-status social category, it may increase in value to observers. Findings from studies examining the impact of sex composition on the evaluation of groups support these hypotheses. For example, in a laboratory experiment, Taylor et al. (1978) had college students rate interacting teacher groups depicted in slide and tape presentations. They found that students' ratings of how competent and organized the groups were became more positive as the percentage of men in the group increased. They also found that, as the percentage of men in the group increased, estimates of the grade level taught by the group increased.

Occupational prestige. Research evidence has demonstrated that gender composition affects status ratings, prestige, and earnings of occupations. Sociologists (Hodge & Hodge, 1965; Kerckhoff, 1984; McLaughlin, 1978), economists (Buckley, 1971), and social psychologists (Suchner, 1979; Touhey, 1974a, 1974b; White, Crino, & De-Sanctis, 1981) have conducted studies in this area, using a wide range of research methodologies. On balance, the research indicates that, as the percentage of female workers in an occupation increases, the status of the occupation declines.

In studying the impact of sex composition on occupational prestige, social psychologists have tended to rely upon studies of college students' perceptions. Typically, college students have been asked to rate the prestige of a number of occupations, some of which are stated to be experiencing a rapid change in sex composition. The earliest studies of this type were reported by Touhey (1974a), who gave 200 students descriptions of five typically "masculine" occupations (architect, college professor, lawyer, physician, and scientist). Occupations described as increasing in female participation received significantly lower prestige ratings (from both male and female students) than occupations described as remaining stable in sex composition. Touhey (1974b) performed a similar experiment using stereotypically "feminine" occupations (home economist, kindergarten teacher, librarian, registered nurse, and social worker), describing some occupations as experiencing a rapid increase in male participation. Both male and female students rated occupations increasing in male participation more positively on prestige and desirability than they rated stable so-called feminine occupations.

Others have attempted to replicate Touhey's findings without success. Suchner (1979) used an experimental design identical to Touhey's (1974a) in every respect, but found that students rated occupations described as increasing in female participation no differently than occupations described as remaining stable in sex composition. White et al. (1981) had 394 male business students rate seven business-related occupations, and again the suggestion that women were entering an occupation in rapidly increasing numbers was found to have no significant effect on prestige or desirability ratings. Finally, Crino, White, and DeSanctis (1983) reported nonsignificant findings in a similar experiment examining the occupations of accountant, banker, engineer, and veterinarian.

Though Touhey's (1974a, 1974b) early findings are provocative, the limitations of this body of research are evident. First, the fact that only professional occupations were used in any of the studies resulted in a restriction of range in the dependent variable. Inclusion of manual and service occupations would have increased the statistical power of the research by increasing the range of prestige and desirability ratings. Second, the experimental manipulation used was rather weak, and students may not have believed statements by the experimenter that the sex composition of an occupation was changing without being shown demographic statistics that substantiated such claims. Fabrication of such demographic tables might have enhanced the strength of the experimental manipulation. Finally, the exclusive use of college students as subjects limits the generalizability of findings from these studies.

Other studies of students ratings have shown some support for the hypothesis that sex composition affects the value people place on an occupation. Feather (1975) found that students' ratings of occupational prestige were strongly positively correlated with their estimates of the percentage of men in the occupation (Spearman rank-order correlation = .64). A study by Buttner and Rosen (1986) suggested that male- and female-dominated occupations may be treated differently by employers under situations of a limited labor supply. These researchers found that students presented with a hypothetical decision situation were more likely to offer an increase in salary for predominantly male jobs than for predominantly female jobs when the labor supply was limited. However, this was only true for entry and midlevel jobs. For professional jobs, students were more likely to suggest salary increases for the female-dominated than for the male-dominated job. This contradictory finding may be due to the fact that the predominantly female profession used in the study (registered nurse) is notorious for its low wages relative to the skill and education levels required.

Earnings of occupational groups. A better way to test the effects of the sex composition of an occupation would be to include a representative sample of occupations at all prestige levels and to use objective measures of the dependent variable (e.g., actual earnings rather than estimates or hypothetical offers). A study meeting these criteria was reported by England (1984). Using 1974 data from the Panel Study of Income Dynamics, she found that women had higher lifetime earnings if they worked in predominantly male occupations than if they worked in predominantly female occupations, even when education and work experience were held constant. England cited 10 previous studies showing the same result. A similar finding was reported by Konrad (1986a). Using data from the 1983 Current Population Survey, she found that the average earnings of both men and women working full-time were positively related to the percentage of men employed in their industries and occupations, even when labor markets and human capital were statistically controlled.

Perhaps the most convincing evidence of the impact of sex composition on occupational earnings can be found in comparisons of work organizations. Pfeffer and Davis-Blake (1987) examined the 1978 and 1983 earnings of administrators in over 1000 institutions of higher education in the United States. They found that, in institutions where the percentage of female administrators was high, the earnings of both male and female administrators were lower than in institutions having fewer female administrators. Buckley (1971) and McDougall-Young (1977) found that the earnings commanded by a number of occupations were substantially higher in businesses employing only men for those occupations than in businesses employing only women for those occupations. These findings were obtained from national representative data bases collected in 1969, 1970, and 1975. It appears that in establishments where an occupation is exclusively "masculine," it is more highly valued (and therefore, highly paid) than in establishments where it is exclusively "feminine."

Subgroup Proportions and Evaluations of Individuals

High-status individuals who enter a group made up predominantly of low-status individuals may be viewed as superior to the normative group member (Francesco & Hakel, 1981). As a member of a high-status group, a lone white man entering a female- or ethnic-dominated group may be hypothesized to receive more positive evaluations than other members unless he proves himself to be incompetent. Research on the evaluation of male and female individuals supports this hypothesis. Crocker and McGraw (1984) found that in ad hoc student groups composed predominantly of the opposite sex, solo males were chosen as the leader twice as often as were solo females. Other researchers have found that men in predominantly female occupations are favored over women for promotion and are overrepresented among upper-level organizational positions (Etzkowitz, 1971; Segal, 1962).

Low-status individuals who enter a group of mostly high-status individuals may be viewed as inferior to the normative group member (Kaschak, 1981; Nieva & Gutek, 1980; Nilson, 1976; Parsons, Adler, & Kaczala, 1982; Wiley & Eskilson, 1982). It may be hypothesized that, as a member of a low-status group in society, an unknown woman or ethnic-minority individual entering a preponderantly white, male group may receive more negative evaluations than the other members, at least until the individual has proven herself or himself to be competent (see Martinko & Gardner, 1983; Nieva & Gutek, 1980; and Ruble, Cohen, & Ruble, 1984, for discussions of the effect of objectively proven competence upon the occurrence of evaluation bias).

A number of research findings support the preceding hypothesis. Izraeli (1983) studied the attitudes of union representatives in preponderantly male and gender-balanced union workers' committees in Israel. She found that women in gender-balanced committees considered women to be just as effective as men in serving as union representatives, while women in preponderantly male committees considered women to be less effective than men. Female students have been found to obtain lower grades and to show lower motivation for study than male students when the academic environment is predominantly male (Lantz, 1985; Spangler, Gordon, & Pipkin, 1978). Female students in predominantly male academic environments have also been found to be excluded from areas of study open to male students, to be taken less seriously than male students, and to have their commitment to the field of study questioned (Holahan, 1979). Finally, women in predominantly male ad hoc groups have been found to have less influence on the group than men. Wolman and Frank (1975) found that women in mostly male T-groups had little influence over the topics discussed by the groups, though they made many suggestions to the group. As mentioned previously, Bradley (1980) found that women who acted incompetent in predominantly male groups had less influence on decisions made by the group than did men who acted incompetent.

Once they have proven their competence in the situation, low-status individuals in the numerical minority in a group have sometimes been found to receive better evaluations than the high-status members of the group. Taynor and Deaux (1973, 1975) have suggested that this phenomenon occurs because a woman's success on a so-called masculine task is so surprising that it deserves special comment. Abramson, Goldberg, Greenberg, and Abramson (1977), who reported similar findings called this effect the "talking platypus" phenomenon, suggesting its perceived rarity. Ruble et al. (1984) have suggested that since men are expected to perform better than women on these masculine tasks, male performance may be devalued when women perform equally well, because the men are then perceived as performing less well than expected.

Low-Status Individuals in the Numerical Minority Versus Majority

While the preceding research compared outcomes of an individual in the numerical minority to those *of other members of his or her group,* a number of studies in the literature have compared the outcomes of low-status individuals in situations where they were in the numerical minority *to situations where low-status individuals were in the majority.* This literature is among the most confusing and contradictory in the area of group composition. Some of these studies show women and ethnic minorities to have more positive outcomes overall when in the numerical minority in a group (South et al., 1982; Taylor et al., 1978), while others show women and ethnic minorities to have more positive outcomes when in the numerical majority (Braddock, 1981; Burnim, 1980; Cohen, Pettigrew, & Riley, 1972; Fleming, 1985; Holahan, 1979; Tidball, 1980), and others show no significant difference between numerical minority and majority status (Hoskins, 1978).

It seems likely that these studies produce mixed findings because the effect of group composition on the evaluation *of individuals* is confounded with its effect on evaluations *of the group itself.* While low-status individuals in the numerical minority may be evaluated more negatively than the high-status majority of a group, low-status individuals may still have better outcomes overall in groups of predominantly high-status individuals because of the relatively positive evaluation of the group. For example, when a predominantly male group (e.g., a group of executives) is valued much more highly than a predominantly female group (e.g., a group of secretaries), a woman may obtain the best outcomes if she enters the mostly male group, especially if women within this group are valued only slightly less than men in the group. Conversely, when a group composed primarily of men (e.g., a group of lab technicians) is valued only slightly more highly than a group composed mostly of women (e.g., a group of social workers), a woman may obtain the best outcomes by entering the mostly female group, especially if women within the mostly male group are valued much lower than men in the group.

Considered according to this logic, the mixed findings of studies examining the effects of numerical minority versus majority standing in a group upon the evaluation of socially low-status individuals become understandable. In all cases, the studies that showed no significant difference or more positive outcomes for women and blacks when in the numerical minority used professionals as the targets for dependent variable ratings (Hoskins, 1978; South et al., 1982; Taylor et al., 1978). In all cases, the studies that showed negative outcomes for women and blacks when in the numerical minority used students as the targets for dependent variable ratings (Braddock, 1981; Burnim, 1980; Cohen,

Pettigrew, & Riley, 1972; Holahan, 1979; Tidball, 1980). Perhaps students from a low-status social category who are in a numerical minority are more likely to be evaluated negatively than professionals with similar characteristics because professionals have already proven their competence in an area to some extent, while students are still developing competencies. Thus while a female or black professional may be valued no differently from a white male professional (or may even be overvalued, for reasons discussed above), a female or black student may be valued less than a white male student.

This logic may also explain Blalock's (1957) enigmatic finding of relatively high levels of economic discrimination against blacks among black-dominated census tracts in the South (in this study discrimination was measured by the size of the black/white earnings differential, the difference between the percentage white in unskilled jobs, and the difference between the percentage black and the percentage white in unskilled jobs, and the differences between black and white unemployment and home-ownership rates). Blalock (1957) found that the percentage of blacks in the census tract accounted for 64% of the variance in black-white economic discrimination in the South. While Blalock's finding has been replicated on more recent data bases (Brown & Fugitt, 1972; Glenn, 1964; Semyonov & Scott, 1983), this effect has been found to be unique to the southeastern United States (Blalock, 1956; Giles, 1972; Glenn, 1964).

Blalock's finding can be considered a case in which being in the numerical majority is detrimental to the outcomes of members of a low-status group. While blacks from mostly white neighborhoods may be economically disadvantaged, blacks from mostly black neighborhoods are even more disadvantaged, as shown by the even higher level of economic discrimination found in these areas. The reason this effect occurs only in the South may be because status differences between blacks and whites are greater in this region than anywhere else in the country. Since Southerners are less likely than other people in the United States to encounter blacks in prestigious positions, they may be most likely to consider blacks an undesirable group and to behave negatively toward them. Blacks wishing to move into a mostly white neighborhood in the South may have to command higher incomes, better education, and more prestigious jobs before being admitted to the community than is necessary for the acceptance of blacks in mostly white neighborhoods in other areas of the country. As a result blacks with lower incomes may tend not to reside in mostly white or mixed-race neighborhoods in the South. Thus if the only blacks residing in Southern white neighborhoods are those with relatively high incomes, this would explain Blalock's (1957) finding of a lower income discrepancy in favor of white families in these neighborhoods.

Subgroup Proportions and the
Social Isolation/Integration of Individuals

Kanter (1977) suggested that unbalanced subgroup proportions should have the effect of heightening subgroup distinctions. She theorized that when individuals of a new social category enter a previously homogeneous group, the group members become consciously aware of the characteristics that make them a group and, consequently, of subgroup differences. The numerically dominant subgroup may then behave in ways that heighten social boundaries between subgroups. Individuals in the minority in these unbalanced groups may therefore experience social isolation. It might be further hypothesized that low-status individuals in the numerical minority are more likely than high-status individuals in the minority to experience social isolation in unbalanced groups. Henley's (1977) findings of greater smiling and attention directed toward high-status individuals than toward low-status individuals suggest that high-status individuals may receive more opportunities for social interaction than low-status individuals when either is in the numerical minority. This hypothesis has received some research support. Women in predominantly male jobs have been found to be treated with hostility by male coworkers (O'Farrell & Harlan, 1982), while men in predominantly female jobs experience almost no hostility from female coworkers (Schreiber, 1979) and have been found to be socially well integrated into the work group (Fairhurst & Snavely, 1983).[2]

Gender effects may be different than other low-status effects in this respect, for women may be more likely to socialize with men than other low-status groups (e.g., blacks or Hispanics) are to socialize with whites. Women have more to gain by socializing with men, in terms of lovers and marriage partners; however, Gutek and Dunwoody (1986) and Gutek (1985) have emphasized that sexual behavior in the workplace seldom benefits women and often penalizes them. Blacks or Hispanics may refuse to socialize with whites, especially when their is ample opportunity to socialize with members of their own ethnic group.

Research has consistently shown that individuals choose to interact more often with members of their own social groups than with other individuals (Cohen, 1975; Sagar, Schofield, & Snyder, 1983; Sagar, Schofield, & St. John, 1975; Stephan, 1978). When they are in the numerical majority, low-status individuals may isolate the few high-status individuals socially because they prefer to interact with members of their own social group. Some evidence for the social isolation of whites in black-dominated groups has been reported by Bynum and Thompson (1983), who found that all five white students entering a predominantly black college as freshmen dropped out before the senior year. However, more research is needed on the social integration of whites as numerical minorities in groups made up largely of blacks or Hispanics.

Heterogeneity and social interaction in groups. Researchers have quantified the distributions of social categories within groups in ways that represent the *heterogeneity* of the group: that is, the relative diversity found among members of the group (Blau, 1977). Such measures of heterogeneity reflect both the number of subgroups represented in a group and the distribution of individuals among those subgroups. Blau (1977) considered heterogeneity to be a fundamental property of groups, and he defined it such that heterogeneity is maximized in a group having many types of subgroups and an equal number of individuals in each subgroup.

Researchers have theorized that the heterogeneity of a group influences the social experiences of individuals within the group. Two types of hypotheses have been examined in the literature. The first line of inquiry has tested the theory that as heterogeneity increases, the probability that two dissimilar individuals will come into contact increases. As the amount of random contact within the group increases, the probability that social interaction between dissimilar individuals will occur also increases (Blau, 1977). Research has generally supported this theory. Blau, Blum, and Schwartz (1982) found that as the ethnic heterogeneity of a census tract increased, the probability of intermarriage between ethnic groups increased. Similarly, Sampson (1984) showed that as the ethnic heterogeneity of a census tract increased, the probability of intergroup crime (i.e., crimes in which the victim and the perpetrator were of different ethnic groups) increased. Sampson (1984) also found that as the heterogeneity of a census tract by age increased, the probability of crimes in which the victim and perpetrator were of different age groups increased.

The second line of inquiry rests upon the large body of literature showing that individuals prefer to interact with similar rather than dissimilar others (Antill, 1983; Bradburn, Sudman, Gockel, & Noel, 1971; Hamilton & Bishop, 1976; Hill, Rubin, & Peplau, 1976; Hill & Stull, 1981; Kandel, 1978; Sagar et al., 1983; Schofield & Sagar, 1977; Singleton & Asher, 1977, 1979). Since people prefer similar others, the average quality of social interactions within a group should decline as the heterogeneity of the group increases (Konrad, 1986b). Konrad (1986b) found that as the sexual and educational heterogeneity of a work group increased, average ratings of social integration within the group declined. This decline in the quality of work-group social relations found among heterogeneous groups has been theorized as producing higher rates of turnover within these groups (Wagner, Pfeffer, & O'Reilly, 1984). O'Reilly and Caldwell (1986) found that increased work-group heterogeneity led to a decline in social integration within the group, and this decline in social integration led to an increase in turnover of group members. Wagner et al. (1984) found that turnover increased as the heterogeneity of executive work groups by age and tenure increased; and McCain, O'Reilly, and Pfeffer (1983) found that turnover increased as the heterogeneity of faculty groups by tenure increased.

Interactions of Group Proportion
Effects at Different System Levels

When a social institution, such as an occupation, becomes numerically dominated by individuals of a given social category, such as women, it may become stereotyped as that category's occupation (e.g., elementary school teaching and nursing are seen as women's occupations). However, when a particular organization in the same society generally hires men in that occupation, gender stereotyping of the occupation should decline among people in that organization. Conversely, when an organization generally hires women in that occupation, gender stereotyping of the occupation should increase among people in that organization. Research in the area of education has typically resulted in findings consistent with these hypotheses. Girls in grade school, as well as women in college, who have science, math, or law classes that are predominantly female have consistently been found to be more likely than other girls and women to perform well in these traditionally male fields and to major in these fields in college (Casserly & Rock, 1985; Finn, 1980; Fox, Brody, & Tobin, 1985; Lantz, 1985; Spangler et al., 1978; Tidball, 1980; Women's College Coalition, 1980).

Conclusion

Social distinctions may be defined as human characteristics along which individuals vary and which elicit predictable responses from other people. A review of the research shows that individuals react systematically to the social characteristics of gender and ethnicity. These reactions of individuals correspond to societal-level status differences between men and women and between ethnic groups. The relationships between gender and status, and ethnicity and status, within organizations interact in predictable ways with societal-level status differences between these social categories. Finally, the proportions of men and women and of ethnic subgroups within groups and organizations have systematic effects, many of which appear to be interrelated with societal-level status differences between these categories.

Directions for Future Research

This review of the existing literature on group composition highlights several areas that deserve more research attention. The present chapter has focused upon the social distinctions of gender and ethnicity, and one main reason for this focus is the abundance of empirical research available on these topics. However, the theoretical conceptualization of group composition presented here may be applied to other types of social distinctions, such as nationality, occupation, religion, and so on. Future research could usefully focus upon the effects of group composition along these other social dimensions, since little of the work that has been done has examined dimensions other than gender and ethnicity.

More generally, research on group composition should focus explicitly on the context in which group processes occur. For example, the impact on individuals of being part of the numerical minority or the majority in a group may depend upon the status characteristics held by the majority of the group (see also Gutek, Larwood, & Stromberg, 1986, pp. 227-228). Being in groups that are mostly composed of low-status individuals may not benefit low-status individuals because the groups themselves become devalued (even though low-status individuals may feel more comfortable there). High-status individuals who are in a numerical minority may receive better evaluations than do low-status group majorities because they are perceived as being more competent. Research also suggests that high-status individuals may have better social experiences when in the numerical minority than do low-status individuals. However, more research is needed on the social experiences of high-status individuals in groups composed mostly of low-status individuals, especially those of whites in groups of ethnic minorities.

Cases in which group composition at a given system level is radically different from the composition of the system at higher levels deserve special consideration (e.g., departments of black workers in a predominantly white company or mostly female departments in a predominantly male university). By examining groups whose composition differs greatly from the organizational norm, researchers can obtain insight into group-composition effects on behavior that may erroneously have been attributed to internal characteristics of the individual. For example, studies of educational institutions having many women or ethnic minorities in upper-level positions have shown major benefits in the outcomes of women or ethnic minority students. These findings suggest that the performance of low-status students may be hampered in the typical educational institution in which most upper-level positions are held by individuals from high-status social groups. Researchers who are inattentive to such composition effects may erroneously attribute the negative outcomes of low-status students in typical educational settings to immutable internal deficiencies in abilities or motivation.

Research on the impact of the composition of organizational hierarchies promises to be one of the most fruitful areas for the study of group composition. The little research that has been conducted in this area has shown consistently large effect sizes. Since this research has been conducted exclusively in educational settings, studies of other types of organizations and groups (e.g., businesses) are needed to determine whether these effects generalize to other settings.

Notes

1. Obviously, before an individual can be treated differently because of his or her membership in a social group, the fact that the individual belongs to the social group must be known to others. In addition to being known, the social group membership of the individual must be salient in the current situation if behavioral effects are to occur. It seems clear that in *any* situation there are *some* social groupings that are not salient and thus become irrelevant to the social behavior that occurs. For example, in many situations, individuals are treated no differently from one another whether they are members of the American Civil Liberties Union (ACLU) or not. However, in some situations, ACLU membership may have important social consequences for the individual. It also seems clear that some social classifications are salient more often than others and thus influence behavior in more situations. For example, race may affect social behavior in many situations, where as ACLU membership may not. McGuire, McGuire, and Winton (1979) and McGuire and Padawer-Singer (1976) provided a list of six conditions under which a social characteristic of an individual becomes salient:

(1) the characteristic is distinctive in that it is somewhat unique;
(2) the characteristic is relevant to the task at hand;
(3) the characteristic is obvious rather than subtle;
(4) the characteristic is available (that is, in awareness) due to recency, familiarity, or prior expectations;
(5) the characteristic is relevant to enduring values; and
(6) the characteristic has been an important determinant of reward and punishment in past experiences.

Social characteristics with one or more of these six qualities should be most salient.

2. The findings of South et al. (1982, 1983) seem to contradict the hypothesis that individuals in a numerical minority in a group experience relative social isolation. These researchers found that as the proportion of a group making up an individual's own sex declines, amount of contact with group members of the opposite sex increases. However, their findings do not indicate whether the *total* amount of contact with coworkers is lower when the individual is in a numerical minority, as is hypothesized here. While women in a predominantly male work group may have more contact with men than do women in a predominantly female work group, due merely to the fact that the probability of contact with men increases when there are more men around (Blau, 1977), they may still have fewer social contacts than do men in the mostly male group.

The quality of contact is also important, and women in predominantly male work groups often receive many derogatory contacts, sexual innuendos (or even sexual harassment), and requests to perform menial service functions (like making the coffee).

References

Abramson, P.E., Goldberg, P. A., Greenberg, J. H., & Abramson, L. M. (1977). The talking platypus phenomenon: Competency ratings as a function of sex and professional status. *Psychology of Women Quarterly, 2,* 114-124.

Antill, J. K. (1983). Sex role complementarity versus similarity in married couples. *Journal of Personality and Social Psychology, 45,* 145-155.

Becker, H. S. (1963). *Outsiders.* New York: Free Press.

Berger, P. L., & Luckmann, T. (1966). *The social construction of reality.* Garden City, NY: Doubleday.

Bielby, W. T., & Baron, J. N. (1986). Men and women at work: Sex segregation and statistical discrimination. *American Journal of Sociology, 91,* 759-799.

Blalock, H. M. (1956). Economic discrimination and Negro increase. *American Sociological Review, 22,* 584-588.

Blalock, H. M. (1957). Per cent non-white and discrimination in the South. *American Sociological Review, 23,* 677-682.

Blau, P. M. (1977). *Inequality and heterogeneity.* New York: Free Press.

Blau, P. M., Blum, T. C., & Schwartz, J. E. (1982). Heterogeneity and intermarriage. *American Sociological Review, 47,* 45-62.

Bradburn, N. M., Sudman, S., Gockel, G. L., & Noel, J. R. (1971). *Side by side: Integrated neighborhoods in America.* Chicago: Quadrangle Books.

Braddock, J. H., II. (1981). Desegregation and black student attrition. *Urban Education, 15,* 403-418.

Bradley, P. H. (1980). Sex, competence, and opinion deviation: An expectation states approach. *Communication Monographs, 47,* 101-110.

Brown, D. L., & Fuguitt, G. V. (1972). Percent nonwhite and racial disparity in nonmetropolitan cities in the South. *Social Science Quarterly, 53,* 573-582.

Brown, G. D. (1976, July). How type of employment affects earnings differences by sex. *Monthly Labor Review, 99,* 25-30.

Brown, G. D. (1978, March). Discrimination and pay disparities between white men and women. *Monthly Labor Review, 101,* 17-22.

Buckley, J. E. (1971, November). Pay differences between men and women in the same job. *Monthly Labor Review, 94,* 36-39.

Burnim, M. L. (1980). The earnings effect of black matriculation in predominantly white colleges. *Industrial and Labor Relations Review, 33,* 518-524.

Buttner, E., & Rosen, B. (1986, August). *The effects of labor shortages on starting salaries for sex typed jobs.* Paper presented at the meeting of the Academy of Management, Chicago.

Bynum, J. E., & Thompson, W. E. (1983). Dropouts, stopouts and persisters: The effects of race and sex composition of college classes. *College & University, 59*(Fall), 39-48.

Casserly, P. L., & Rock, D. (1985). Factors related to young women's persistence and achievement in advanced placement mathematics. In S. F. Chipman, L. R. Brush, & D. M. Wilson (Eds.), *Women and mathematics: Balancing the equation* (pp. 225-248). Hillsdale, NJ: Lawrence Erlbaum.

Cohen, D. K., Pettigrew, T. F., & Riley, R. T. (1972). Race and outcomes of schooling. In T. Mosteller & D. P. Moynihan (Eds.), *On equality of educational opportunity.* New York: Random House.

Cohen, E. (1975). The effects of desegregation on race relations. *Law and Contemporary Problems, 39,* 271-299.

Corcoran, M., & Duncan, G. J. (1978). Work history, labor force attachment, and earnings differences between the races and sexes. *Journal of Human Resources, 14,* 3-20.

Crino, M. D., White, M. C., & DeSanctis, G. L. (1983). Female participation rates and the occupational prestige of the professions: Are they inversely related? *Journal of Vocational Behavior, 22,* 243-255.

Crocker, J., & McGraw, K. M. (1984). What's good for the goose is not good for the gander. *American Behavioral Scientist, 27,* 357-369.

Diab, L. N. (1970). A study of intragroup and intergroup relations among experimentally produced small groups. *Genetic Psychology Monographs, 82,* 49-82.

Dudycha, G. J. (1942). The attitudes of college students toward war and the Germans before and during the Second World War. *Journal of Social Psychology, 15,* 317-324.

Eagly, A. H., & Steffen, V. J. (1984). Gender stereotypes stem from the distribution of women and men into social roles. *Journal of Personality and Social Psychology, 46,* 735-754.

Eagly, A. H., & Wood, W. (1982). Inferred sex differences in status as a determinant of gender stereotypes about social influence. *Journal of Personality and Social Psychology, 43,* 915-928.

England, P. (1984). Wage appreciation and depreciation: A test of neoclassical economic explanations of occupational sex segregation. *Social Forces, 62,* 726-749.

Etzkowitz, H. (1971). The male sister: Sexual separation of labor in society. *Journal of Marriage and the Family, 34,* 431-434.

Fairhurst, G. T., & Snavely, B. K. (1983). A test of the social isolation of male tokens. *Academy of Management Journal, 26,* 353-361.

Feather, N. T. (1975). Positive and negative reactions to male and female success and failure in relation to the perceived status and sex-typed appropriateness of occupations. *Journal of Personality and Social Psychology, 31,* 536-548.

Finn, J. D. (1980). Sex differences in educational outcomes: A cross-national study. *Sex Roles, 6,* 9-26.

Fleming, J. (1985). *Blacks in college: A comparative study of students' success in black and in white institutions.* San Francisco: Jossey-Bass.

Fox, L. H., Brody, L., & Tobin, D. (1985). The impact of early intervention programs upon course-taking and attitudes in high school. In S. F. Chipman, L. R. Brush, & D. M. Wilson (Eds.), *Women and mathematics: Balancing the equation* (pp. 249-274). Hillsdale, NJ: Lawrence Erlbaum.

Frances, S. J. (1979). Sex differences in nonverbal behavior. *Sex Roles, 5,* 519-535.

Francesco, A. M., & Hakel, M. D. (1981). Gender and sex as determinants of hierability of applicants for gender-typed jobs. *Psychology of Women Quarterly, 5,* 747-757.

Frieze, I. H., & Ramsey, S. J. (1976). Nonverbal maintenance of traditional sex roles. *Journal of Social Issues, 32*(3), 133-141.

Giles, M. W. (1972). Percent black and racial hostility: An old assumption reexamined. *Social Science Quarterly, 53,* 412-417.

Glenn, N. D. (1964). The relative size of the Negro population and Negro occupational status. *Social Forces, 43,* 42-49.

Goffman, E. (1969). Mental illness and the insanity of place. In D. H. Wrong & H. L. Gracey (Eds.), *Readings in introductory sociology* (3rd ed.). New York: Macmillan.

Gutek, B. A. (1985). *Sex and the workplace: Impact of sexual behavior and harassment on women, men and organizations.* San Francisco: Jossey-Bass.

Gutek, B. A., & Dunwoody, V. (1986). Understanding sex in the workplace and its effects on women, men, and organizations. In A. Stromberg, L. Larwood, & B. A. Gutek, *Women and work: An annual review* (Vol. 2, pp. 249-269). Newbury Park, CA: Sage.

Gutek, B. A., Larwood, L., & Stromberg, A. (1986). Women at work. In C. L. Cooper & I. Robertson (Eds.), *Review of industrial and organizational psychology* (pp. 218-234). Chichester, England: John Wiley.

Gutek, B. A., & Morasch, B. (1982). Sex ratios, sex-role spillover, and sexual harassment of women at work. *Journal of Social Issues, 38*(4), 55-74.

Hacker, H. M. (1981). Blabbermouths and clams: Sex differences in self-disclosure in same-sex and cross-sex friendship dyads. *Psychology of Women Quarterly, 5,* 385-401.

Hamilton, D. L., & Bishop, G. D. (1976). Attitudinal and behavioral effects of initial integration of white suburban neighborhoods. *Journal of Social Issues, 32*(2), 47-67.

Henley, N. M. (1977). *Body politics: Power, sex, and nonverbal communication.* Englewood Cliffs, NJ: Prentice-Hall.

Hill, C. T., Rubin, Z., & Peplau, L. A. (1976). Breakups before marriage: The end of 103 affairs. *Journal of Social Issues, 32*(1), 147-168.

Hill, C. T., & Stull, D. E. (1981). Sex differences in effects of social and value similarity in same-sex friendship. *Journal of Personality and Social Psychology, 71,* 249-263.

Hodge, R. W., & Hodge, P. (1965). Occupational assimilation as a competitive process. *American Journal of Sociology, 71,* 249-263.

Hoffman, S. D. (1981, July). On-the-job training: Differences by race and sex. *Monthly Labor Review, 104,* 34-36.

Holahan, C. K. (1979). Stress experienced by women doctoral students, need for support, and occupational sex typing: An interactional view. *Sex Roles, 5,* 425-436.

Hoskins. R. L. (1978). *Black administrators in higher education: Conditions and perceptions.* New York: Praeger.

Howard, J. W., & Rothbart, M. (1980). Social categorization and memory for in-group and out-group behavior. *Journal of Personality and Social Psychology, 38,* 301-310.

Hurwitz-Inwald, R., & Bryant, N. D. (1981). The effect of sex of participants on decision making in small teacher groups. *Psychology of Women Quarterly, 5,* 532-542.

Instone, D., Major, B., & Bunker, B. B. (1983). Gender, self confidence, and social influence strategies: An organizational simulation. *Journal of Personality and Social Psychology, 44,* 322-333.

Izraeli, D. N. (1983). Sex effects or structural effects? An empirical test of Kanter's theory of proportions. *Social Forces, 62,* 153-165.

Juni, S., & Brannon, R. (1981). Interpersonal touching as a function of status and sex. *Journal of Social Psychology, 114,* 135-136.

Kandel, D. B. (1978). Similarity in real-life adolescent friendship pairs. *Journal of Personality and Social Psychology, 36,* 306-312.

Kanter, R. M. (1977). *Men and women of the corporation.* New York: Basic Books.

Kaschak, E. (1981). Another look at sex bias in students' evaluations of professors: Do winners get the recognition that they have been given? *Psychology of Women Quarterly, 5,* 767-772.

Katz, D., & Kahn, R. L. (1978). *The social psychology of organizations.* New York: John Wiley.

Katz, P. A. (1976). The acquisition of racial attitudes in children. In P. A. Katz (Ed.), *Toward the elimination of racism* (pp. 125-154). New York: Pergamon.

Kaufman, R. L. (1983). A structural decomposition of black-white earnings differentials. *American Journal of Sociology, 89,* 585-611.

Kerckhoff, A. C. (1984). The current state of social mobility research. *Sociological Quarterly, 25,* 139-153.

Kipnis, D. (1984). The use of power in organizations and in interpersonal settings. In S. Oskamp (Ed.), *Applied social psychology annual: Vol. 5. Applications in organizational settings* (pp. 179-210). Newbury Park, CA: Sage.

Konrad, A. M. (1986a). *Explaining the male-female earnings differential.* Manuscript submitted for publication.

Konrad, A. M. (1986b). *The impact of work group composition on social integration and evaluation.* Unpublished doctoral dissertation, Claremont Graduate School, Claremont, CA.

Krefting, L. A., Berger, P. K., & Wallace, M. J., Jr. (1978). The contribution of sex distribution, job content, and occupational classification to job sextyping: Two studies. *Journal of Vocational Behavior, 13,* 181-191.

Lantz, A. (1985). Strategies to increase mathematics enrollments. In S. F. Chipman, L. R. Brush, & D. M. Wilson (Eds.), *Women and mathematics: Balancing the equation* (pp. 329-354). Hillsdale, NJ: Lawrence Erlbaum.

Latane, B., & Wolf, S. (1981). The social impact of majorities and minorities. *Psychological Review, 88,* 438-453.

Lavine, L. D. (1982). Parental power as a potential influence on girls' career choice. *Child Development, 53,* 658-663.

Leffler, A., Gillespie, D. L., & Conaty, J. C. (1982). The effects of status differentiation on nonverbal behavior. *Social Psychology Quarterly, 45*(3), 153-161.

Lockheed, M. E. (1985). Sex and social influence: A meta-analysis guided by theory. In J. Berger & M. Zelditch, Jr., *Status, rewards, and influence: How expectations organize behavior.* San Francisco: Jossey-Bass.

Locksley, A., Ortiz, V., & Hepburn, C. (1980). Social categorization and discriminatory behavior: Extinguishing the minimal intergroup discrimination effect. *Journal of Personality and Social Psychology, 39,* 773-783.

Martinko, M. J., & Gardner, W. L. (1983). A methodological review of sex-related access discrimination problems. *Sex Roles, 9,* 825-839.

McCain, B. E., O'Reilly, C., & Pfeffer, J. (1983). The effects of departmental demography on turnover: The case of a university. *Academy of Management Journal, 26,* 626-641.

McDougall-Young, A. (1977, June). Year-round full-time earnings in 1975. *Monthly Labor Review, 100,* 36-41.

McDougall-Young, A. (1979, June). Median earnings in 1977 reported for year-round full-time workers. *Monthly Labor Review, 102,* 35-39.

McGuire, W. J., McGuire, C. V., & Winton, W. (1979). Effects of household sex composition on the salience of one's gender in the spontaneous self-concept. *Journal of Experimental Social Psychology, 15,* 77-90.

McGuire, W. J., & Padawer-Singer, A. (1976). Trait salience in the spontaneous self-concept. *Journal of Personality and Social Psychology, 33,* 743-754.

McLaughlin, S. D. (1978). Occupational sex identification and the assessment of male and female earnings inequality. *American Sociological Review, 43,* 909-921.

Milner, D. (1975). *Children and race.* Harmondsworth, England: Penguin.

Milner, D. (1981). Racial prejudice. In J. C. Turner & H. Giles (Eds.), *Intergroup behavior* (pp. 102-143). Oxford, England: Blackwell.

Moore, H. A., & Johnson, D. R. (1983). A reexamination of elementary school teacher expectations: Evidence of sex and ethnic segmentation. *Social Science Quarterly, 64,* 460-475.

Nieva, V. F., & Gutek, B. A. (1980). Sex effects on evaluation. *Academy of Management Review, 5,* 267-276.

Nilson, L. B. (1976). The occupational and sex-related components of social standing. *Sociology and Social Research, 60,* 328-336.

O'Farrell, B., & Harlan, S. L. (1982). Craftworkers and clerks: The effect of male coworker hostility on women's satisfaction with non-traditional jobs. *Social Problems, 29,* 252-264.

O'Reilly, C. A., III., & Caldwell, D. F. (1986, July). *Work group demography, social integration, and turnover.* University of California, Berkeley, Working Papers.

Parsons, J. E., Adler, T. F., & Kaczala, C. M. (1982). Socialization of achievement attitudes and beliefs: Parental influence. *Child Development, 53,* 310-321.

Perry, R. W. (1980). Social status and the black violence hypothesis. *Journal of Social Psychology, 111,* 131-137.

Persell, C. H. (1983). Gender, rewards and research in education. *Psychology of Women Quarterly, 8,* 33-47.

Petersik, J., & Schneir, S. (1980). Sex role dynamics in the grade book. *SASP Newsletter, 6*(1), 7-8.

Pfeffer, J. (1981). Some consequences of organizational demography: Potential impacts of an aging work force on formal organizations. In S. B. Kiesler, J. N. Morgan, & V. K. Oppenheimer (Eds.), *Aging: Social change* (pp. 291-329). New York: Academic Press.

Pfeffer, J., & Davis-Blake, A. (1987). The effect of the proportion of women on salaries: The case of college administrators. *Administrative Science Quarterly, 32:* 1-24.

Piacente, B. A., Penner, L. A., Hawkins, H. L., & Cohen, S. L. (1974). Evaluation of the performance of experimenters as a function of their sex and competence. *Journal of Applied Social Psychology, 4,* 321-329.

Porter, J. N. (1974). Race, socialization, and mobility in educational and early occupational attainment. *American Sociological Review, 39,* 303-316.

Pugh, M. D., & Wahrman, R. (1983). Neutralizing sexism to mixed-sex groups: Do women have to be better than men? *American Journal of Sociology, 88,* 746-762.

Pushkin, I., & Veness, T. (1973). The development of racial awareness and prejudice in children. In P. A. Katz (Ed.), *Toward the elimination of racism* (pp. 23-42). New York: Pergamon.

Ramirez, A., & Soriano, F. (1982). Social power in educational systems: Its effect on Chicanos' attitudes toward the school experience. *Journal of Social Psychology, 118,* 113-119.

Rosenhan, D. L. (1973). On being sane in insane places. *Science, 179,* 250-258.

Rovner-Pieczenik, R. (1976). Labeling in an organizational context: Adjudicating felony cases in an urban court. In M. P. Golden (Ed.), *The research experience* (pp. 447-464). Itasca, IL: Peacock.

Ruble, T. L., Cohen, R., & Ruble, D. N. (1984). Sex stereotypes. *American Behavioral Scientist, 27,* 339-356.

Rytina, N. F. (1982, April). Tenure as a factor in the male-female earnings gap. *Monthly Labor Review, 105,* 32-34.

Rytina, N. F. (1983, April). Occupational segregation and earnings differences by sex. *Monthly Labor Review, 106,* 32-34.

Sagar, H. A., & Schofield, J. W. (1980). Racial and behavioral cues in black and white children's perceptions of ambiguously aggressive acts. *Journal of Personality and Social Psychology, 39,* 590-598.

Sagar, H. A., Schofield, J. W., & St. John, N. (1975). *School desegregation: Outcomes for children.* New York: John Wiley.

Sagar, H. A., Schofield, J. W., & Snyder, H. N. (1983). Race and gender barriers: Preadolescent peer behavior in academic classrooms. *Child Development, 54,* 1032-1040.

Sampson, R. J. (1984). Group size, heterogeneity, and intergroup conflict: A test of Blau's *Inequality and Heterogeneity. Social Forces, 62,* 618-639.

Schofield, J. W., & Sagar, H. A. (1977). Peer interaction patterns in an integrated middle school. *Sociometry, 40,* 130-138.

Schreiber, C. T. (1979). *Changing places: Men and women in transitional occupations.* Cambridge, MA: MIT Press.

Seago, D. W. (1947). Stereotypes: Before Pearl Harbor and after. *Journal of Psychology, 23,* 55-63.

Segal, B. E. (1962). Male nurses: A case study in status contradiction and prestige loss. *Social Forces, 41,* 31-38.

Semyonov, M., & Scott, R. I. (1983). Percent black, community characteristics and race-linked occupational differentiation in the rural South. *Rural Sociology, 48,* 240-252.

Sherif, M., Harvey, O. J., White, B. J., Hood, W. E., & Sherif, C. W. (1961). *The robber's cave experiment.* Norman: University of Oklahoma Book Exchange.

Sieling, M. S. (1984, June). Staffing patterns prominent in female-male earnings gap. *Monthly Labor Review, 107,* 29-33.

Singleton, L. C., & Asher, S. R. (1977). Peer preferences and social interaction among third-grade children in an integrated school district. *Journal of Educational Psychology, 69,* 330-336.

Singleton, L. C., & Asher, S. R. (1979). Racial integration and children's peer preferences: An investigation of developmental and cohort differences. *Child Development, 50,* 936-941.

Sinha, A.K.P., & Upadhyaya, O. P. (1960). Change and persistence in the stereotypes of university students toward different ethnic groups during Sino-Indian border dispute. *Journal of Social Psychology, 52,* 31-39.

South, S. J., Bonjean, C. M., Markham, W. T., & Corder, J. (1982). Social structure and intergroup interaction: Men and women of the federal bureaucracy. *American Sociological Review, 47,* 587-599.

South, S. J., Bonjean, C. M., Markham, W. T., & Corder, J. (1983). Female labor force participation and the organizational experiences of male workers. *Sociological Quarterly, 24,* 367-380.

Spangler, E., Gordon, M. A., & Pipkin, R. M. (1978). Token women: An empirical test of Kanter's hypothesis. *American Journal of Sociology, 84,* 160-170.

Stake, J. E., Walker, E. F., & Speno, M. V. (1981). The relationship of sex and academic performance to quality of recommendations for graduate school. *Psychology of Women Quarterly, 5,* 515-522.

Stephan, W. G. (1978). School desegregation: An evaluation of predictions made in "Brown v. Board of Education." *Psychological Bulletin, 85,* 217-238.

Stevens, G. (1980). Bias in attributions of positive and negative behavior in children by school psychologists, parents, and teachers. *Perceptual and Motor Skills, 50,* 1283-1290.

Stevens, G. (1981). Bias in the attribution of hyperkinetic behavior as a function of ethnic identification and socioeconomic status. *Psychology in the Schools, 18,* 99-106.

Suchner, R. W. (1979). Sex ratios and occupational prestige: Three failures to replicate a sexist bias. *Personality and Social Psychology Bulletin, 5,* 236-239.

Suter, L. E., & Miller, H. P. (1972). Income differences between men and career women. *American Journal of Sociology, 78,* 962-974.

Tajfel, H. (1982). Social psychology of intergroup relations. In M. R. Rosenzweig & L. W. Porter (Eds.), *Annual review of psychology* (Vol. 33, pp. 1-39).

Tajfel, H., Billig, M. G., Bundy, R. P., & Flament, C. (1971). Social categorization and intergroup behavior. *European Journal of Social Psychology, 1,* 149-178.

Taylor, S. E., Fiske, S. T., Etcoff, N. L., & Ruderman, A. J. (1978). Categorical and contextual bases of person memory and stereotyping. *Journal of Personality and Social Psychology, 36,* 778-793.

Taynor, J., & Deaux, K. (1973). When women are more deserving than men. *Journal of Personality and Social Psychology, 28,* 360-367.

Taynor, J., & Deaux, K. (1975). Equity and perceived sex differences: Role behavior as defined by the task, the mode, and the actor. *Journal of Personality and Social Psychology, 32,* 381-390.

Tidball, M. E. (1980). Women's colleges and women achievers revisited. *Signs: Journal of Women in Culture and Society, 5,* 504-517.

Touhey, J. C. (1974a). Effects of additional women professionals on ratings of occupational prestige and desirability. *Journal of Personality and Social Psychology, 29,* 86-89.

Touhey, J. C. (1974b). Effects of additional men on prestige and desirability of occupations typically performed by women. *Journal of Applied Social Psychology, 4,* 330-335.

Treiman, D. J., & Roos, P. A. (1983). Sex and earnings in industrial society: A nine-nation comparison. *American Journal of Sociology, 89,* 612-650.

Turner, J. C., Sachdev, I., & Hogg, M. A. (1983). Social categorization, interpersonal attraction, and group formation. *British Journal of Social Psychology, 22:* 227-239.

Turner, J. H. (1982). *The structure of sociological theory.* New York: Dorsey.

Wagner, W. G., Pfeffer, J., & O'Reilly, C. A., III. (1984). Organizational demography and turnover in top-management groups. *Administrative Science Quarterly, 29,* 74-92.

White, M. C., Crino, M. D., & DeSanctis, G. L. (1981). Ratings of prestige and desirability: Effects of additional women entering selected business occupations. *Personality and Social Psychology Bulletin, 7,* 588-592.

Wicker, A. W. (1969). Attitudes versus actions: the relationship of verbal and overt behavioral responses to attitude objects. *Journal of Social Issues, 25*(4), 41-78.

Wiley, M. G., & Eskilson, A. (1982). Coping in the corporation: Sex role constraints. *Journal of Applied Social Psychology, 12,* 1-11.

Wolman, C., & Frank, H. (1975). The solo woman in a professional peer group. *American Journal of Orthopsychiatry, 45,* 164-171.

Women's College Coalition. (1980). *A profile of women's colleges: Analysis of the data.* (Available from the Women's College Coalition, 1725 K St., N.W.—Suite 1003, Washington, DC 20006).

5

Toward a Taxonomy
of Interpersonal
Conflict Processes

HAROLD H. KELLEY

I believe that patterns of interaction process, which we may call interaction sequences, constitute the basic phenomena of an *interpersonal science*. This is an important science, lying as it does at the intersection of clinical, developmental, personality, and social psychology, drawing on and contributing to all of these areas and to their interplay. For its development, this strategically located science needs a collection of its basic phenomena, a collection of interaction sequences. Just as other sciences (e.g., geology, zoology, botany) have, for their development, required collections—in museums and botanical and zoological gardens—of the entities they try to understand and explain, so we interpersonal scientists need a collection of our focal entities—a collection of interaction sequences.

One of my goals for interpersonal science is that we may develop a collection of this sort and come to realize the scientific benefits to be derived from it. I anticipate that a collection of interaction sequences will serve, first, to make more real and concrete the phenomena that are the target of our scientific efforts. Next, the collection will serve to stimulate the classification, measurement, and description of our phenomena. Finally, it will promote the development of theory to account for the variety of sequences and for the conditions of their occurrence.

From an applied perspective, I would expect this collection to be useful for interpersonal practitioners, that is, for applied social psychologists who deal with problems of the family, marriage, and small groups. For example, I can imagine an atlas of sequences, somewhat like the MMPI Atlas, in which an interpersonal therapist can look up an observed husband-wife scenario and quickly obtain information about its occurrence, its implications, the conditions of its change, and so on.

From a theoretical perspective, assembly of information about interaction sequences reflects my long-standing interest in establishing the conceptual links among the three major domains of interpersonal phenomena: *situations* of interdependence, the actors' interpersonal *dispositions,* and the *interaction process* resulting from the interplay of situation and dispositions. The theoretical works of John Thibaut and myself (Kelley & Thibaut, 1978; Thibaut & Kelley, 1959) have focused on the structure of interdependence; but from the very first we have also been interested in the processes deriving from those structures, as illustrated by our analysis of the process occurring in the minimal social situation (Kelley, Thibaut, Radloff, & Mundy, 1962). What has changed over the intervening years is the increasing study of *natural* interaction process by scientists outside of social psychology, particularly in child development, clinical psychology, and sociology. It is now becoming possible to compare natural processes with those produced in laboratory studies (largely by experimental social psychologists) and, as in this chapter, to apply social psychological theory to both bodies of evidence. More important, it becomes possible to shift away from the past preoccupations with situational, structural, and personality factors in interpersonal relations and to give equal attention to the processes that constitute the ongoing functioning of those relations—the processes by which relationships become alive, develop, change, and die.

In this chapter, I have made an attempt to draw together some of the existing evidence about patterns of interpersonal conflict. My survey is very far from complete. "Conflict" probably defines the category of process about which there exists the most varied and extensive body of evidence, so I present only a small sample of what is thought and known about conflict processes. My original goal in preparing this chapter was to develop a taxonomy of conflict processes. However, I have found it necessary to clear away some conceptual underbrush and settle for a broad overview of the domain of interpersonal conflict. My two purposes in what follows, then, are (1) to gain a sense of how to go about assembling this sort of information, and (2) to get a general idea of the insights it is likely to yield.

Definition of Conflict

Defining conflict seems like an essential first step in my effort. I worry about getting bogged down on this point, because I can remember more than one seminar that never got beyond this sort of initial definitional question. However, some preliminary thoughts on the matter seem necessary.

There is a general distinction in the literature between three aspects of conflict: (1) the structure, (2) the content or topic, and (3) the process. I will have more to say about these below. Here, it is simply necessary to make clear that my focal concern is with the last. Having the goal of constructing a taxonomy of process, I need not *directly* consider the kinds of structures and content involved in conflict. So the question is: "What features of process are essential if we are to identify a specific interaction sequence as one of *conflict*?" An answer to this question is necessary, of course, if we are to distinguish conflict process from other classes of process.

Are we to look for certain words or certain kinds of motor behavior as defining conflict? Name-calling? Hitting? Probably not, because we can think of conflicts that are conducted without such events, for instance, the wordless exchange of hateful glares. Should we look for negative effect (anger, fear, sadness) as the criterion? This would certainly not suffice unless we were able unequivocally to attribute the negative affect to the interaction. We might do a little better by resorting to affect terms that have strong interpersonal implications, such as hostility, antagonism, hatred, antipathy. From Fink's (1968) broad survey of problems in conflict theory, it is clear that a variety of other terms are possible definers of conflict: *competition, rivalry, active opposition, struggle, antagonistic interaction.* However, it must be noted that these terms are often proposed as labels for classes of process to be *distinguished from* conflict. Alternatively, these terms seem to be merely possible synonyms for "conflict," or worse, labels for subclasses of it. They do not help us zero in on the paradigmatic instances of our broad and fuzzy category.

To escape this morass, I will provisionally adopt the definition provided by Donald Peterson in our recent book, *Close Relationships: "Conflict is an interpersonal process that occurs whenever the actions of one person interfere with the actions of another"* (Peterson, 1983, p. 365, italics in original). For a number of reasons, this definition is very useful: It focuses our attention on something happening between two or more people (i.e., it is clearly interpersonal); it does not concern itself with *why* it might be that the one person is acting or *why* the other's actions are being interfered with (i.e., it doesn't contaminate the definition of process with inter- or intrapersonal structural factors); it links interpersonal conflict with negative affect (via George Mandler's conception of affect as stemming from interruption of an organized behavior sequence—a conception applied to interaction by Ellen Berscheid, 1983); and it is general enough to cover all sorts of actions and types of causal links between the two persons.

Peterson's (1983) definition can be illustrated by his example, shown in Figure 5.1, of a quarrel between a husband and wife during their drive home from a visit to his parents. As she drives and he studies, he shifts his position in a manner that blocks her view through the rearview mirror. Made anxious, she asks him to move, which interrupts his studying and annoys him. Thinking she can adjust to the situation, he tells her to use the side mirror. That annoys her, and so on down the sequence of exchanges until he takes over the driving. In Figure 5.1 (which follows the general mode of analysis suggested in our book, Kelley et al., 1983), each person is pictured as generating multistrand chains of affect, thought, and action, which are organized via intrastrand causal links. Interaction consists of causal connections between the two chains. Conflict, according to Peterson's definition, exists when the *inter*chain connections provide interference with the *intra*chain organization of events, as illustrated by his blocking her vision and her interrupting his studying.

Framework for Locating Different Aspects of Conflict

Let us return to the three-way distinction between structure, content, and process. The structure-process distinction runs throughout discussions of conflict, and many empirical studies provide evidence on the

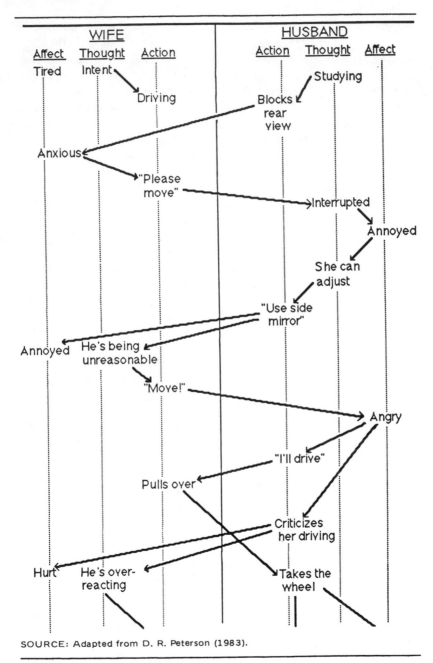

SOURCE: Adapted from D. R. Peterson (1983).

Figure 5.1: Illustration of Conflict

content. Because my goal is not merely to classify the processes but also to understand them, I believe it is necessary to examine them in the light of the other two aspects of conflict. Both the structural and the topical aspects of conflict would seem, on logical grounds, to be relevant to the form and the conditions of occurrence of conflict.

These three categories provide a broad framework for assembling ideas and information about conflict. Thus the headings at the top of Figure 5.2 provide the outline we must eventually fill in. *Structure* refers to the more or less stable causal factors that give rise to and provide the context for any particular conflict process. *Content* refers to what the conflict is about—the topics or issues. *Process* refers to the conflictual interaction—the sequence of events that includes what we have tentatively proposed as the distinctive feature, namely, one person's actions interfering with those of another person.

Conflict Structure

In order to reflect more fully the literature and phenomena of confict, under "structure" in Figure 5.2 it is necessary to distinguish between *situation* and *persons*. The literature is replete with terms that suggest one category or the other. Suggested by Fink's (1968) review are the *situation* terms shown in Figure 5.2: conflict situation, competitive social situation, scarce resources, competitive marketplace, conflicting group interests. Terms referring to the *persons* include conflict of personalities, incompatible difference in objectives, inharmonious like interests, unlike attitudes, conflicting interests, and competing desires.

It is not always clear where to make this distinction. For there to be a *situation* of conflict of interest, there must be *persons* with incompatible interests. It seems that the conflict-promoting nature of the situation can always be traced to something about the persons. Yet two persons with certain interests may find their goals in conflict under certain external circumstances (e.g., scarcity of resources, which renders their interests incompatible) but not under other circumstances (e.g., a plenitude of means for satisfying their similar needs). The situation-persons distinction also comes up in the recurrent question, particularly common in debates about international conflict: Are the contending parties the victims of their external circumstances, of scarcity of resources and objective conflict of interest? Or is their conflict of their own making, a

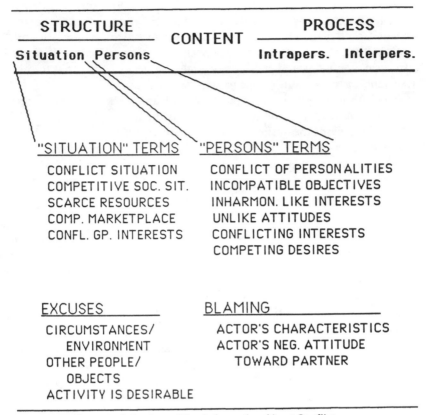

Figure 5.2: Framework for Assembling Information About Conflict

result of their wrong-headedness, short-sightedness, and unnecessary hostility?

The situation-persons issue also appears in the attributional aspect of interpersonal conflict, where there is often an implicit or explicit debate about the reasons for one person's offensive behavior. The terms of this debate are shown in the lower portion of Figure 5.2. The offender often makes excuses by reference to causal factors that are situational and more or less external to himself or herself, asserting that the behavior is explainable by reference to the circumstances, other people, or its intrinsic desirability. The victim of the offense more often points the finger of blame at the offender as a person, by reference to his or her personal traits or attitudes (Orvis, Kelley, & Butler, 1975).

I have some ideas about how to resolve the conceptual question of "situation" versus "persons," but they are too lengthy to explain here. I am convinced that the situation-persons distinction is an important psychological reality for the conflicting parties, as revealed in attributional conflict, *and,* furthermore, that a clear drawing of the distinction is not only possible but essential in our theoretical analysis.

Conflict Content

Table 5.1 lists the results from a few of the many studies that have described the content of conflict. Included are examples from a variety of ages and relationships. We may note in advance that these content categories are not cleanly separable from the other categories. These topical lists sometimes include clear references to structure (e.g., conflicting preferences) or process (e.g., blocking, interference).

Dawe's (1934) categories reflect her observers' judgments of the kind of difficulty over which a quarrel began between preschoolers during outdoor free play. Hartup's (1974) list, also based on observations, is a coding of three broad classes of action that led to a child's aggressive act at school. Kounin's (1970) list is a coding of children's answers to the question, "What is the worst thing a kid can do at home (at school)?" Whereas Kounin's list suggests what children do that annoys adults (at least, as the kids view it), Patterson's (1982) observation categories define aversive stimuli a child can receive from his or her parents and siblings and that serve as antecedents for the child's negative behavior.

My list (Kelley, 1979) is a categorization of young couples' reports of the problems they encountered in their relationships. Finally, Toch's (1969) list is coded from arrest reports that include police officers' descriptions of the events leading up to their being assaulted by a person they had stopped and questioned.

These lists show the variety of things that trigger conflict, that give rise to annoyance, that lead to active argument or even violent combat. They are the events to which people react with anger and attack, they are the subject matter of hot arguments and quarrels. They are the "content" of interpersonal conflict.

Of the many ideas stimulated by these lists, I will note only one. Our criterion for conflict, one person's actions interfering with the actions of another, sometimes appears as one specific item among others: for example, interference with activity, blocking, interference with partner's

Table 5.1
Classifications of Content of Conflict

Dawe (1934): Preschoolers
  Possessions
  Physical violence
  Interference with activity
  Social adjustment

Hartup (1974): Preschoolers, first, and second graders
  Blocking (involving possessions, space, activity)
  Bodily contact
  Derogations (negative social comparisons, ridicule, criticism)

Kounin (1970): first and third graders
  Breaking objects
  Nonconformance with adults
  Assaults on children
  Rule violation
  Inconvenient acts (disturbing, not harmful)

Patterson (1982): Parents' and sibs' actions to child
  Expressing disapproval of child
  Teasing child
  Humiliating child
  Hitting child
  Yelling at child

Kelley (1979): Young heterosexual couples
  Inadequate and poor communication
  Aggressive behavior and temper
  Influence attempts, nagging, making decisions
  Failure to give appreciation, understanding, affection
  Independence, external involvements
  Dependence, possessiveness
  Passivity, lack of confidence, lack of ambition
  Excessive worry, compulsivity, moodiness
  Carelessness, sloppiness, impulsivity
  Conflicting preferences concerning leisure time, where to live, and so on
  Division and fulfillment of responsibility
  Interference with partner's study, work, and so on
  Inappropriate behavior in social situations
  Attitudes and behavior toward parents
  Attitudes and behavior toward friends

Toch (1979): Persons stopped and arrested by police officers
  Assault in defense of autonomy (touching, orders)
  Assault as expression of contempt or disapproval
  Assault in effort to escape
  Assault to prevent being moved
  Assault to protest captivity
  Assault as extension of other violence
  Assault in defense of others

study and work, efforts to escape, or to prevent being moved. "Interference with actions" has appeared to these various investigators to be a feature of only one type of conflict. Perhaps it is not the *general* distinguishing feature of conflict, after all. This problem can be resolved by giving "intereference" a very broad interpretation, so that it includes such things as (1) failing to provide expected contextual support for ongoing activity (as in failing to give attention, or failing to fulfill responsibilities), or (2) producing disruption of ongoing chains of positive feelings and thoughts about one's self (as in ridicule, disapproval, criticism). This broad interpretation is consistent with the notion of the multistrand chains of intraperson organization of affect, thought, and action, and with the fact that interpersonal linkages can go from one person's action to any portion of the other person's chain. Perhaps, then, our criterion must be a broad one, of *any interchain interference or disruption,* and not merely one of interference with *action.*

Conflict Process

Now we come to the focus of our problem, which is conflict process. The example from Peterson in Figure 5.1 suggests that a distinction be made between *intrapersonal* process and *interpersonal* process. This follows the schematic analysis of interaction presented in our book, *Close Relationships* (Kelley et al., 1983). *Intra*personal process refers to the *psychological mechanisms* involved in the conflict. They are characterized by such terms as *rational* versus *irrational, strategic logic, tension relief, catharsis, affective or emotional process, instigation to aggression, elicitation of reactions,* and *cognitive mediation.* These terms refer to the psychological mechanisms by which one person's actions cause or promote disturbances within another's chain of events, and to the linkages within the second chain that mediate between stimulus input and reaction.

The *inter*personal processes are the focus of our analysis. They are the processes for which we would hope to create a useful taxonomy. On examining the evidence and commentary on these processes, we are immediately faced with a problem of *levels,* or size of units of description. There are many proposals on this matter, but I think the distinctions outlined by Evie McClintock (1983) serve our purpose very well. These are schematized in Figure 5.3

As shown there, a Relationship consists of many episodes, each of the sort illustrated by the earlier example from Peterson. Each Episode represents a particular problem the pair encounters. Among the many episodes a couple experiences only some involve conflict, but those are the ones that concern us here. Each episode consists of a number of Phases or stages; each phase consists of a number of interaction Sequences, and a sequence consists of a number of interlinked Events. Some of the common labels for these five levels of phenomena, as they involve conflict, are given at the bottom of Figure 5.3. These will suggest the meaning of the five levels. On the left, they are labels for different kinds of relationships, distinguished as to conflict features. Then, in successive columns, they are labels for various kinds of conflict episodes, for various phases within a conflict episode, for various sequences within a conflict phase, and finally, for the events distinguishable within a conflict sequence.

Conflict Process in Distressed Relationships

The different levels can be illustrated by research on distressed relationships (i.e., married couples seeking counseling and characterized by low marital satisfaction). Such relationships have been compared with normal ones in terms of the frequency of phenomena at each of these levels of analysis. In terms of *episodes*, distressed couples have been found to be more likely to have an argument on any given day, to be less likely to have had sexual intercourse, and to have spent less time together, thereby having had fewer opportunities for interaction episodes of any sort (Birchler & Webb, 1977; Christensen & King, 1982).

At the level of *phases* within conflict episodes, Gottman (1979) reports differences between distressed and normal couples in their laboratory discussions of conflict issues. His results are summarized in Table 5.2. Like Bales and Strodtbeck (1951), Gottman divided the total conflict discussion into thirds. On the basis of the frequency of various events during each third, he characterized the first as the "agenda building" phase, the second as the "arguing" phase, and the third as the "negotiation" phase. As Table 5.2 shows, two of these phases include sequences for the distressed couples that are different from those for the normal ones. The agenda building phase for the distressed couples includes more cross-complaining sequences (complaint followed by

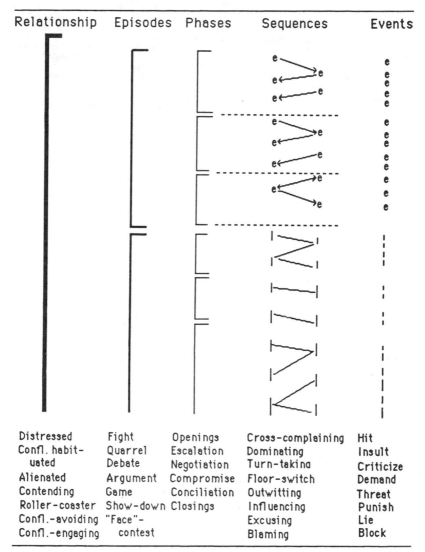

Relationship	Episodes	Phases	Sequences	Events
Distressed	Fight	Openings	Cross-complaining	Hit
Confl. habit-	Quarrel	Escalation	Dominating	Insult
uated	Debate	Negotiation	Turn-taking	Criticize
Alienated	Argument	Compromise	Floor-switch	Demand
Contending	Game	Conciliation	Outwitting	Threat
Roller-coaster	Show-down	Closings	Influencing	Punish
Confl.-avoiding	"Face"-		Excusing	Lie
Confl.-engaging	contest		Blaming	Block

Figure 5.3: Levels of Analysis of Conflict Process

countercomplaint) and fewer validation sequences (complaint followed by acknowledgment). Similarly, the distressed couples' negotiation phase includes more counterproposal sequences (proposal followed by counterproposal) and fewer contracting sequences (proposal followed by agreement).

Table 5.2

Three Phases of Discussion of a Marital Issue

Phase	Nonclinic Couples	Clinic Couples
Beginning phase: agenda building	Validation sequences	Cross-complaining sequences
Middle phase: arguing	(Difficult to discriminate the two kinds of couples; disagreement is typical of both.)	
Last phase: negotiation	Contracting sequences	Counterproposal sequences
(Throughout)	Sequences with *low* reciprocation of negative affect	Sequences with *high* reciprocation of negative affect

SOURCE: Adapted from Gottman (1979).

In addition to what the above phase differences imply about differences between distressed and normal couples in their typical interaction *sequences* during conflict, they differ in the frequency of other sequences. Throughout their discussions, distressed couples show more reciprocation of negative affect (sequences in which one person's negative affect is followed by the other's similar affect), more disagreement and interruption, and less agreement and approval. Finally, in terms of *events,* distressed couples report a higher ratio of displeasing to pleasing acts (Wills, Weiss, & Patterson, 1974), and in observations of their interaction they are seen more often to criticize, complain, and be sarcastic, and less often to smile, laugh, and make physical contact (Gottman, 1979).

Bases for a Taxonomy of Conflict Processes

Figure 5.2 outlined the broad framework that seems necessary for assembling information about conflict. The literature contains many ideas and data about the underlying structure, the content (topic or issue), and the process of conflict, both *intra-* and *inter*personal. Figure 5.3 expanded on the interpersonal process category and indicated the distinctions among levels of analysis that it seems necessary to make. Where do these frameworks and analyses leave us in the task of constructing a taxonomy of conflict process?

It is clear that our taxonomy must eventually deal with all the levels of interaction process. It will probably be easiest to construct taxonomies for each level separately, but in any case, the levels conception indicates the importance of not intermingling levels—for example, by trying to place in the same taxonomy phases and sequences. However, the levels concept also suggests that our deeper problem is to develop an understanding of each level that will enable us to mesh it with the other levels. Our essential problem is to understand the *organization* of conflict interaction, that is, how the sequences are organized into phases, how phases are organized within various kinds of episodes, and, most important, how various episodes are organized within and, indeed, constitute the life processes of an ongoing relationship. Our taxonomic efforts on the specific levels must not stand in the way of attaining an understanding of their overall organization.

One way to ensure that we will come to understand the total organization of interaction is to conduct the process analysis in the light of theory that cuts across the structure, content, and process realms. Such theory must begin with the situational and personal factors that underlie conflict. A full statement of a theory of conflict would be out of place in this chapter. A brief formulation is that *the process of conflict reflects (1) the structure of the situation in which the actors find or place themselves and (2) the personal dispositions (attitudes, motives, values) they bring to that situation or that are evoked within it.* This formulation takes for granted the situation-persons distinction shown in Figure 5.2. That distinction reflects the importance that closely related persons place upon their personal attitudes and motives, and their tendencies to scan their interaction for clues about such factors and to be sensitive to their display (Kelley, 1979). The formulation implies a dynamic interactive process in which initial situational and personal factors are likely to undergo modification, through processes of situational selection and restructuring and of dispositional arousal and adjustment. The course of conflict, then, reflects initial situational and personal conditions that contain potentialities for conflict and a process of modifying and adjusting those conditions to a state in which the potentialities for conflict dominate the causal system.

In applying this view of conflict process, we have available various concepts for describing situations and the processes of their selection and restructuring (for example, see Kelley, 1984; Kelley & Thibaut, 1978). Additionally, in the content of conflict we find clues about the nature of the conflict-relevant personal factors. In lists such as those in

Table 5.1, we can identify the attitudes and motives about which people are concerned in their conflicts. Some of these, along with examples of actions that evoke or implicate them, include: (1) *respect or esteem* (Hartup: derogations; Patterson: disapproval); (2) *autonomy* (Kelley: dependence; Toch: defense of personal autonomy); (3) *fairness* (Dawe; Hartup: conflict over possessions; Kelley: division and fulfillment of responsibility); (4) *loyalty* (Kelley: independence, external involvements); (5) *considerateness* (Patterson: humiliating, teasing; Kelley: failure to give appreciation, understanding); and (6) *conventionality* (Kounin: inconvenient acts; Kelley: carelessness, sloppiness, impulsivity; inappropriate behavior).

A list such as this provides one possible starting point for a taxonomy of process. Conflict about a particular dispositional issue implies that the persons are encountering some particular kind of situation and are finding that their attitudes and motives relevant to that situation are incompatible. For example, issues of autonomy give rise to conflict when the persons are interdependent to some considerable degree but they disagree about how great that interdependence, with its closeness and exclusivity, should become. According to our brief formulation above, the conflict process—with its flow of influence, debate, pressures, threats, and so on—will take a form that reflects both the situational and the dispositional factors that lie at its base. This idea is illustrated below by process research relating to the first item in the list above, the dispositional issue of respect or esteem.

Aggression and Personal Issues of Esteem

We may first consider some ideas and evidence from developmental psychology. Following an earlier distinction between hostile, "person-directed" versus instrumental, "object-directed" aggression, Hartup (1974) proposed that, with advancing age, children display more of the person-directed type, and that this person-oriented aggression is particularly responsive to threats to self-esteem. Hartup's data and several related studies are consistent with his hypothesis. As children become older, more of their aggressive behavior occurs in episodes in which they seem to be seeking to restore their self-esteem, as in trying to get back at peers who have insulted them. Most striking is Hartup's evidence that another person's blocking of a concrete goal—a provocation that at an earlier age would have occasioned an instrumental, physical response—becomes, with increasing age, the occasion for a personal, derogatory counterattack.

These results lend themselves to various interpretations, but Hartup suggests that age changes in social-cognitive processes are responsible for this shift, with the personal aspects of conflict becoming increasingly important as children become able to make attributions of intention to an agent of frustration and thereby are able to recognize the possible ego-threatening implications of concrete, blocking actions. The other side of the coin, documented by Shantz and Voydanoff (1973), is that older children are better able to recognize accidental provocations and react to them with less aggression.

However, older children who have reputations among their peers and teachers of being "aggressive" seem to have problems with the intentional-accidental discrimination. This is well illustrated by Dodge's (1985) work on aggressive boys. His results support the important role of attributions of intentionality as mediating, in the intraperson chain, aggressive conflict actions. Figure 5.4 provides a schematic picture of the sequence that Dodge's work identifies. When, for ambiguous reasons, his puzzle is knocked over by the peer partner, the aggressive boy thinks it was done on purpose. He then acts to destroy the peer's puzzle and is verbally hostile to him. These actions and reactions are supported and accompanied by the aggressive boy's beliefs that other kids are hostile to him, and by the peer's expectation that the boy will be aggressive. The latter reflects the reputation the aggressive boy has acquired, presumably through repeated sequences of the sort shown in Figure 5.4.

Dodge's work is a good example of research aimed at teasing out the details of the intraperson processes that are involved in the interpersonal sequence of provocation and attack. It ties in neatly with applied research on teaching people to avert conflict situations by avoiding states of arousal and attributions of personal intent to provocative behavior, as illustrated by Novaco's (1979) procedures for training police officers to deal with personal confrontations, and by various studies of training children to talk and think aloud in order to process social information more slowly and accurately (Kendall & Finch, 1979).

Developmental studies such as Dodge's have provided fascinating information about the conflict sequences created and participated in by highly aggressive children. Without pretending to cover all of this literature, I may mention several other useful findings. Among the

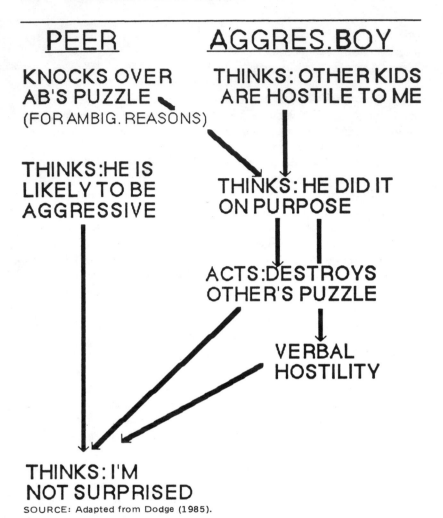

Figure 5.4: Sequence of Aggressive Boy's (ABs) Reaction to Ambiguously Caused Interference

sequences are those in which the highly aggressive boy punishes another, "trainee" child *more* severely if he believes the other will be able later to retaliate against him (Peterson, 1971). This is consistent with the aggressive boy's belief that others are hostile toward him and they have to be shown who is boss. Other work suggests that when they attack others out of anger, highly aggressive boys perceive the suffering of their victims as evidence of the success of their aggression (Perry & Perry, 1974) and fail to experience the negative self-reactions to the victims' pain that normal boys do (Perry & Bussey, 1977). One might conclude that highly aggressive boys have an instrumental orientation to their interpersonal attacks, with others' consequent pain serving merely to show the success of their efforts and not to occasion guilt.

Another literature relevant to the esteem- and power-related personal aspects of aggression is provided by students of adult violence. In many ways, these provide a portrait of the aggressive boy who has grown in physical size but has not changed much in his role in conflict sequences. Toch's (1969) study of sequences leading to assaults on police yields the schematic view of the typical scenario shown in Figure 5.5. Although his outline of the elements in the sequence does not reveal the personal attitudes it includes, these are made clear by Toch's analysis of the offender's "approach" to the arrest situation. In his sample of the arrest records of 69 violent offenders, the most frequent "approaches" include "self-image defending" (aggression as retribution against persons seen to cast aspersions on the self-image), "self-image promoting" (violence as a demonstration of worth, toughness, or status), and "reputation defending" (aggressive violence in order to sustain public recognition). These categories show that "personal" feelings, feelings of being personally attacked or challenged, are extremely important in the violence scenario. The sequence outline in Figure 5.5 is substantially mediated by intrachain events on the offender's side related to cognitions of the self and to affective responses to being touched, given orders, or subjected to restraint.

A more explicit view of the "personal feelings" intrachain mediators of the violence sequence is provided by Luckenbill (1977). From analysis of public records and interviews with the participants and observers of 94 instances of criminal homicide, Luckenbill has drawn up the outline of the episode summarized in Table 5.3. In the second stage, the offender (the one who ultimately does the killing) interprets the earlier actions of the victim as a challenge to his esteem—as "personally offensive." As the scenario proceeds, the offender takes steps to restore "face" and demonstrate his toughness. The sequence moves on toward its disastrous conclusion as the victim takes up the challenge and accepts the situation as a contest of reputations for courage.

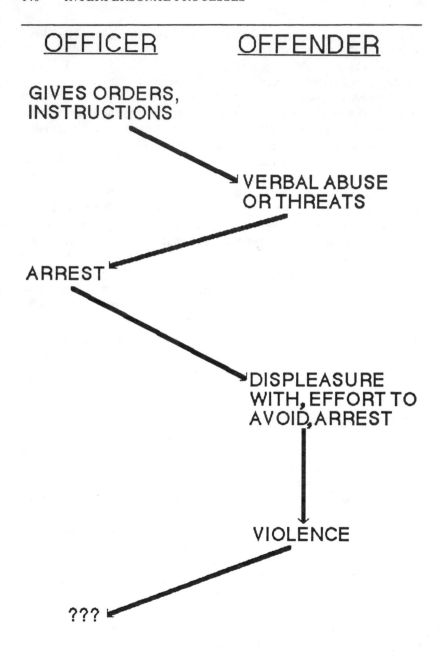

SOURCE: Adapted from Toch (1969).

Figure 5.5: Sequence Leading to Assault on Police Officer

Table 5.3

Stages of an Episode of Criminal Homicide

Stage I: Event is performed by victim (and subsequently is defined by offender as an offense to "face").
—victim's insult, disparagement
—victim's refusal to cooperate or comply with offender
—victim's physical or nonverbal gesture

Stage II: Offender interprets victim's previous move as personally offensive.
—offender learns meaning of victim's move from inquiries made of victim or audience
—offender imputes meaning on basis of victim's prior behavior

Stage III: Offender makes retaliatory move aimed at restoring face and demonstrating strong character.
—offender expresses anger/contempt signifying victim is regarded as unworthy person.
—offender issues a verbal or physical challenge to victim

Stage IV: Victim comes to a "working agreement" with proferred definition of situation as one suited for violence.
—victim does not comply, continues performance of offensive activity
—victim physically retaliates against offender
—victim issues counterchallenge

Stage V: Offender and victim are committed to, and do, battle (54% are one-sided; 46% two-sided). Victim is killed.

SOURCE: Adapted from Luckenbill (1977).

Personal Dispositions and Their Associated Situations

The preceding evidence bears on the special subclass of conflict process that revolves around personal feelings about self-esteem, deservingness of respect, reputation, and so on. Our earlier formulation of conflict leads us to examine the situational and personal factors that give rise to this particular process. We may say that the persons either are in, or create for themselves, a situation of the type described by the outcome matrix for the game of Chicken (Kelley & Thibaut, 1978)—a game structure that takes its name from the macho adolescent contest in which two opponents drive straight at each other, attempting to force the other to turn aside first. This situational structure affords each one a means of action that constitutes a challenge to the other *either* to enter into a mutually destructive course of action *or* to accept an inferior, demeaning position in their relationship. At the outset of their interaction, this situation exists as a potential one, by virtue of the social and physical circumstances and their respective abilities and resources (fighting skills, weapons, etc). In the course of their interaction, this situation becomes activated or even exacerbated by their respective dispositions—their self-esteem sensitivities, values placed on courage, competitive attitudes toward each other, and so on. The interplay between situational and personal factors is a two-way street: A particular situation tends to call forth the dispositions relevant to its opportunities and constraints, but once activated, particular dispositions also lead to selecting or restructuring the current situation so that it becomes an appropriate setting for their expression.

The top line of Table 5.4 summarizes the situational and personal factors that, according to the preceding argument, are generative of violence scenarios. The situation is one of relatively equal dependence (equal control over each other's outcomes) but it affords sizable negative outcomes, such as those incurred at the mutually destructive conclusion of the game of Chicken. This situation lends itself to the working out of personal issues of esteem and courage.

The lower lines of Table 5.4 highlight some of the other personal issues we identified earlier in the content of conflict, along with the situational structures to which each is relevant. Dispositions relating to autonomy (independence) versus closeness (interdependence, intimacy) are relevant when two persons are interdependent but differ in their attitudes about that state. (Their interdependence can be said to be "positive" because both persons gain mainly positive outcomes from their interaction.) The one more desirous of closeness is likely to become more dependent than the other, so the situation is one of some asymmetry in dependence. This situation is not uncommon in heterosexual relationships, particularly during their formative stages, and is a source of considerable discomfort for the more dependent person. A conflict scenario plausibly derivative from this situation is the one described by Sullaway and Christensen (1983) as the "demand-withdraw" conflict. One partner demands a closer relationship (more attention, more contact) and the other feels "crowded" and responds with less contact or withdrawal.

Fairness and loyalty issues have been shown by Thibaut (1968) and his colleagues to arise in situational structures corresponding to the Threat game (Kelley & Thibaut, 1978). Here, the two persons are equally dependent on the continuation of the relationship, and it yields positive outcomes for both. However, within the relationship, one has

Table 5.4
Some Situational and Personal Structures and Their
Associated Conflict Processes

Structure		Conflict Process
Situational Factors	*Personal Factors*	
Symmetric negative interdependence (Chicken)	Esteem, courage	Violence; fight-not fight (Luckenbill, 1977)
Asymmetric positive interdependence	Autonomy	Demand-withdraw (Sullaway & Christensen, (1983)
Symmetric positive interdependence, but unequal resource control (Threat game)	Fairness, loyalty	Engage-avoid (Kelley, 1979, Komarovsky, 1964)
Exchange problems (Prisoner's Dilemma)	Considerateness	Moral transgressions and desist responses (Nucci & Turiel, 1978)
versus		
Coordination problems (Mutual Behavior Control)	Conventionality	Conventional transgressions and desist responses (Nucci & Turiel, 1978)

greater control over the allocation of its resources (one controls the purse strings, so to speak). The partner's only recourse in the event of the controller's unfair allocations is to threaten to leave the relationship. Accordingly the controller's fairness becomes an issue and, given less than equitable allocations, the partner's loyalty also comes into question. A conflict scenario plausibly derivative from this configuration of situational factors is one between engaging in conflict versus avoiding it. If a controller is mildly exploiting the other's loyalty, it is in the controller's interests not to enter into discussion of the matter, and instead to let it go unresolved. To the contrary, it is in the partner's interests to engage in conflictual discussions in order to gain full justice. This conflict pattern of engaging-avoiding has been noted by many observers of marital conflict. Evidence in Komarovsky (1964) and Kelley (1979) suggests that men are more often the avoiders and women are more often the engagers, which is consistent with the general pattern in American couples for the man to control resource allocations.

The distinction just drawn, between the demand-withdraw sequence and the engage-avoid sequence, is probably not as clear as the commentary suggests. The reason is that in real social relationships, the situational structures that we can distinguish conceptually and experimentally become combined or intermixed. In this particular case, the situational pattern of unequal dependence tends to become one that also includes unequal resource control. This conclusion is suggested by the considerable evidence that the less dependent partner is likely to wield greater power—to have more say—than the more dependent one. As a consequence, the person who "demands" more closeness (out of discomfort with his or her greater dependence), and tries to increase the partner's involvement, is also likely to be the one who is subject to the other's control over allocations and therefore the one who is more interested in "engaging" issues in the relationship that arise from unfair allocations. Christensen (in press) presents evidence that seems consistent with this view.

The bottom rows of Table 5.4 describe the situational structures that can give rise to personal issues of considerateness and conventionality. Exchange problems, aptly characterized by the conflicting motives of competition versus cooperation found in the Prisoner's Dilemma game, raise questions about the actors' considerateness (cooperativeness, concern about each other's welfare). In contrast, coordination problems, described by the game pattern that Kelley and Thibaut (1978) label "correspondent, mutual behavior control," raise questions about the actors' readiness to follow rules of order, such as conventions about when and where certain behaviors are appropriate. Nucci and Turiel (1978) identify the different conflict sequences that result when one person interferes with another in these two types of situation. In exchange situations, the interference constitutes a moral transgression inasmuch as it hurts or fails to help the other person. The response, intended to cause the transgressor to desist, is a strong one, calling attention to the harm done the other and punishing or threatening punishment for further transgression. The transgression in the coordination situation is more harmless (as illustrated in Table 5.1 by Kounin's category of inconvenient acts, disturbing but not harmful) and the desist response is milder, with attention being called to the disorder the transgression has created and some ridicule of the transgressor's inept performance. In sum, Nucci and Turiel's (1978) work identifies two different scenarios of transgressions and the reactions to them, and these two types of conflict process are plausibly based on the different types of situational and personal factors shown in the lower portion of Table 5.4.

Table 5.4 illustrates the kind of organized understanding of interpersonal phenomena that a systematic analysis of types of conflict can stimulate. For applied psychologists, information assembled in this format can be useful in dealing with interpersonal conflicts. A priori assessments of the way in which people are interdependent and of the dispositions they bring to their relationship afford a basis for anticipating the kinds and patterns of conflict they are likely to experience. Alternatively, observations of the pattern of conflict a couple experiences afford a basis for systematic hypotheses about their underlying interdependence and relevant personal factors. This kind of understanding can obviously contribute to the prevention of conflict and to amelioration of ongoing conflict.

Summary

Our examples suggest that different types of conflict process originate in different structures defined by situational and personal factors. The development of a taxonomy of conflict processes can be guided not only by distinguishable features of the process itself but also by distinctions among various combinations of situations and their related personal dispositions. The structural basis of conflict has obvious implications for the content of conflict—for instance, the nature of the attributional issues raised, or the kinds of normative considerations invoked. More important, the structural basis has implications for the organization of conflict processes—the nature of the instigating events, the possible escalation of conflict, the potential crucial junctures or turning points in the sequences, and the various possible outcomes of the process. Thus analysis of the structural basis of the process promises to provide us with the perspective necessary to understand how the various levels of conflict are interarticulated.

The overall organization of conflict process is implied by our earlier formulation, with its emphasis on the interplay between the situational and the personal factors. In conflict, persons partly react to the concrete problems of their interdependence but they also redefine those problems. Their behavior is partly guided by their initial dispositions but also by the accommodation of those dispositions to their partner's similar or complementary ones. Interdependent in both the concrete aspects of their situation and in the dispositions they bring to bear upon it, they make adjustments and counteradjustments in both their specific behaviors and their dispositional guidelines for that behavior. In doing so, they develop a scenario that bears some relation to where they started but that also reflects the dynamics of their adjustment and counteradjustment process.

References

Bales, R. F., & Strodtbeck, F. L. (1951). Phases in group problem-solving. *Journal of Abnormal and Social Psychology, 46,* 485-495.

Berschied, E. (1983). Emotion. In H. H. Kelley, E. Berscheid, A. Christensen, J. H. Harvey, T. L. Huston, G. Levinger, E. McClintock, L. A. Peplau, & D. R. Peterson, (Eds.), *Close relationships.* New York: W. H. Freeman.

Birchler, G. R., & Webb, L. J. (1977). Discriminating interaction behavior in happy and unhappy marriages. *Journal of Consulting and Clinical Psychology, 45,* 494-495.

Christensen, A. (in press). Detection of conflict patterns in couples. In K. Halweg & M. J. Goldstein (Eds.), *The impact of family research on our understanding of psycho-pathology.* Heidelberg, Germany: Springer-Verlag.

Christensen, A., & King, C. E. (1982). Telephone survey of daily marital behavior. *Behavioral Assessment, 4,* 327-338.

Dawe, H. C. (1934). An analysis of two hundred quarrels of preschool children. *Child Development, 5,* 139-157.

Dodge, K. A. (1985). Attributional biases in aggressive children. In P. C. Kendall (Ed.), *Advances in cognitive-behavioral research and therapy* (Vol. 4). New York: Academic Press.

Fink, C. B. (1968). Some conceptual difficulties in the theory of social conflict. *Journal of Conflict Resolution, 12,* 412-460.

Gottman, J. M. (1979). *Marital interaction: Experimental investigations.* New York: Academic Press.

Hartup, W. W. (1974). Aggression in childhood: Developmental perspectives. *American Psychologist, 29,* 336-341.

Kelley, H. H. (1979). *Personal relationships: Their structures and processes.* Hillsdale, NJ: Lawrence Erlbaum.

Kelley, H. H. (1984). Affect in interpersonal relations. In P. Shaver (Ed.), *Review of personality and social psychology* (Vol. 5). Newbury Park, CA: Sage.

Kelley, H. H., Berscheid, E., Christensen, A., Harvey, J. H., Huston, T. L., Levinger, G., McClintock, E., Peplau, L. A., & Peterson, D. R. (1983). *Close relationships.* New York: W. H. Freeman.

Kelley, H. H., & Thibaut, J. W. (1978). *Interpersonal relations: A theory of interdependence.* New York: Wiley-Interscience.

Kelley, H. H., Thibaut, J. W., Radloff, R., & Mundy, D. (1962). The development of cooperation in the "minimal social situation." *Psychological Monographs, 76,* No. 19 (Whole No. 538).

Kendall, P. C., & Finch, A. J., Jr. (1979). Developing nonimpulsive behavior in children: Cognitive-behavioral strategies for self control. In P. C. Kendall & S. D. Hollon (Eds.), *Cognitive-behavioral interventions: Theory, research, and procedures.* New York: Academic Press.

Komarovsky, M. (1964). *Blue-collar marriage.* New York: Random House.

Kounin, J. S. (1970). *Discipline and group management in classrooms.* New York: Holt, Rinehart & Winston.

Luckenbill, D. E. (1977). Criminal homicide as a situated transaction. *Social Problems, 25,* 176-186.

McClintock, E. (1983). Interaction. In H. H. Kelley et al., *Close relationships.* New York: W. H. Freeman.

Novaco, R. W. (1979). The cognitive regulation of anger and stress. In P. C. Kendall & S. D. Hollon (Eds.), *Cognitive-behavioral interventions: Theory, research, and procedures.* New York: Academic Press.

Nucci, L. P., & Turiel, E. (1978). Social interactions and the development of social concepts in preschool children. *Child Development, 49,* 400-407.

Orvis, B. R., Kelley, H. H., & Butler, D. (1975). Attributional conflict in young couples. In J. H. Harvey, W. J. Ickes, & R. E. Kidd (Eds.), *New directions in attribution research* (Vol. 1). Hillsdale, NJ: Lawrence Erlbaum.

Patterson, G. R. (1982). *Coercive family process.* Eugene, OR: Castalia.

Perry, D. G., & Bussey, K. (1977). Self-reinforcement in high- and low-aggressive boys following acts of aggression. *Child Development, 48,* 653-657.

Perry, D. G., & Perry, L. C. (1974). Denial of suffering in the victim as a stimulus to violence in aggressive boys. *Child Development, 45,* 55-62.

Peterson, D. R. (1983). Conflict. In H. H. Kelley, E. Berscheid, A. Christensen, J. H. Harvey, T. L. Huston, G. Levinger, E. McClintock, L. A. Peplau, & D. R. Peterson (Eds.), *Close Relationships.* New York: W. H. Freeman.

Peterson, R. A. (1971). Aggression as a function of expected retaliation and aggression level of target and aggressor. *Developmental Psychology, 5,* 161-166.

Shantz, D. W., & Voydanoff, D. A. (1973). Situational effects on retaliatory aggression at three age levels. *Child Development, 44,* 149-153.

Sullaway, M., & Christensen, A. (1983). Assessment of dysfunctional interaction patterns in couples. *Journal of Marriage and the Family, 45,* 653-660.

Thibaut, J. W. (1968). The development of contractual norms in bargaining: Replication and variation. *Journal of Conflict Resolution, 12,* 102-112.

Thibaut, J. W., & Kelley, H. H. (1959). *The social psychology of groups.* New York: John Wiley.

Toch, H. (1969). *Violent men: An inquiry into the psychology of violence.* Chicago: Aldine.

Wills, T. A., Weiss, R. L., & Patterson, G. R. (1974). A behavioral analysis of the determinants of marital satisfaction. *Journal of Consulting and Clinical Psychology, 42,* 802-811.

6

Interpersonal Influence: Being Ethical and Effective

ROBERT CIALDINI

Although my topic is the general interpersonal influence process, I want to focus on a specific feature of influence, a specific form of influence—compliance. Compliance refers to the process of getting other people to say "yes" to a request. In other words, it is the science of getting what you ask for. With that said, let me take a moment to explain how it was that I got interested in studying the compliance process in the first place.

It has to do, I think, with the fact that all my life I had been a pushover for the appeals of salespeople and fundraisers of various sorts. Much too frequently I would find myself saying "yes" to requests to buy products that I really didn't want or to contribute to causes that I had hardly heard about. Although this was a frustrating experience for me, in part, it was also an intriguing one because I recognized that there must be a psychology to the techniques that got me to say "yes" to such requests. And in my role as an experimental social psychologist, I decided to begin a research program that was designed to identify which factors cause one person to say "yes" to the requests of another. I will spend the majority of this chapter describing the results of some of that research. But before I do, I think it is important to discuss briefly the social context in which we can best understand these results.

We currently live in what is unquestionably the most complicated stimulus environment that has ever existed on this planet. The world has become so overloaded with information, so complex, so rapidly moving that people have had to adjust; and one of the fundamental adjustments that they have made to this avalanche of information in their environment is in the way that they make their decisions. Citizens of modern Western society no longer have the time, the energy, or even the mental ability to weigh carefully the pros and cons of the majority of decisions that face them. Instead, people have had to resort to shortcuts in their decision making (Kahneman, Slovic, & Tversky, 1982). Rather than trying to identify and analyze each of the many relevant pieces of information when making a decision, someone using the shortcut approach picks out just one usually reliable piece of information and responds automatically to it. In my work (Cialdini, 1985), I have referred to these single, reliable pieces of information as *trigger features.* This shortcut approach can be very effective and economical because the trigger features are normally very informative in telling us how to behave correctly in a situation. In fact, they are so informative that often people feel that they can safely stop considering the other information in that situation and rely solely on the information that comes from the single, trigger feature that they focus on.

For the last few years, my interest has centered on the question, "What are the triggers of compliance?—that is, what are the factors that cause an individual to stop a careful consideration of the merits of a request and move instead toward an unthinking 'yes'?" It turns out that there are very few such trigger principles, and that each one can be described in terms of a fundamental, powerful principle of psychology that directs human behavior. I'll discuss several of these principles in this chapter.

Reciprocation

Let us start by turning to the first important trigger principle: the principle of reciprocation. There is a rule in our society, in fact in every human society, that says that we are obligated to give back to others the kind of behavior that they have given to us (Gouldner, 1960). So, gifts are to be met with return gifts, favors are to be met with return favors, and so on. Therefore, when someone asks for a favor, we will often comply simply because that person has done us a prior favor, thereby creating an obligation to repay (Regan, 1971). This feeling of obligation is a trigger feature for compliance. The interesting thing about the rule for reciprocation is that it obligates us, it indebts us, *even in those situations where what we have been given is not something we asked for or not something we wanted in the first place.* We still feel uncomfortable receiving without giving in return. Let's take an example that most people who travel through airports have encountered.

Though the Hare Krishna society is an ages-old religious organization with roots traceable to the Indian city of Calcutta, in Western society it has a relatively recent history. Nonetheless, the Krishnas have had a very profitable and successful record in the United States in terms of getting people to give them funds. The way they do it is first to give people something before asking for a contribution in return. Sometimes it is the *Back to Godhead* magazine of the organization, sometimes it is a book, but in the most cost-effective version it is a flower. They walk up and pin a flower on your lapel and if you say, "No, I don't want this. Here, please take it back," they *refuse* to take back the gift. "No, no," they say, "that is our gift to you; however, if you would like to give a contribution for the good works of the society, that would be greatly appreciated."

For an entire day in the O'Hare airport in Chicago, I watched how people reacted to the Krishnas, and it was a remarkable demonstration of the power of the rule for reciprocation. People who didn't want the flower, who had it forced on them, still did not feel that they could walk away from the situation, taking something without giving something in return, because that goes against all of our upbringing. We have been taught from childhood that we should not take without giving in return. It makes us feel uncomfortable, it makes us feel guilty, it makes us feel indebted. We don't like those kinds of feelings. So what these people did—not all of them, but many of them—was reach in their pockets, come up with a couple of dollars and give them to the Krishna solicitor. And *then* they felt free to walk away. It was not until they had paid for this thing they did not want, had repaid the gift, that they could break the bonds of that social interaction. That is very instructive!

Another thing that I saw that was informative was that some people tried to avoid the pressures of the rule for reciprocation by refusing to keep the flower. If the Krishna solicitor would not take it back, they did not simply leave; instead they said, "All right, look, I'm throwing this flower on the ground. I don't have it anymore. I have not accepted it." and then they felt free to walk away. Now, isn't *that* interesting! While they possessed this thing that they never wanted or requested, the bonds of the reciprocity rule still held them there. But when they threw it on the ground, they could walk away. However, true to form, the Krishnas have found a way to counteract this strategy. In the United States, they have started pinning small American flags on people's lapels because they know that most Americans will not throw an American flag on the ground. They want people locked in the rule of reciprocation. They want us all in the jaws of that rule because we are much more willing to say "yes" to their request after we have received something from them. As I indicated before, they have been very successful in using the trigger of obligation to gain an advantage. In fact, they have become wealthy enough in the process to own property, businesses, and temples in 108 centers, worldwide.

It is precisely this trap of obligation that many companies try to avoid by refusing to accept gifts. IBM is a good example of that. IBM is very careful not to allow its employees to accept gifts and favors from its vendors. Consequently, they keep themselves and their company from becoming obligated. This makes it more likely that decisions for contracts or sales will be made for business reasons, free of the pressures of obligation.

Ethical Applications. We saw that the Krishnas have decided to use the principle of reciprocation in an illegitimate way. But this is not necessary. In applied settings, it is possible to engage the power of this principle in an honest and ethical fashion. For example, the principle of reciprocation has particular significance within management. In the old school of management, managers were depersonalized, they stayed separate from their people, who stayed apart from them. But influential managers today are team players, which means they must use the "give and take" method. They must learn how to give something so that by the power of reciprocation they will get something they want in return. For instance, one of the important things a manager can obtain is information from employees. A good manager must learn to give certain information in order to get needed information in return. This creates a beneficial information exchange. It works because there is an unwritten law making it work (Jourard, 1971).

Reciprocal Concessions

I have been describing the repayment of gifts, favors, and information, but the rule for reciprocity is not limited merely to such things. Reciprocity governs another kind of behavior that also lends itself to the compliance process. It governs the making of concessions in a negotiation with someone else (Chertkoff & Conley, 1967). If two people start out with incompatible positions on some issue—one person wants this, the other person wants that—and one of those individuals makes a concession, saying "All right, I'll retreat from my extreme position here to a more moderate one; I'll make a concession to you," the second party should feel a need to reciprocate that concession, to provide a retreat in return. A few years ago, I saw some firsthand evidence of exactly how that process works.

As I was walking on campus in front of my university's library, I was approached by a young boy about 11 or 12 years old, who said that he was a Boy Scout. He was selling tickets to the Boy Scout circus that was going to be held that Saturday night. He wanted me to buy a pair of his tickets at $5 each. I declined. But before I could walk away, he said, "Well, if you can't do that, would you be willing to buy a couple of our big chocolate bars here? They're only $1 apiece." So, I bought a couple of his chocolate bars, and I immediately recognized that something important had happened, because I do not like chocolate. But I do like dollars, and he had done something to make me give him my dollars for his chocolate. Clearly, something other than the value of his offer pushed me to say "yes."

The principle he had used, I think, involved the need to reciprocate the concession he had made to me. He started out by requesting an extreme favor—buy these tickets, $5 apiece—and my response was "no." He replied, in effect, "Well, if you can't do that, I'll retreat to requesting only $1 apiece for what I'm offering." If I was going to live up to the rule for reciprocation, I had to respond with a reciprocal concession. I had to comply and say "yes." So, I bought his chocolate bars. And I scratched my head and went back to my office, where I called a meeting of my research assistants to try to understand what had happened, and where they devoured the evidence in the process. We decided that perhaps there was a technique here that would work not just on me—since we already know I'm a pushover—but on other people, too. The technique works as follows: If you want something from someone, you first ask for a large request that you're likely to have rejected; then after the large request has been turned down, you retreat to the more moderate request that you were interested in all along. To test this technique, we decided we would do the following experiment:

We stopped people who were passing by and said that we were from the County Juvenile Detention Center and we wondered if they would be willing to chaperone a group of juvenile delinquents on a day trip to the zoo. As you might expect, the great majority of these individuals declined when that was the only request we made of them. Only 17% complied. For other, randomly selected individuals who were passing by, we said that we were from the County Juvenile Detention Center and we were interested in their willingness to serve as a counselor to one of the children down at the center. "This would require two hours of your time every week for the next three years." Of course, everyone said, "No, I can't agree to that kind of request." Then, taking our lead from the Boy Scouts, we said, "Oh. Well, if you can't do that, would you be willing to chaperone a group of juvenile delinquents on a trip to the zoo for just one day?" The results were quite dramatic. When we made the zoo trip request by itself, recall that only 17% of the subjects were willing to say "yes." But when we retreated to that request from a still larger one, 50% of the people volunteered. Think of it! We tripled willingness to comply with a sizable request by adding a few more words. But those words were crucial because they triggered the obligation to reciprocate a concession.[1]

Scarcity

Let us move on to a second principle that triggers the tendency to comply with requests—the principle of scarcity. People try to seize those items and opportunities that are scarce or are becoming unavailable. Therefore, sometimes all that is necessary to make people want something more is to tell them that before long they cannot have it. That is why advertisers love to use the kinds of advertising lines such as "limited supply," "limited time only," "last chance offer." They know that people will want a product or service more under those conditions.

Furthermore, research shows that people are most motivated to possess a scarce item when they are in competition for it with other people; the kind of scarcity that is most effective is that produced by social demand (Worchel, Lee, & Adewole, 1975). Direct rivalry for a rare commodity can make people lose all sense of value, and this can occur even at the highest levels of organizational leadership. Consider, for example, what happened in New York City in 1973 when, for the first time in history, the three American TV networks bid directly against one another for the rights to a single showing of a motion picture. They became so frenzied in their attempts to outbid one another that the "winner" of the competition, ABC-TV, spent $3.3 million, assuring itself of a million dollar loss on the showing (MacKenzie, 1974).

Of course, the effects of competition for a scarce resource can be seen in situations far more commonplace than multimillion dollar struggles for motion picture rights. For instance, my brother, Richard, worked his way through school by selling used cars in a way that made use of this trigger for compliance. When he needed money, he would buy a car advertised for sale in the newspaper by its owner and, adding little but soap and water, would advertise and sell it the following week for a $200-$300 profit. Aside from knowing how to find an underpriced car and how to write a good newspaper ad for it, my brother's secret for success was quite simple. Let us say that on a given Sunday morning four prospective buyers called to arrange to see the car. Richard would schedule them all for the same time—2 o'clock that afternoon. By the time the last prospect arrived to see the car, it would seem clear to all that there was a substantial social demand for this particular automobile. Nearly always, a hurried appraisal of the car would ensue, and one of the rivals would offer to buy at my brother's price to "beat out" the others. Although the tactic was repeatedly effective, it contained genuine ethical issues. That is, prospects were responding to a level of social demand that was intentionally made to appear larger than it truly was. Consequently, a normally trustworthy trigger for compliance had become misleading.

Exclusivity of Information

Most of us recognize that scarcity affects the desire to want things such as commodities. What we might not recognize, however, is that this principle also works on our desire to want and to believe information that is scarce. Information that is exclusive, that not everyone has access to, is more persuasive and has more impact than information that is available to everyone (Brock, 1968; Fromkin & Brock, 1971). Let us take an example from a study that was done by a student of mine (Knishinsky, 1982). This was a student who had been in one of my classes and was, in fact, a successful businessman who had returned to school to get his degree in marketing. He wanted to do an experiment; so he came into my office and we talked about the principle of scarcity and how research indicated that exclusive information and scare commodities can cause people to want to say "yes" more quickly and more frequently. It happened that he was the owner of a business that imported beef from South America and Australia. He then sold his beef to large supermarket chains here in the United States. He decided to do the following experiment to show how connecting a request to the scarcity principle could increase the willingness of people to buy.

He had his salespeople call 90 buyers of large retail supermarkets and give them one of three sales presentations, so that each sales presentation was heard by one-third of the sample of buyers. In one condition, the sales presentation went as follows: "We have a certain amount of beef for sale; this is the price; we think that it's a good time to buy. How many carloads would you be willing to buy?" That was the standard condition, the way that the request was usually made. In a second condition, for a second group of buyers, his salespeople added the information that because of unexpected circumstances there was an impending shortage of Australian beef in the near future. Then these contacts were asked to buy the product. Using just the standard request, the total number of carloads that were bought was 10. In the second condition, when the request also included scarcity, the number of carloads that were bought more than doubled to 24. But there was a third condition in this experiment. In this one, the salespeople not only said that there was an impending beef shortage in Australia, but they said that this information came to them through their exclusive sources in Australia; no one else had this information. In this procedure, then, not only was the beef scarce, but the information about the beef's scarcity was scarce itself. What happened to the buying patterns under those conditions? Six times as much beef (61 carloads) was purchased.

Ethical issues. It is important to note that the beauty of this procedure was that it was performed in a completely ethical way. There really *was* an impending beef shortage in Australia and the information really *did* come from the company's exclusive sources down there. So everyone—company and customer alike—benefited from the use of this technique. Afterwards, my student remarked to me that these circumstances (exclusive information about scarcity) had existed several times before in the history of his company. But because he did not know what the research said, he had not made use of it. This is a good example of how much more effective (and still ethical) an influence agent can be by integrating social psychological research findings into organizational procedure.

Authority

Let us move on to yet another principle that influences compliance: the principle of authority. There is a lot of expert worship in our culture. People are very willing to follow the suggestions of someone whom they see as a legitimate authority (e.g., Milgram, 1974). This represents another shortcut that people can use to decide what to do without having to think too much about the situation that they are in. Often, then, when an authority speaks, people stop searching for additional information in the situation and simply comply with the authority's directive. This kind of unthinking compliance or deference to an authority can be seen in a variety of situations in our society.

Let us consider one situation that is very important: In the medical context, we all know that the physician is the recognized authority on health matters, not only to the rest of us who serve as his or her patients but also to the medical staff in a hospital. Frequently, staff members in a hospital do not assess the merits of what a physician has directed them to do but instead merely respond automatically. Some medical researchers (Cohen & Davis, 1981) have suggested that this accounts for a startling and distressing statistic in our society: 12% of all of the medication that is given in a hospital every day of the year is given in error. These medical researchers have suggested that this occurs because sometimes the physician makes an error, an obvious error (physicians are human), but the medical staff and the patients who are the recipients of this error do not think to challenge it because, in the context of an authority's directives, nobody is thinking. People are simply reacting; they are not analyzing the situation anymore. They are simply responding to the fact that an authority has spoken.

This can be a very dangerous trap in management settings when employees stop thinking about the wisdom of a superior's directive and just respond to it. Sometimes, because of a human mistake or an error in communication, an obviously wrongheaded action is taken by someone who is not thinking since the boss has spoken. That is why it is important to train managers to avoid the air of rigid authority and to encourage employees to see them as human beings who will occasionally make mistakes.

Perhaps nowhere is this last point driven home more dramatically than in the consequences of a phenomenon that airline industry officials have termed "Captainitis." Frequently, in the operation of multipilot aircraft, obvious and potentially dangerous errors by the flight captain can go unmentioned by crew members, who either ignore the possibility of such errors occurring or who recognize the problem but fail to challenge the captain's judgment. Furthermore, some aviation psychologists have argued that this tendency is strongest among crews dominated by an authoritarian leadership style in which input from crew members is discouraged (Foushee, 1984). Frightening evidence of the breadth of the problem can be seen in a study conducted by a major airline company on its personnel (Harper, Kidera, & Cullen, 1971). In flight-simulator trials involving harsh weather and poor visibility, the captains pretended to be experiencing subtle symptoms of incapacitation. The results showed that in 25% of the instances, ones where the first officers did not take over control, the flights would have crashed.

Credibility

In addition to understanding the trap that authority can sometimes produce, it is also important to understand how the authority principle can be used productively. The sort of authority who is most influential has credibility. Research tells us that credibility consists of two separate features: knowledge, on the one hand, and trustworthiness, on the other (Myers, 1983). A credible expert is a person who is, first of all, knowledgeable about the issues at hand; second, the expert is a person who can be trusted to provide information in a way that is not self-serving, in a way that is honest. Both of these factors are important to establish but, of the two, it is usually more difficult to establish trustworthiness; research in several countries has shown that even acknowledged experts will not be persuasive unless they are viewed as trustworthy (McGuinnies & Ward, 1980). But, how does one go about persuading people of one's trustworthiness? One way is through a procedure that has been validated in experimental work (Walster, Aronson, & Abrahams, 1966) and that is frequently used by advertisers to get the audience to believe that they are being honest. These advertisers first say something that seems to be contrary to their own interests—perhaps they mention that the competitor has a good product or that their own product has some minor drawback. This non-self-serving statement establishes their honesty. Let me give you a set of examples from national ad campaigns—"Avis, we're number 2, but we try harder"; "Listerine, the taste you hate three times a day"; "L'Oreal, expensive but worth it"; "Peace Corps, the toughest job you'll ever love." You get the idea. By first saying something negative about their own product, the advertisers make the audience much more likely to believe all of the positive things that they say afterwards.

A while ago, I saw a list of the 10 most effective advertising campaigns in American history. It was very instructive to me that of the top 5 advertising campaigns, 3 had this character of starting with something negative and then moving to the positive features of the product. I will describe two of them. One was the Avis commerical that we just considered—"We're number two, but we try harder." But do you know what was rated as the most effective advertising campaign of all time in the United States? It was the Volkswagen campaign in the very early 1960s when the Volkswagen corporation decided to import its "beetle" into the United States. At that time, the average American was buying great big boatlike cars—chrome and metal and fins. That was the trend. How could an advertising agency get the public to turn its attention to this oddly shaped, little car? They started out their early ads with the line "We're ugly, but . . ." Thus, they first said something mildly negative. This got the agreement and trust of the populace, and *then* they mentioned the many positive features, such as the reliability, the economy, the availability of parts, and so on; and you know the success story that followed.

Let us consider one more example of how the credibility factor can be used to get people to comply with requests. It is an example that comes from a setting that most people do not recognize as an influence setting—the restaurant. One thing that the server wants to influence us to do is to leave a large tip. Another thing that the server and the manager of the restaurant want us to do is to buy a lot of food so that the basic bill on which the tip is figured is larger. There is a strategy that certain very effective waiters and waitresses use to enhance the chance that we will, first of all, leave them a larger tip and, second, buy more food. It goes as follows. Suppose you are part of a large party of people, say 10 individuals, out to dinner at a fine continental restaurant. Suppose further that I am your waiter, Roberto. And I come up to the table and ask the first person what she would like. Let us say that she orders the salmon. I go into the following act: My hand freezes above the pad. I look over my shoulder conspiratorily and I lean down so that everyone at the table can hear, and I say, "That's not as good tonight as it usually is. I wouldn't recommend that. Let me recommend . . ." And then I will suggest something a dollar or so *less* expensive than whatever the woman ordered.

What have I done with that single maneuver? By telling everyone at the table that the salmon is not good tonight, I have done everybody a favor; and we know what the rule for reciprocation says about returning favors. When it comes time for the tip, you should give me a larger tip because I have done you a favor. But, as well, I have produced an image of credibility for myself. I am, first, knowledgeable about the wares of the house; I obviously know what is good and what is bad. But, most of all, I am a trustworthy source of information about that food because I did not make the self-serving suggestion that you buy something more expensive. I suggested that you take something a dollar or so less expensive from the menu, thereby seeming to argue against my own interests. Of course, the loss from my tip—15% or 20% of a dollar—is trivial.

But also, now that I have generated a public image as a credible source of information, when it comes time to recommend a wine to the table, I can say, "And would you like me to suggest a wine or to choose one?" And, if all has gone well, you are likely to nod and say, "Yes, Roberto. You know what's good and you're on our side. Tell us what to get." And the same thing is likely to happen when, later, I make suggestions about the glories of the chocolate mousse or the baked Alaska. You should be more likely to believe me and to comply with my recommendations because of my perceived credibility.

Ethical issues. Although in our story the waiter, Roberto, made profitable use of the factor of credibility, he did so in a regrettably dishonest fashion because, no matter what the first person at the table ordered, he would have said, "That's not good tonight." He misrepresented the situation so that he could generate a perception of his own credibility. Notice how, in contrast to Roberto's tactics, the Volkswagen advertisement established a similar kind of knowledge and trustworthiness without being deceptive at all.

These two examples reflect a fundamental difference in approach to the influence process. The distinction is between being a *smuggler* of influence triggers into a situation where they do not actually exist versus being a *detective*, by finding the triggers of influence that naturally exist there. The detective versus the smuggler. To be effective as an influence agent and at the same time ethical, it is not necessary to import illicitly one of these features that does not exist in the situation. All that is necessary is to find a principle that naturally exists there, point to it, and bring it to the surface. This detective approach should be just as effective as the smuggler approach, but much more ethical.

Ethical Influence

The question of what constitutes ethical conduct has concerned and confounded writers and thinkers for centuries. The span of the issues involved is so large and the inherent problems are so multifaceted that anyone offering simple answers seems hopelessly naive. Like most people, I am loath to seem hopelessly naive. Consequently, I won't attempt to provide a simple solution to the grand conundrum of ethics. However, perhaps by reconstituting the question and greatly restricting its scope, it might be possible to offer a straightforward way to decide about the ethical quality of certain actions of an influence agent.

Let us set our question as follows, "If an influence agent is aware of a particular psychological principle of influence (a trigger feature) that causes influence targets to say 'yes' to an offer with little consideration of the merits of the offer, when is it ethically acceptable or objectionable to use that trigger?" I have already hinted several times at what I think is the answer: It is acceptable to use the trigger if it resides naturally in the existing setting; it is objectionable, however, to import and use the trigger if it is not an inherent part of the setting.

It should be clear from this question and answer that by focusing on the ethical *use* of certain influence principles, I have not tried to answer the larger question of what constitutes overall ethical conduct in an influence setting, for I have left out such important considerations as the purposes and consequences of that conduct. For instance, a legitimate charity organization may raise hundreds of thousands of dollars for needed medical research by smuggling into the communication channel one or another trigger of influence (for example, by employing the actor Robert Young as its spokesperson in order to exploit the impression of medical authority he brings to the situation via his longtime role as "Dr. Marcus Welby, M.D."). The issue of whether the charity organization's actions are or are not ethical, in total, is simply not addressed by the system I have proposed. The system merely concerns whether one component of those actions—the way in which an influence principle was employed—can be considered ethical. And, in this hypothetical example, I would argue that the authority principle was employed unethically because it was artificial to the medical setting rather than springing naturally from it.

The Most Powerful Triggers

A second feature of this system that is worthy of further consideration involves the crucial evolutionary assumption that a powerful trigger of influence normally steers people correctly when it is a natural part of the existing setting. That is, any principle that is regularly able to cause people to agree to an offer with little consideration of the merits of the offer must have gained this ability by directing people properly most of the time. Thus the reason that the use of naturally occurring trigger principles is ethical is that such principles usually do a good job of informing people of when to say "yes."

What are these trigger principles that, except when counterfeited, make for highly effective and ethical influence? We have already identified three of them—reciprocity, scarcity, and authority. In some earlier work (Cialdini, 1985, 1987), I have argued that three others also belong in this category—consistency, liking, and social validation. I also argued in that work that the property that most visibly distinguishes these six from other influence principles is their pervasiveness in practice. These are the principles that are most ubiquitously employed by compliance professionals, those individuals whose business it is to get others to say "yes" to their requests (e.g., salespeople, fundraisers, advertisers, recruiters, lobbyists, negotiators, con artists). These six principles are noteworthy by virtue of the fact that they have been regularly employed by a broad spectrum of compliance professionals, in a variety of forms and versions, across a wide range of compliance professions, and under many sets of economic and social conditions.

The reason compliance professionals have chosen to apply these principles so regularly is precisely because they are the most general and potent principles of psychological influence. For the targets of influence attempts, it has always made great sense to repay favors, to value scarce resources, to listen to authorities, to behave consistently, to favor the requests of those they like, and to take heed of the actions of similar others.

Ethical Versus Unethical Uses of Triggers

I have noted that because influence targets normally find these principles so useful as guides to compliance, influence agents can be effective *either* by pointing to those trigger principles that exist naturally in the situation at hand or (at least in the short term) by artificially injecting into the situation principles that do not inhere there. It is my present argument that these two approaches to the use of influence triggers define ethically acceptable and objectionable use of the triggers, respectively. They are, according to the characterizations offered earlier in this chapter, the *detective's* approach and the *smuggler's* approach. The first requires the influence agent to hone his or her abilities to uncover, bring into focus, and engage resident trigger principles, while the second requires the abilities to counterfeit or fabricate the presence of such triggers.

To make the issues more concrete, let's reexamine the case of Roberto the waiter who, by using a frequent tactic of clever servers, was able to inject an artificial sense of credibility into his interactions with dinner patrons. By recommending against the first main course selection made at a table and urging instead a slightly less expensive menu option, Roberto not only gained from larger tips left for him, to reciprocate the "favor" he had done, but he also gained from the increased willingness of patrons to accept his suggestions for wine and dessert choices. Because neither the favor he provided nor the credibility he acquired were genuine, he used both of the trigger principles of reciprocation and authority unethically; that is, he smuggled them into a situation where they did not naturally reside.

But there was no good reason for Roberto to act this way. By taking the detective approach instead, he could have engaged the principles of reciprocation and authority in a wholly ethical fashion that benefited himself and his customers. He could have come into work a few minutes early to examine the kitchen and check with the staff to determine what truly was bad or good that night, paying special attention to inexpensive menu items that looked good. Then, armed with this valuable information about the stores of the house, he could dispense it to everyone's advantage. At the outset of the interaction, he could describe which dishes were below par and which were better than usual, making sure to mention the less expensive items in this latter category. As a consequence, he would have provided a genuine favor to the diners in the form of authoritative, trustworthy information about their options. No doubt, he would have been able to reap the accompanying benefits but, it is important to note, so would his customers. Not only would they have been done a valuable favor at the outset—one worth repaying— but when he later made wine and dessert recommendations, they could count on the veracity of that information, too, because it would be based on his prior investigation of that night's kitchen. As long as Roberto stayed true to the system of using only those triggers of influence that sprang naturally from the situation, he would be able to achieve the coveted "win-win" arrangements so sought after in human management circles these days.

What's more, he would not have to stop with just the reciprocation and authority principles. He could use any others that arose naturally from the setting. If one dessert had been getting appreciative comments from patrons, he need only say so to subsequent diners to benefit as a detective from the social validation principle. (Once again, because the social validation principle—which urges an individual to follow the lead of many similar others—usually steers people correctly, those diners would benefit as well from his detective approach.) And when that particular dessert began to diminish in supply because of the social demand for it, Roberto could mention that fact when making his dessert presentation, thereby using the power of the scarcity principle in an ethical fashion.

The important point to recognize in all this is that most influence situations that one would be likely to encounter will allow for the natural functioning of one or more of the six influence triggers we have discussed. Thus the decision to use the triggers ethically becomes substantially less difficult to make. The detective approach does not restrict one's ability to use powerful influence principles. It only restricts the choice of which powerful influence principles to use—those principles that are grounded in the reality of the situation and can therefore be ethically employed. Fortunately, this restriction has great potential advantages. An influence agent who, over time, systematically adheres to such constraints is likely to be labeled as ethical by influence targets (which should enhance substantially the chance of future influence) and is likely to self-apply a similar label (which should bolster self-regard). These two probable advantages of increased long-term effectiveness and of heightened self-concept are enough to give me hope for the detective approach to influence as the wave of the future.

Note

1. For a full description of the conditions and methods of this study, see Cialdini, Vincent, Lewis, Catalan, Wheeler, and Darby (1975).

References

Brock, T. C. (1968). Implications of commodity theory for value change. In A. G. Greenwald, T. C. Brock, & T. M. Ostrom (Eds.), *Psychological foundations of attitudes* (pp. 243-273). New York: Academic Press.

Chertkoff, J. M., & Conley, M. (1967). Opening offer and frequency of concessions as bargaining strategies. *Journal of Personality and Social Psychology, 7,* 185-193.

Cialdini, R. B. (in press). Compliance principles of compliance professionals: Psychologists of necessity. In M. P. Zanna, J. M. Olson, & C. P. Herman (Eds.), *Social influence: The Ontario Symposium* (Vol. 5, pp. 165-184). Hillsdale, NJ: Lawrence Erlbaum.

Cialdini, R. B. (1985). *Influence: Science and practice.* Chicago: Scott, Foresman.

Cialdini, R. B., Vincent, J. E., Lewis, S. K., Catalan, J., Wheeler, D., & Darby, B. L. (1975). Reciprocal concessions procedure for inducing compliance: The door-in-the-face technique. *Journal of Personality and Social Psychology, 31,* 206-215.

Cohen, M., & Davis, N. (1981). *Medication errors: Causes and prevention.* Philadelphia: G. F. Stickley.

Foushee, M. C. (1984). Dyads and triads at 35,000 feet: Factors affecting group process and aircraft performance. *American Psychologist, 39,* 885-893.

Fromkin, H. L., & Brock, T. C. (1971). A commodity theory analysis of persuasion. *Representative Research in Social Psychology, 2,* 47-57.

Gouldner, A. (1960). The norm of reciprocity. *American Sociological Review, 25,* 161-178.

Harper, C. R., Kidera, C. J., & Cullen, J. F. (1971). Study of simulated airline pilot incapacitation: Phase II, Subtle or partial loss of function. *Aerospace Medicine, 42,* 946-948.

Jourard, S. M. (1971). *The transparent self.* New York: Van Nostrand.

Kahneman, D., Slovic, P., & Tversky, A. (Eds.). (1982). *Judgment under uncertainty: Heuristics and biases.* New York: Cambridge University Press.

Knishinsky, A. (1982). *The effects of scarcity of material and exclusivity of information on industrial buyer perceived risk in provoking purchase decisions.* Unpublished doctoral dissertation, Department of Marketing, Arizona State University.

MacKenzie, B. (1974, June). When sober executives went on a bidding binge. *TV Guide.*

McGuinnies, E., & Ward, C. D. (1980). Better liked than right: Trustworthiness and expertise as factors in credibility. *Personality and Social Psychology Bulletin, 6,* 467-472.

Milgram, S. (1974). *Obedience to authority.* New York: Harper.

Myers, D. G. (1983). *Social psychology.* New York: McGraw-Hill.

Regan, D. T. (1971). Effects of a favor and liking on compliance. *Journal of Experimental Social Psychology, 7,* 627-639.

Walster (Hatfield), E., Aronson, E., & Abrahams, D. (1966). On increasing the effectiveness of a low prestige communicator. *Journal of Experimental Social Pyschology, 2,* 325-342.

Worchel, S., Lee, J., & Adewole, A. (1975). Effects of supply and demand on ratings of object value. *Journal of Personality and Social Psychology, 32,* 906-914.

7

A Theory of Individual Encounters with the World

SANDRA SCARR

Two metaphors for personality can be found in "the bad seed" and the blank slate. The themes of emergent but preestablished personality versus the tabula rasa have infected debates over the ages about how personality differences come to be. In a version of the nature/nurture debate, personality theory has not been spared the crazy Cartesian dualism that pits mind against body, environments against genes, human against animal, and generally makes a mess of our thinking. In this chapter I address issues of theory and research on the genetic bases of personality and the role of experience in its development. The theory avoids, I hope, the pitfalls of our Cartesian heritage. I will focus on how people come to develop individuality in their personal ways of being and doing, across time and space. This chapter will explore what is known about sources of individuality in personality and propose a theory to account for the individuality of persons as responders, evokers, and selectors of their own experiences.

Author's Note: This chapter is adapted from a paper delivered at the Henry A. Murray Lectures in Personality, Michigan State University, April 12-13, 1985.

Ignoring Individuality

We have to admit that the study of personality, particularly Murray's (1938) brand of personology, has been a sideline activity of psychology. In fact, concern with individual differences in general has been relegated to the more applied fields, such as clinical and school psychology, where individual cases actually matter. The historical roots of this neglect of individual and species variability are not hard to find: They resulted from the rejection of evolutionary theory by the founders of experimental psychology, who came to be more influential in the English-speaking world than the followers of an evolutionary view (Boakes, 1984).

In the nineteenth century, there was a fight between advocates of models of mind drawn from evolutionary theory and those drawn from physics. Unfortunately for personality research, the experimental physicalists won on the principle of parsimony: If the animal mind could be explained on the basis of simpler rather than more complex processes, the simpler explanation was to be preferred (Boakes, 1984). Parsimony is the greatest reductionist scam of all time. The legacies of parsimony are the general, now discredited, laws of learning and a research tradition that considers only those processes so general to mammalian species that even a rat can learn them under deprived rearing conditions. From John Watson to B. F. Skinner, the same principles of learning and reinforcement were said to explain the behaviors of all species. Whatever the religiously motivated metaphysics of that tradition, it is clearly inappropriate to our understanding of animal behavior today and inapplicable to the study of individual variation in human personality.

We still suffer a nostalgia for simplicity, even if such simplicity masks and distorts species and individual variation in patterns of being and doing, which are the heart of personality. The contemporary residue of the physical tradition in the study of human behavior is a preference for the simplest models—ones that toss individual differences into the trash bin of error terms and fail to account for more than a trivial portion of personality variation. Most often, group differences are the focus of investigations; for example, sex differences in aggression, age differences in identity, and all sorts of family and other so-called environmental classifications crossed with average differences between groups.

If the developmental psychology literature on personality were to be read literally, one would think that investigators have theories with only main effects. That is, environmental agents or events hypothesized to influence personality development are supposed to act on everyone in the same way. For example, children who have been through divorce, had unemployed parents, been abused, or been reared by authoritarian methods are said to have unfavorable personality outcomes from those experiences. Similarly, children from intact homes, with employed parents, not abused, or reared by authoritative methods are considered to develop more adaptive personalities, *because* of their more favorable rearing experiences.

Actually, most intelligent investigators do not believe that such theories of main effects answer all questions about personality development. They recognize that their results apply to groups who differ *on average* and that within every group there is more individual variation than there is mean variation between groups. Developmentalists may even acknowledge informally that they try to predict average differences between groups, variously defined, because that is the only variance that their theories *can* predict. They may not recognize, however, how very small a portion of the total personality variance is actually addressed by theories with main effects.

Siblings and Strangers

Let me illustrate the problem of accounting for individuality with data from family studies of personality. Studies of sibling similarities and differences reveal that siblings, reared together all of their lives and sharing about half of their genes, are barely more similar on personality inventories than randomly paired members of the same population. Adopted children are slightly less similar to each other than are biological siblings and a little more similar than randomly paired members of the population.

The typical sibling correlation for self-report personality measures is about .20 (Ahern, Johnson, Wilson, McClearn, & Vandenberg, 1982; Carey & Rice, 1983; Grotevant, 1978; Grotevant, Scarr, & Weinberg, 1977; Loehlin, Horn, & Willerman, 1981; Rowe & Plomin, 1981; Scarr, Webber, Weinberg, & Wittig, 1981). If the personality correlation between biological siblings is .20 and the standard deviation of the personality measure is 4.5 (which is typical of the measures used in these studies), then the average absolute difference between siblings is 4.54

points on the scales, a difference of one standard deviation. This value is calculated by a general formula that assumes a normal distribution, an assumption that is met by IQ and personality scales (Jensen, 1980, p. 459):

$$|\bar{d}| = (2\,\sigma\sqrt{1-r}\,/\sqrt{\pi})\tag{1}$$

where $|\bar{d}|$ is the average absolute difference between siblings' scores, σ is the standard deviation of the scores, r is the correlation between the siblings, and π is 3.1416.

Given that randomly paired people in the population have scores that are not correlated, their average difference is 5.08 points, compared to the sibling difference of 4.54 points—hardly a *jnd* (just noticeable difference) on a personality scale.

Adopted adolescent siblings, reared together since infancy, have negligible correlations (median = .07) on the same personality scales, so that their average difference of 4.90 points is closer to that of the general population.

To quote myself from an earlier discussion of these surprising findings:

> Lest the reader slip over these results, let us make explicit the implications of these findings: Upper middle class brothers who attend the same schools and whose parents take them to the same plays, sporting events, music lessons, and therapists, and who use similar child rearing practices on them are little more similar in personality measures than they are to working class or farm boys, whose lives are totally different. (Scarr & Grajek, 1982, p. 361)

Brothers and sisters who have had objectively similar experiences with divorce, parental unemployment, abuse, and authoritarian child-rearing practices (or lack of same) do not turn out to have similar personalities. If the siblings are unrelated but reared together, there is a 3.6% reduction in their average difference over randomly paired people. If the siblings are genetically related, there is an 11% reduction in their differences—statistically significant in most studies, but not very impressive. Somehow, there is a mismatch between the nature of personality theories and the data about individuality.

Trivializing Individuality

Most standard psychological and sociological concepts about families represent environments that siblings share and that therefore *cannot* account for the vast differences among them. Parental occupations, parental beliefs about child rearing, parental education and intelligence, family size, rural-urban residence, income, and so forth are measures of characteristics that are common to all children in the family. If the goal of the research is to explain individual differences in personality, the theories do not even contain concepts that can address the majority of the variance to be explained.

Unfortunately, investigators do not always make clear what variance they are attempting to explain. A prime example of this confusion between group and individual variances is found in the birth order literature. Ironically, theories about the effects of sibling constellations (birth order, age spacing, age, and sex of siblings) are the only well-developed theories of individual differences between siblings (Scarr & Grajek, 1982). The confluence model (Zajonc & Markus, 1975; Zajonc, Markus, & Markus, 1979) is the only operational model that has attempted prediction of sibling IQ scores by a set of constellation variables, most notably birth order. The spectacular fits in these regression models of IQ and birth order are achieved with *average* IQ scores for thousands of young men at each birth order. Thus the model eliminates individuality by averaging out all other sources of individual differences.

However, in models where family constellation variables are fit to *individual* IQ values, birth order accounts for 2%-4% of the total IQ variation (Brackbill & Nichols, 1982; Galbraith, 1982; Grotevant, Scarr, & Weinberg, 1977). Thus the confluence model can account for 90+% of the 2%-4% of the individual IQ variation. Whoopee! In personality variation, even the confluence model cannot make any claims, as the world's literature generally shows no association between birth order or any other sibling constellation variables and personality variation (Ernst & Angst, 1983).

One crafty strategy to produce seemingly impressive results is the universal practice in developmental psychology of studying only one member per family and attributing the results to differences in parenting practices or other parental characteristics. On the face of it, attributing causality to environments that are shared by siblings but that differ among families would seem to require a test of within-family *versus* between-family models. So far, investigators have largely escaped the logical consequences of this non sequitur. Of course, investigators of personality variation in college sophomores and police recruits are also guilty of sampling one child per family, but they less often attribute personality variation back to the parental environment. The variance they seem to want to account for is a small portion of the total variance, anyway. Again, these studies account for only tiny fractions of the total personality variation.

A morality tale. An old tale about the drunk and the lost coin has him looking for the coin on the pavement in the light cast by a street lamp, even though he knows the coin is lost somewhere in the dark alley. When asked why he is looking on the pavement if he knows the coin is in the alley, he replies that that's where he can see.

And so it is, I fear, with research on individual differences in personality; we explore those places where our theories illuminate the terrain, and not the dark areas where the important data lie but where there are no ideas to light the search. If you are now persuaded that most of the variance in personality can be found *within* families (that is, among siblings), why then do we study variation *between* families? The problem is that we have no adequate theories about the causes of individuality among members of the same family. There is no light to guide the search, even if we know the coin is there. At this time, however, some investigators are trying to find a light for the sources of individuality.

Sources of Personality Differences

Although most investigators would agree that siblings experience somewhat different environments when growing up in the same family, there is little theory to guide research on the critical features of those environmental differences. Rowe and Plomin (1981) reviewed the causes of environmental variation among siblings and classified them into five types: accidental factors of each sibling's experiences, like Bandura's (1982) random experiences; sibling interaction in which each affects the other; family compositions; differential parental treatment; and extrafamilial sources, such as teachers, peers, and TV. The correlation between any one of these potential sources of sibling differences and any behavioral difference is very small, however. Even more discouraging is their finding that no common environmental factor can be extracted to account for more than a tiny fraction of the vast differences that siblings display on all behavioral measures.

Rather than despair, Rowe and Plomin (1981) and Scarr and McCartney (1983) advise that understanding how family environments affect individual members will require behavior-genetic designs with more than one sibling per family and more than one degree of genetic relatedness. Recent research on siblings' perceptions of family relations and parental treatment (Daniels & Plomin, in press) shows that children in the same families perceive different parental treatment, especially in affection and, to a lesser extent, in control. There are "his" and "her" parents, just as there are "his" and "her" marriages.

Of course, research on children's perceptions of family treatment and relations is just one way to examine within-family effects. We have not yet begun to explore how differences in family environments, measured by an observer, relate to personality differences. Nor have we considered seriously the possibility (in my mind, the probability) that differences in parental treatment are instead largely *caused* by differences in children's personalities or by the match or mismatch between parental and child characteristics (Buss & Plomin, 1984; Scarr, 1985; Thomas & Chess, 1977).

Parents may be differentially responsive to their children, depending on the children's characteristics and depending on the flexibility of parents in dealing with children of different temperaments (Bugental & Shennum, 1984). Some "difficult" children may be hard for most parents to foster to normal personality development, while other "easy" children in the same families may escape parental irascibility and despair (Plomin & Daniels, 1984). Corroborating data are hard to find, however (Daniels, Plomin, & Greenhalgh, 1984).

Children are also likely to differ in the degree of their vulnerability (Garmezy, 1983) to environmental presses, making parental treatment more of an issue for some children than others. For all of these reasons, family environments need to be conceptualized in finer grain than is now the mode (Wachs, 1983; Wachs & Gruen, 1982). And, more important, children need to be conceptualized as providing different events for parental treatment and as being differentially responsive to those treatments.

Behavior-Genetic Challenges
to Personality Theory

Seemingly unbeknown to most personality researchers, behavior geneticists who study personality have arrived at a startling consensus about two major points:

(1) The heritable portion of personality variation is a modest but demonstrable 25% to 40% of the total variance; and

(2) Most of the nonerror variance in personality is due to *individual experiences*—those not shared by members of the same family, neighborhood, or social class—and therefore unaccounted for by any contemporary theory of personality.

The basis for estimations of heritable variation in personality is twin and family studies of parents and children (genetic $r = .50$), brothers and sisters who are related as identical twins (genetic $r = 1.00$), as fraternal twins and ordinary siblings (genetic $r = .50$), and as adopted siblings (genetic $r = .00$). Assuming that all of the members of families have been reared together and that there is little assortative mating between parents for personality traits, the formula for calculating the heritability of personality measures in the population is straightforward:

$$h^2 = 2 (r_{ia} - r_{ib}) \qquad [2]$$

where r_i is the correlation coefficient for pairs of persons on any given personality trait; and h is the estimate of heritability based on the comparison of r_{ia} for pairs of persons genetically related by 1.00 and r_{ib} for pairs related by 0.5, or, alternatively, r_{ia} for pairs genetically related by 0.5 and r_{ib} for pairs genetically unrelated, 0.0.

Each comparison controls for environmental similarity (for twins, see Scarr & Carter-Saltzman, 1980; for adoptees, see Scarr, Scarf, & Weinberg, 1980) and estimates half of the genetic variance; hence, the multiplier. The effect of assortative mating is usually very small, for the correlations on most measured personality traits are below .20. However, if there is significant assortative mating for personality (as in

Buss, 1984), adjustments can be made in the multiplier to reflect the lower genetic variance within the family and the greater genetic variance between families.

Comparisons of family resemblances can also take differences in rearing environments into account, as when identical monozygotic twins (MZs) reared apart are compared to MZs reared together. From comparisons of family resemblances by genetic and environmental relatedness, models can be designed to estimate the degree of genetic and environmental variability in personality measurements. Furthermore, the genetic and environmental components of variance can be divided into within-family and between-family components, to reflect the degree to which assortative mating and common rearing environments affect the sources of personality variation in the population.

Twins and Siblings, Together and Apart

In a previous paper (Scarr & McCartney, 1983), we reviewed evidence about how monozygotic (MZ) twins come to be more similar than dizygotic (DZ) twins, and biological siblings become more similar than adopted siblings on nearly all measurable characteristics, at least by the end of adolescence (Scarr & Weinberg, 1978). We also reviewed the evidence on the unexpected similarities of MZ twins reared in different homes. All of these data are explained nicely by our theory of declining family influences and increasing individuality, which is described below.

Representative findings from twin and family studies of personality are presented in Table 7.1. Twins' and siblings' resemblances on typical personality scales show a pattern that parallels their genetic resemblances. Minor variations on the genetic pattern are apparent in the slightly higher correlation of DZ twins than ordinary siblings (but then twins are the same ages when tested) and the slightly higher correlations of MZ twins raised in different homes than those reared in the same home. What, you ask? Twins reared apart have more similar personality scores than twins reared *together*?

For laypeople, the most fascinating results are the unexpectedly great similarities between identical twins reared in different homes. Bouchard and colleagues have reported on the personality resemblance of their sample of 30 pairs of adult identical twins reared apart for most or all of

Table 7.1
Correlations of Twins and Siblings for Personality Test Scores
in Late Adolescence

	Twins			Siblings	
Personality Scale	MZ Reared Together	MZ Reared Apart	DZ	Biological	Adopted
Genetic r =	1.00	1.00	.50	.50	.00
Introversion-extraversion	.52	.61	.25	.20	.07
Neuroticism	.52	.55	.22	.28	.05
Impulsivity	.48	—	.29	.20	.05
Median	.52[a]	.65[b]	.25[a]	.20[c]	.07[c]

a. 27 CPI scales from Nichols (1978).
b. 11 DPQ scales from Bouchard (1984) and EPI scales from Shields (1962).
c. 10 EPI, DPQ, and APQ scales from Scarr et al. (1981).

their lives (Bouchard, 1981, 1984). They find, as did James Shields (1962) before them, that identical twins reared largely apart are *at least as similar* in personality as identical twins reared together. The correlations on multiple personality scales, including the MMPI, the CPI, and the DPQ, average .65. In fact, in both studies, twins reared apart have slightly greater correlations on personality tests than those reared together. The reason for this seems to be an environmental press on MZs to develop individuality when reared together (Hopper & Culross, 1983). When reared apart, of course, there is no press for contrast or differentiation to deter them from their genotypic similarity in responsiveness to their environments.

In contrast to the considerable similarity of identical twins reared apart or together, fraternal (DZ) twins are little more similar than ordinary siblings. The average personality correlation of DZ twins is .25 and of siblings is .20. For adopted siblings, common rearing from the early months after birth to adolescence results in a median correlation of .07 on personality scales.

There is a range of values for heritabilities calculated from the twin and family data. If the MZs reared in different homes are compared to the genetically unrelated adopted siblings reared in the same home, the comparison is between individuals with all of their genes but none of their rearing environment in common and individuals with none of their genes but all of their rearing environment in common. The difference in their correlations is an estimate of heritability (.65 – .07 = .58); since this comparison estimates the full genetic variance, it does not require the multiplier of formula 2.

The comparison of identical (MZ) and fraternal (DZ) median correlations of .52 and .25, respectively, yields a heritability coefficient of .54. So far, so good. By contrast, the comparison of the biological siblings' with adopted siblings' median correlations yields an estimated heritability of only .26. How can this be? Others in addition to the present author (Carey & Rice, 1983) have pondered this discrepancy between the twin and family data. We wondered about the possibly reduced within-family environmental variance that MZ twins may experience, being the same sex, same age, and looking and acting much alike. DZ twins and siblings, on the other hand, are not so similar in appearance or behaviors, nor are their correlations markedly different. Adopted siblings, as predicted, bear little resemblance to each other in personality. None of this speculation about sibling versus twin results really addresses the unusual similarity of MZs reared in different homes or the lack of similarity of adopted children reared together. However, our theory of declining family effects and increasing individuality does address these observations.

Similar to heritability estimates, one can calculate the effects of being reared in the same home, neighborhood, and social class by holding genetic resemblance constant and varying the degree of shared environment. A comparison of identical twins reared together with others reared apart yields a negative effect for common rearing environments $(.52 - .65 = -.13)$. A comparison of fraternal twins' resemblance with that of ordinary siblings gives an estimate of the effects of "twinness" for unusually similar environments $(.25 - .20 = .05)$, a slightly positive effect. The small effect of "twinness" is about the same as that created for adopted children reared together (.07), compared to genetically unrelated members of the population reared apart (.00). In all cases, environmental differences have a small effect on personality.

An environmental theory of main effects cannot possibly account for the stunning resemblances of identical twins reared apart or the lack of resemblance of adopted adolescents reared in the same homes since infancy. On the other hand, a theory of genetic determinism does not speak to the less than perfect resemblance of identical twins or the slight resemblance of adopted siblings. But it is certainly more correct than an environmental theory of main effects that relies on proximal family influences. Our theory of genotype → environment effects (described in the next sections) *can* account for all of these data by predicting the degree of environmental similarity that is experienced by twins and sibs, whether they live together or not.

Individual Differences in Experience

Each of us encounters the world in different ways. We are individually different in the ways we process information from the environment, which makes our experiences individually tailored to our interests, personality, and talents. Human beings are also developmentally different in their ability to process information from the environment. Preschool children do not glean the same information from a football game as older children or adults. Preschoolers may wonder why grown men are mauling each other, while adults accept the rules of the competition and forget to ask why players are rewarded for being so aggressive toward one another. Each of us, at every developmental stage, gains different information from the same environments, because we attend to some aspects of our environments and ignore other opportunities for experience. Each individual also processes information against a background of previously different experiences—not different environments but different experiences gleaned from the same environments.

I propose that these differences in experience—both developmental changes and individual differences—are caused by genetic differences. Over development, different genes are turned on and off, creating maturational changes in the organization of behavior, as well as maturational changes in patterns of physical growth. Genetic differences among individuals are similarly responsible for determining what experiences people do and do not have in their environments. What is attended to and what is ignored are events that are correlated with individual differences in interests, personality, and talents. Thus I argue that individual and developmental differences in behavior are more a function of genetic differences in individuals' patterns of development than of differences in the *opportunities* available in most environments.

In an earlier article (Scarr & McCartney, 1983) I proposed a theory of environmental effects on human development that emphasized the role of the genotype in determining not only which environments are experienced by individuals but also which environments individuals seek for themselves. To show how this theory addresses the process of becoming an individual, the theory was used to account for seemingly anomalous findings from deprivation, adoption, twin, and intervention studies. I will first review the theory and, in the last section, apply it more specifically to personality development.

Personality *development* depends on both a genetic program and a suitable environment for the expression of the human, species-typical program for development. Personality *differences* among people can arise from both genetic and environmental differences. The process by which differences arise is better described as genotype → environment effects. The genotype determines the *responsiveness* of the person to those environmental opportunities.

I distinguish here between objective environments to which a person is exposed and subjective environments that are actively experienced or "grasped" by the person. Individuals simply do not learn the same material given equal exposure. In addition, individuals *prefer* to spend time in different settings. Given leisure time, some people gravitate to the sports field or the television set, others to libraries, still others to concerts, films, self-help groups, gardening, horse races, butterfly collecting, and so forth. The environments they choose from the vast array of possibilities are determined in part by their individual personalities, interests, and talents. The development of the Strong-Campbell Interest Inventory (Campbell, 1974) is based on the idea that different personalities are more and less satisfied with different occupations. The Holland Scales (Holland, 1966) are even more explicit about the connection between personality and the nature of the work environment. Any theory of individuality must take into account the selective nature of experience and the compatibilities and incompatibilities of persons and environments.

A Model of Genotypes and Environments

Figure 7.1 presents the model of behavioral development. In this model, the child's phenotype, P_c (that is, her observable characteristics), is a function of both the child's genotype, G_c, and her rearing environment, E_c. There will be little disagreement on this. The parents' genotypes, G_p, determine the child's genotype, which in turn influences the child's phenotype. Again, there should be little controversy over this

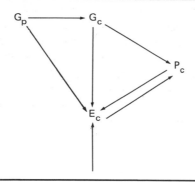

Figure 7.1   A Model of Behavioral Development

point. As in most developmental theories, transactions occur between the organism and the environment; here they are described by the correlation between phenotype and rearing environment. In most models, however, the source of this correlation is ambiguous. In this model, both the child's phenotype and rearing environment are influenced by the child's genotype. Because the child's genotype influences both the phenotype and the rearing environment, their correlation is a function of the genotype. The genotype is *conceptually prior* to both the phenotype and the rearing environment.

I argue that developmental changes in the genetic program prompt new experiences through maturation. Before the full phenotype is developed, the person becomes attentive to and responsive to aspects of the environment that previously were ignored or had other meanings. Just before puberty, many children become attentive to the attractiveness of the opposite sex. Little do they know what is to come, but they are responding to preliminary, changing relationships with peers that will change their biological and social lives for many years to come. What is "turned on" in the genotype affects an emerging phenotype both directly through maturation and through prompting new experiences.

It follows from the preceding argument that the transactions we observe between phenotypes and environments are merely correlations, determined by developmental changes in the genotype. The correlation of phenotype and environment is represented by the double arrows between P_c and E_c. The theory states that developmental changes in phenotypes are prompted both by developmental changes in the effective genotype and by changes in the salience of environments.

Genotypes and environments are then correlated. I recognize that this is not a popular position, but it accounts for data discussed in the final sections of this chapter far better than any other theory.

The path from the G_c to P_c represents maturation, which is controlled primarily by the genetic program. New structures arise out of maturation, from genotype to phenotype. Behavioral development is elaborated and maintained, in Gottlieb's (1976) sense, by the transactions of phenotype and environment, but it cannot arise de novo from this interaction. Thus in this model the course of development is a function of genetically controlled, maturational sequences, although the rate of maturation can be affected by some environmental circumstances, such as the effects of nutrition on sexual development (Watson & Lowry, 1967).

Separation of Genetic and Environmental Effects on Development

At any one point in time, personality differences may be analyzed into variances that can be attributed more or less to genetic and environmental sources (see Plomin, DeFries, & Loehlin, 1977; Scarr & Kidd, 1983). Depending on the amount of genetic variation and the amount of environmental variation for the characteristic of interest in the population studied, sources of individual differences can be estimated. But such an account does not describe how development of those differences occurred.

The theory that we proposed does not attempt to allocate variance but to describe how individuals evoke and select their own environments to a great extent. There may appear to be arbitrary events of fate—such as falling ill (perhaps due to a personal lifestyle that lowers resistance to disease?) or one's spouse running off with another mate (but how friendly and rewarding were you?)—but even these may not be entirely divorced from personal characteristics that have some genetic variability. Please understand that I do not mean that one's environmental fate is *entirely* determined by one's genotype—only that some genotypes are more likely to receive and select certain environments than others. The theory is not deterministic but probabilistic (see Scarr, 1981).

An Evolving Theory
of Behavioral Development

Plomin et al. (1977) described three kinds of genotype-environment correlations that I believe form the basis for a developmental theory. The theory of genotype → environment effects proposed has three propositions that I will now expand on.

(1) The process by which children develop is best described by three kinds of genotype → environment effects: a *passive* kind whereby the genetically related parents provide a rearing environment that is correlated with the genotype of the child (sometimes positively and sometimes negatively); an *evocative* kind whereby the child receives responses from others that are influenced by his genotype; and an *active* kind that represents the child's selective attention to and learning from aspects of his environment that are influenced by his genotype, and indirectly correlated with those of his biological relatives.

(2) The relative importance of the three kinds of genotype → environment effects changes with development. The influences of the passive kind declines from infancy to adolescence, and the importance of the active kind increases over the same period.

(3) The degree to which experience is influenced by individual genotypes increases with development and with the shift from passive to active genotype → environment effects, as individuals select their own experiences.

Three Genotype → Environment Effects

The first, *passive* genotype → environment effect arises in biologically related families and renders all of the research literature on parent-child socialization uninterpretable. Because parents provide both genes and environments for their biological offspring, the child's environment is necessarily correlated with her genes, because her genes are correlated with her parents' genes, and the parents' genes are correlated with the rearing environment they provide. It is impossible to know *what* about the parents' rearing environment for the child determines *what* about the child's behavior, because of the confounding effect of genetic transmission of the same characteristics from parent to child. Not only can we *not* interpret the direction of effects in parent-child interaction, as Bell (1968) argued, we also cannot interpret the *cause* of those effects in biologically related families.

An example of a positive passive kind of genotype-environment correlation can be found in social skills. Parents who are very sociable, who enjoy and need social activity, will expose their child to more social situations than parents who are socially inept and isolated. The child of sociable parents is likely to become more socially skilled, for both genetic and environmental reasons. The child's rearing environment is positively correlated with the parents' genotypes and therefore with the child's genotypes as well.

An example of a negative passive genotype-environment correlation can also be found in sociability. Parents who are socially skilled, faced with a child who is a social isolate, may exert more pressure and do more training than they would with a more socially adept offspring. The more enriched environment for the less able child represents a negative genotype → environment effect (see also Plomin et al., 1977). There is thus an unreliable, but not random, connection between genotypes and environments when parents provide the opportunities for experience.

The second kind of genotype → environment effect is called *evocative* because it represents the different responses that different genotypes evoke from the social and physical environments. Responses to the person further shape development in ways that correlate with the genotype. Examples of such evocative effects can be found in the research of Lytton (1980) and the review of Maccoby (1980). For instance, smiling, active babies receive more social stimulation than fussy, difficult infants (Wachs & Gandour, 1983). Cooperative, attentive preschoolers receive more pleasant and instructional interactions from the adults around them than uncooperative, distractable children. Individual differences in responses evoked can also be found in physical attractiveness; people who are considered attractive by others receive more positive attention, are thought to be more pleasant, desirable companions, and so forth (Bersheid & Walster, 1974).

The third kind of genotype → environment effect is the *active,* niche-picking or niche-building sort. People seek out environments they find compatible and stimulating. We all select from the surrounding environment some aspects to respond to, learn about, or ignore. Our selections are correlated with motivational, personality, and intellectual aspects of our genotypes. The active genotype → environment effect, we argue, is the most powerful connection between people and their environments and the most direct expression of the genotype in experience.

Examples of active genotype → environment effects can be found in the selective efforts of individuals in sports, scholarship, relationships— in most aspects of life. Once experiences occur, they naturally lead to further experiences. Buss (1984) argues that mate selection is a niche-selection process by which personal similarities make for compatibility and lead to further environmental shaping of personal characteristics. I agree that phenotypes are elaborated and maintained by environments, but the impetus for the experience comes, I think, from the genotype.

Developmental Changes in
Genotype → Environment Effects

The second proposition of our theory is that the relative importance of the three kinds of genotype → environment effects changes over development from infancy to adolescence. In infancy, much of the environment that reaches the child is provided by adults. When those adults are genetically related to the child, the environment they provide, in general, is positively related to their own characteristics and their own genotypes. Although infants are active in structuring their experiences by selectively attending to what is offered, they cannot do as much seeking out and niche-building as older children; thus *passive* geno-type → environment effects are more important for infants and young children than they are for older children, who can extend their experiences beyond the family's influences and create their own environments to a much greater extent. Thus the effects of passive genotype → environment effects wane when the child has many extra-familial opportunities.

In addition, parents can provide environments that are negatively related to the child's genotype, as illustrated earlier with respect to social opportunities. Although parents' genotypes usually affect the environ-ment they provide for their biological offspring, that environment is sometimes positive and sometimes negative, and therefore not as direct a product of the young child's genotype as later environments will be. Thus, as stated in proposition 3, genotype → environment effects increase with development, as active forms replace passive forms.

Genotype → environment effects of the *evocative* sort persist throughout life, as we elicit responses from others based on many personal, genotype-related characteristics, from appearance to personality and intellect. Those responses from others reinforce and extend the directions our development has taken. High intelligence and adaptive skills in children from very disadvantaged backgrounds, for example, evoke approval and support from school personnel who might otherwise despair of the child's chances in life (Garmezy, 1983). In adulthood, personality and intellectual differences evoke different responses in others. Similarities in personal characteristics evoke similar responses from others, as shown in the case of identical twins reared apart (Bouchard, 1981). These findings are also consistent with the third proposition.

Genetic Resemblance
Determines Environmental Similarity

The expected degree of environmental similarity for a pair of relatives can be thought of as the product of a person's own genotype → environment path and the genetic correlation of the pair. Figure 7.2 presents a model of the relationship between genotypes and environments for pairs of relatives who vary in genetic relatedness. G_1 and G_2 symbolize the two genotypes, E_1 and E_2 their respective environments. The similarity in the two environments (path *a*) is the product of the coefficient of each genotype with its own environment (path *x*) and the genetic correlation of the pair (path *b*). On the assumption that individuals' phenotypes are equally influenced by their own genotypes, the similarity in the environments of two individuals becomes a function of their genetic correlation.

This model can be used to describe the process by which MZ twins come to be more similar than DZ twins, and biological siblings more similar than adopted siblings. For identical twins, for whom path $b = 1.00$, the relationship of one twin's environment with the other's genotype is the same as the correlation of the twin's environment with his or her own genotype. Thus one would certainly predict what is often observed: that the hobbies, food preferences, choices of friends, academic achievements, and so forth of the MZ twins are very similar

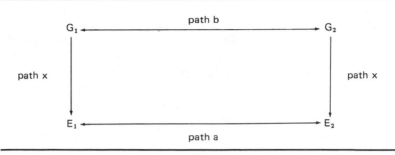

Figure 7.2: A Model of Environmental Similarity Based on Genetic Resemblance

(Scarr & Carter-Saltzman, 1980). Kamin (1974) proposed that all of this environmental similarity is imposed on MZ twins because they look so much alike, a proposal that fails utterly to account for the personality findings on identical twins reared apart. Theories of genetic resemblance do not speak to how close resemblances arise. We propose that the responses that the MZ twins evoke from others and the active choices they make in their environments lead to striking similarities through genotypically determined correlations in their learning histories.

The same explanation applies, of course, to the greater resemblance of biological than adopted siblings. The environment of one biological sib is correlated to the genotype of the other as one-half the coefficient of the sibling's environment to his or her own genotype, because path b = 0.50, as described in Figure 7.2. The same is true of DZ twins. The slightly higher correlation of DZ twins than of biological siblings reflects the additional fact that DZ twins are the same age at the same time in the same family constellation. There is virtually no correlation in personality characteristics between the sets of parents of unrelated children adopted into the same household, so that their genetic correlation is effectively zero. And thus their resemblance in behavioral characteristics are also predicted to be low because they will not evoke from others similar responses, or choose similar aspects of their environments to which to respond.

Shifts in Family Resemblance

Living within the same family seems to increase intellectual similarity and decrease resemblance in personality. There is a small *positive* effect of common family environments in nearly all studies of intelligence; that is, siblings are more similar when reared in the same family than when reared in different families. This is also true for the comparison of identical twins reared together and apart; the IQ correlation of MZs together is about .82 and for MZs reared apart about .76. But for personality scales, estimates of the small effects of common family environment are frequently *negative*; that is, living in the same family makes siblings and twins slightly less similar than they are when living apart (Bouchard, 1981; Hopper & Culross, 1983; Loehlin, 1982).

There are good theoretical reasons for predicting different effects of common family environment on intellectual talents and personality traits. There is only one desirable end to the IQ scale, and presumably everyone knows that to be smarter is better than to be dumber. On personality scales, being extreme at either end is undesirable, and there is a great deal of room in the middle for normal but variant personality scores. Thus there is also room for siblings and twins to differentiate themselves and for parents to create negative passive genotype → environment effects.

It is commonly observed by twin researchers that parents of MZs stress how different their twins are. They tell the investigator that twin A is the dominant one or the outgoing one, whereas twin B is more submissive or retiring. Parents of twins have no difficulty differentiating their children by contrasting them. On the other hand, when asked to rate each child independently on behaviorally anchored personality scales, parents of MZs usually rate them as quite similar. In the range of personality variation that exists in a population, small differences between MZ twins are magnified as important within-family differences— significant within the family but small in relation to the total variation. Parents of DZ twins also have no difficulty differentiating their twins' personalities. On objective, behavioral measures, however, DZ twins are usually rated as far less similar than MZs.

The data on personality resemblance among siblings in childhood and between parents and their children—measurement problem aside— show negligible correlations, regardless of the genetic relatedness of the family members (Loehlin et al., 1981; Scarr et al., 1981). Some evidence for increasing sibling resemblance in personality during middle childhood is found in a large twin study in Sweden (Fischbein, 1984). Behavioral adjustment ratings by teachers and by the twins themselves showed greater MZ than DZ correlations in both grades, but the sixth-grade twins were more similar in personality than fourth graders. By the end of adolescence, data on family members show the patterns of correlation reported in Table 7.1. Thus there are data to support the hypothesis that personality resemblance between genetic relatives increases as the influence of the family decreases and as the active genotype → environment effect increases.

If one were to guess what future studies will show, the best bet would be for increased resemblance among biological relatives when they no longer live together or when they have never lived together. As the present theory predicts, they will choose niches correlated with their own genotypes, environments that are also correlated with their family members' environments to the extent of their genetic correlations with those relatives.

Identical Twins Reared Apart

The most interesting observation is of the unexpected degree of resemblance between identical twins reared mostly apart. With the theory of genotype → environment effects, their resemblance is not surprising. Given opportunities to attend selectively to and choose from varied opportunities, identical genotypes are expected to make similar choices. They are also expected to evoke similar responses from others and from their physical environments. The fact that they were reared in different homes and different communities is not important; differences in their development could arise only if the experiential opportunities of one or both were very restricted, so that similar choices could not have been made.

According to previous studies (Newman, Freeman, & Holzinger, 1937; Juel-Nielsen, 1980; Shields, 1962) and the recent research of Bouchard and colleagues at the University of Minnesota (Bouchard, 1981), the most dissimilar pairs of MZs reared apart are those in which one was severely restricted in environmental opportunity. Extreme deprivation, and perhaps unusual enrichment, can diminish the influence of genotype on environment and therefore lessen the resemblance of identical twins reared apart.

Summary

In summary, the theory of genotype → environment effects proposed by Scarr and McCartney (1983) describes the usual course of human development in terms of three kinds of genotype-environment correlations that posit cooperative efforts of nature *and* nurture. Both genes and environments are constituents in the developmental system, but they have different roles. Genes determine much of human experience, but experiential opportunities are also necessary for development to occur. Individual differences can arise from restrictions in environmental opportunities to experience what the genotype would find compatible. With a rich array of opportunities, however, most differences among people arise from genetically determined differences in the experiences to which they are attracted and which they evoke from their environments.

The theory relies on the idea of individual differences in responsiveness to environments. This seems to me the essence of individuality. It is not just the familiar idea of reaction range, but includes more active kinds of transactions between people and their surrounds. In addition, the theory accounts for seemingly anomalous results from previous research on twins and families. Most important, the theory addresses the issue of process in personality development. Rather than presenting a static view of individual differences through variance allocation, or relying on between-family differences that cannot possibly constitute the major sources of individuality, this theory hypothesizes processes by which genotypes and environments combine across development to make all of us both members of the human species and unique individuals.

References

Ahern, F. M., Johnson, R. C., Wilson, J. R., McClearn, G. E., & Vandenberg, S. G. (1982). Family resemblances in personality. *Behavior Genetics, 12,* 261-280.

Bandura, A. (1982). The psychology of chance encounters and life paths. *American Psychologist, 37,* 747-755.

Bell, R. Q. (1968). A reinterpretation of the direction of effects in studies of socialization. *Psychological Review, 75,* 871-95.

Bersheid, E., & Walster, E. (1974). Physical attractiveness. In L. Berkowitz (Ed.), *Advances in experimental social psychology* (Vol. 7). New York: Academic Press.

Boakes, R. (1984). *From Darwin to behaviorism.* New York: Cambridge University Press.

Bouchard, T. (1981, August). *The Minnesota study of twins reared apart: Description and preliminary findings.* Paper presented at meeting of the American Psychological Association, Los Angeles.

Bouchard, T. J., Jr. (1984). Twins reared together and apart: What they tell us about human diversity. In S. W. Fox (Ed.), *Individuality and determinism* (pp. 147-184). New York: Plenum.

Brackbill, Y., & Nichols, P. (1982). A test of the confluence model of intellectual development. *Developmental Psychology, 18,* 192-198.

Bugental, D. B., & Shennum, W. A. (1984). "Difficult" children as elicitors and targets of adult communication patterns: An attributional-behavioral transactional analysis. *Monographs of the Society of Research in Child Development, 49*(1).

Buss, D. M. (1984). Toward a psychology of person-environment (PE) correlation: The role of spouse selection. *Journal of Personality and Social Psychology, 47,* 361-377.

Buss, A. H., & Plomin, R. (1984). *Temperament: Early developing personality traits.* Hillsdale, NJ: Lawrence Erlbaum.

Campbell, D. P. (1974). *Manual for the Strong-Campbell Interest Inventory T325 (Merged Form).* Palo Alto, CA: Stanford University Press.

Carey, G., & Rice, J. (1983). Genetics and personality temperament: Simplicity or complexity? *Behavior Genetics, 13,* 43-63.

Daniels, D., & Plomin, R. (in press). Differential experience of siblings in the same family. *Developmental Psychology.*

Daniels, D., Plomin, R., & Greenhalgh, J. (1984). Correlates of difficult temperament in infancy. *Child Development, 55,* 1184-1194.

Ernst, C., & Angst, J. (1983). *Birth order.* New York: Springer-Verlag.

Fischbein, S. (1984). Self- and teacher-rated school adjustment in MZ and DZ twins. *Acta Genetica Medica et Gemellologica, 33,* 205-212.

Galbraith, R. (1982). Sibling spacing and intellectual development. *Developmental Psychology, 18,* 151-173.

Garmezy, N. (1983). Stress-resistant children: The search for protective factors. In J. E. Stevenson (Ed.), *Recent research in developmental psychopathology.* Oxford: Pergamon.

Gottlieb, G. (1976). The role of experience in the development of behavior in the nervous system. In G. Gottlieb (Ed.), *Studies in the development of behavior and the nervous system* (Vol. 3): *Development and neural and behavioral specificity.* New York: Academic Press.

Grotevant, H. D. (1978). Sibling constellations and sex typing of interests. *Child Development, 49,* 540-542.

Grotevant, H. D., Scarr, S., & Weinberg, R. A. (1977). Patterns of interest similarity in adoptive and biological families. *Journal of Personality and Social Psychology, 35,* 667-676.

Holland, J. L. (1966). *The psychology of vocational choices: A theory of careers.* Waltham, MA: Ginn.

Hopper, J. L., & Culross, P. R. (1983). Covariation between family members as a function of cohabitation history. *Behavior Genetics, 13,* 459-471.

Jensen, A. R. (1980). *Bias in mental testing.* New York: Free Press.

Juel-Nielsen, N. (1980). *Individual and environment: Monozygotic twins reared apart.* New York: International University Press.

Kamin, L. J. (1974). *The science and politics of IQ.* Hillsdale, NJ: Lawrence Erlbaum.

Loehlin, J. C. (1982). Are personality traits differentially heritable? *Behavior Genetics, 12,* 417-428.

Loehlin, J. C., Horn, J. M., & Willerman, L. (1981). Personality resemblance in adoptive families. *Behavior Genetics, 11,* 309-330.

Lytton, H. (1980). *Parent-child interaction: The socialization process observed in twin and single families.* New York: Plenum.

Maccoby, E. E. (1980). *Social development.* New York: Harcourt, Brace, Jovanovich.

Murray, H. A. (1938). *Explorations in personality.* London: Oxford University Press.

Newman, H. G., Freeman, F. N., & Holzinger, K. J. (1937). *Twins: A study of heredity and environment.* Chicago: University of Chicago Press.

Nichols, R. C. (1978). Heredity and environment: Major findings from twin studies of ability, personality, and interests, *Homo, 29,* 158-173.

Plomin, R., & Daniels, D. (1984). The interaction between temperament and environment: Methodological considerations. *Merrill-Palmer Quarterly, 30,* 2.

Plomin, R., DeFries, J. C., & Loehlin, J. C. (1977). Genotype-environment interaction and correlation in the analysis of human behavior. *Psychological Bulletin, 84,* 309-322.

Rowe, D. C., & Plomin, R. (1981). The importance of nonshared (E1) environmental influences in behavioral development. *Developmental Psychology, 17,* 517-531.

Scarr, S. (1981). *Race, social class, and individual differences in IQ: New studies of old issues.* Hillsdale, NJ: Lawrence Erlbaum.

Scarr, S. (1985). Constructing psychology: Facts and fables for our times. *American Psychologist, 40,* 499-512.

Scarr, S., & Carter-Saltzman, L. (1980). Twin method: Defense of a critical assumption. *Behavior Genetics, 9,* 527-542.

Scarr, S., & Grajek, S. (1982). Similarities and differences among siblings. In M. E. Lamb & B. Sutton-Smith (Eds.), *Sibling relationships* (pp. 357-381). Hillsdale, NJ: Lawrence Erlbaum.

Scarr, S., & Kidd, K. K. (1983). Behavior genetics. In M. Haith & J. Campos (Eds.), *Manual of child psychology: Infancy and the biology of development* (Vol. 2, pp. 345-433). New York: John Wiley.

Scarr, S., & McCartney, K. (1983). How people make their own environments: A theory of genotype → environment effects. *Child Development, 54,* 424-435.

Scarr, S., Scarf, E., & Weinberg, R. A. (1980). Perceived and actual similarities in biological and adoptive families: Does perceived similarity bias genetic influence? *Behavior Genetics, 10,* 445-458.

Scarr, S., Weber, P. L., Weinberg, R. A., & Wittig, M. A. (1981). Personality resemblance among adolescents and their parents in biologically-related and adoptive families. *Journal of Personality and Social Psychology, 40,* 885-898.

Scarr, S., & Weinberg, R. A. (1978). The influence of "family background" on intellectual attainment. *American Sociological Review, 43,* 674-692.

Shields, J. (1962). *Monozygotic twins brought up apart and brought up together.* London: Oxford University Press.

Thomas, A., & Chess, S. (1977). *Temperament and development.* New York: Bruner/Mazel.

Wachs, T. D. (1983). The use and abuse of environment in behavior-genetic research. *Child Development, 54,* 396-407.

Wachs, T. D., & Gandour, M. J. (1983). Temperament, environment, and six-month cognitive-intellectual development: A test of the organismic specificity hypothesis. *International Journal of Behavioral Development, 6,* 135-152.

Wachs, T. D., & Gruen, G. (1982). *Early experience and human development.* New York: Plenum.

Watson, E. H., & Lowry, G. H. (1967). *Growth and development of children.* Chicago: Yearbook Medical Publishers.

Zajonc, R. B., & Markus, G. B. (1975). Birth order and intellectual development. *Psychological Review, 82,* 74-88.

Zajonc, R. B., Markus, H., & Markus, G. B. (1979). The birth order puzzle. *Journal of Personality and Social Psychology, 37,* 1325-1341.

8

Applying Social Psychology to Interpersonal Processes: Theory and Practice

STUART OSKAMP
ARTHUR OLGUIN
MERRY A. CARLSON
ALEXANDRIA SOBOLEW-SHUBIN
SHIRLYNN SPACAPAN

Where and how can social psychological knowledge be applied? One definition of the field of applied social psychology includes application of social psychological methods, theories, principles, or research findings to the understanding or solution of social problems (Oskamp, 1984). Such a definition gives a wide latitude for application since it includes use of psychological methods as well as theories and research data. An even broader scope is offered by Mayo and LaFrance (1980), who suggest using the term *applicable* social psychology, which can include aspects of the field with a potential for application as well as those that have been successfully applied. In their model of the field, theory and research both contribute to *knowledge* *building,* while *utilization and intervention* take that knowledge and use it to promote the goal of a better *quality of life.* All three of these elements, they say, should be linked in a continuing circular relationship, with feedback from each stage affecting each of the other two stages. Their emphasis on the goal of improving people's lives is very compatible with the American Psychological Association's (1981) official declaration that psychologists are committed to utilizing their knowledge for the promotion of human welfare.

The relationship between theory and application can follow several alternative paths, as pointed out by McGrath and Brinberg (1984) in their "validity network schema." Two of these paths are particularly important, the first of which uses theory as a foundation for application. This is the approach suggested by Kurt Lewin's famous quotation, "There is nothing so practical as a good theory" (1944/1951, p. 169). Other authors, too, have noted that scientific theories can serve as our guides to understanding the world, and that they are just as important in practical affairs as in scientific research (Deutsch & Krauss, 1965; Oskamp, 1984; Varela, 1971). Though we seldom stop to think about it, in our daily lives we all use many established scientific principles— involving, for instance, medical treatments, psychological persuasion techniques, economic principles of supply and demand, sociological understanding of social norms and roles—and these principles were first suggested by theorists. While the typical layperson thus applies scientific principles with little awareness of their origin, the work of applied scientists and scientific practitioners needs to be based on conscious use of the theoretical principles underlying their field of activity. The often cited contrast between theory and application is much overstated. Correct theoretical knowledge can be a powerful tool to help unravel applied questions and find solutions for social problems. In contrast, *incorrect or incomplete* theoretical understanding often leads to applications and social interventions that fail to improve or even worsen the problem they were designed to solve. Thus theory is an essential foundation for applied work in any field.

The relationship between theory and application can also take another major form, although we emphasize it less in this volume. This pattern uses substantive real-world observations as a foundation for constructing what has often been called *grounded theory* (Glaser & Strauss, 1967). McGrath and Brinberg (1984) refer to this as developing "system-driven hypotheses," a process in which the substantive area of interest determines the theoretical concepts and structures that are chosen as interpretive aids in understanding particular real-world phenomena. This approach can combine relevance with rigor in a pattern that is just as scientifically respectable, though less common, than the reverse relationship discussed above. Since most of the authors in this volume adopt an inductive approach to theorizing, much of the work reported in the preceding chapters follows this pattern. Consequently, in this chapter, we mainly adopt the other approach, which uses theoretical principles and concepts as a point of departure for developing practical applications.

The two sections of this chapter discuss in some detail, first, the theoretical contributions of the preceding chapters concerning various aspects of interpersonal processes, and second, their applicability to several different areas of practical affairs. The importance of good theories is just as great in the area of interpersonal processes as in any field, and in turn, a more comprehensive knowledge and understanding of interpersonal processes can be a first step in suggesting interventions that will help to resolve important social problems. So interpersonal processes represent an area in which theory and application can have important social consequences.

Dimensions for Theoretical Analysis

First, let us consider some of the major functions that theories serve in science, which have been categorized in different ways by various authors (e.g., Marx & Hillix, 1979; Reynolds, 1971). Rychlak (1981a) characterizes these functions as descriptive, delimiting, integrative, and generative. The *descriptive* function refers to the information provided by the theory about behaviors and situations and the conditions under which they vary. Through the formulation of a few theoretical propositions, which specify relationships between constructs, large amounts of information can be summarized and more easily understood. However, no theory can explain all phenomena, and in the process of defining constructs, the area under consideration is necessarily narrowed. Thus the *delimiting* function clarifies the boundaries and scope of topics covered by the theory and suggests the degree of generalizability of relevant research findings. The *integrative* function ties together current knowledge and research findings in a unified and consistent framework, which includes the concepts of the theory itself as well as disparate theoretical concepts and data from other sources. The final function is *generative,* referring to the basis that the theory provides for development of new theories, research, and/or practical programs.

None of the chapters in this volume represent full-fledged theories of social behavior, and they should not be analyzed as such. Nevertheless, they can be assessed on several theoretical dimensions to demonstrate both their heuristic strengths (which might be the basis for successful applications) and their less developed aspects, which might profit from further thought and research. Accordingly, in this section we will discuss them briefly on the following theoretical dimensions: breadth or scope, causal assumptions, formal structure, and generativity. These four dimensions seem most relevant both to the functions of theory noted above and to the issue of potential applicability. Other criteria commonly used to evaluate theories, for example, predictive ability, degree of rigor, empirical versus rational origin, and degree of empirical support (Marx & Hillix, 1979; Reynolds, 1971), seem less relevant and are omitted here.

Theoretical Breadth

Theoretical breadth refers to the degree that a model or theory is comprehensive—that is, the extent to which it includes all relevant factors and levels of analysis. It bears on the descriptive and delimiting functions of a theory. Other things being equal, science prefers a general explanation to a more specific one, and a simple explanation to a more complex one. Broad theories tend to have a higher level of abstraction than do those more narrowly framed, and they are often referred to as general theories (Hall & Lindzey, 1978). In terms of their applicability, broad theories are likely to have a greater number of potential areas for application than do narrow theories. By contrast, mini-theories or single-domain theories are limited to specific phenomena, and thus they cover only a narrow range of variables. Consequently, their areas of potential application are more limited, but this limitation may be offset by their greater specificity and hence ease of applicability.

As we mentioned in the first chapter, the presentations in this volume differ in their theoretical breadth or scope, and we have arranged them in an approximate descending order of breadth. Thus Werner's chapter on transactional worldview in science provides a very broad framework that can be utilized in approaching any research topic or applied issue. Essentially, what it does is to orient us to the types of variables that are important for us to consider. One reason for the breadth of this framework is that it includes not only the social environment but also the physical environment and temporal factors as major influences on social behavior. Another aspect of its breadth is that it emphasizes patterns of variables rather than the effects of single variables; however, this also makes it more of a descriptive account of behavior than an explanatory one.

Next in order of breadth we have placed Zander's chapter because it discusses the broad social phenomenon of group formation and development, and it presents principles applicable to all types of groups. This is true even though Zander here delimits his interest primarily to formal groups that have some kind of explicit organizational structure and concentrates specifically on how their purposes may guide their activities. Another aspect of breadth in his treatment of group-level phenomena is his inclusion of variables at the interpersonal and even intrapersonal levels of analysis, such as individual desires, expectations, values, and motives.

The chapter by Konrad and Gutek also deals with groups and organizations, as well as involving broad social categories such as men and women and ethnic minorities. However, it delimits its attention to a narrower aspect of groups, namely their composition in terms of subgroups (based on gender or ethnic characteristics) and the resulting consequences for the evaluation and treatment of subgroup members. It includes levels of analysis ranging from the societal level (socioeconomic and occupational patterns) through group variables (e.g., group composition and norms) to individual-level variables of personal evaluative judgments, social behavior, and treatment of other individuals.

Moving from the group to the interpersonal level, Kelley's chapter deals specifically with the interaction of dyads or other very small groups, and it uses the special case of conflict interactions as its topic. However, his approach on this level is a comprehensive one, for he is aiming at the construction of a taxonomic system to classify all possible interpersonal interaction sequences. He incorporates three dimensions of interaction (structure, content, and process), and he includes discussion of five different levels of analysis from single actions or events up through long-term personal relationships.

Cialdini's chapter also focuses primarily on dyadic relationships, and it is limited to the special dyadic relationship between the compliance professional and the target person for his or her influence attempts. Despite this specificity, however, it analyzes several key principles of social influence that are based upon the higher-level phenomenon of strongly inculcated cultural norms of behavior, such as reciprocity. Thus within this limited social setting, it aims at describing relatively broad and universally applicable scientific principles.

Finally, Scarr's approach is narrower in the sense that it focuses primarily at the individual level of analysis, and it gives heavy emphasis to biological, genetic factors affecting the processes by which an individual's personality is formed. However, it also discusses the environmental and interpersonal factors involving interaction with family, friends, and peers, and how these patterns of interaction change over time. In its chosen area, it is stating scientific principles that seem to have broad applicability across different times and cultures.

Causal Assumptions

As "intuitive scientists," human beings seek to understand the determinants of a situation, event, or process. These causal explanations are particularly important for practitioners who (although they may have to deal with social "symptoms") must uncover the causes of any phenomenon in order to intervene successfully and effect desired changes. Understanding the causal assumptions underlying a given theory or research approach is often one of the most important theoretical issues from the standpoint of application.

The word "cause" is related to the Greek word meaning responsibility. Hence, causal explanations describe the factors that "are responsible for" the phenomenon under observation (Rychlak, 1981a, 1981b). As noted in Werner's chapter, four types of cause were elaborated by Aristotle: efficient, material, formal, and final cause. All four types of cause are considered necessary in order to describe any phenomenon fully (Russell, 1972).

Efficient cause is closely related to the notion of movement or action, and is seen in descriptions of antecedent-consequent relations. For example, the presumed causal relationship in experimental research means that the independent variable moved, influenced, or changed the dependent variable. In Cialdini's chapter, the specific trigger events in the influence context operate in an efficient-causal manner. For example, receiving a lapel-flag from a Hare Krishna member causes an influenced person to donate money. Similarly, Konrad and Gutek discuss five possible factors (e.g., visible characteristics, institutional labels) that cause one to treat members of a particular subgroup differently.

Aristotle noted, however, that movement is not the only cause of phenomenon. Any phenomenon also has a substance or mass that, in another sense, is also "responsible" for the occurrence; for instance, a light turns on because electrons flow through its filament. An explanation involving matter, chemical substances, genes, or any similar concept that possesses a physical composition is a *material-cause* explanation. Scarr emphasizes material cause in her explanation of the responsiveness of children to their environment, for her theory assigns most weight to genetic factors, which lead children to seek and respond to certain environmental stimuli. However, Scarr notes that a material-cause explanation does not account fully for the data, since the correlation in personality of MZ twins is less than perfect and since there appears to be some resemblance in personality, however small, of adopted siblings. To explain this discrepancy, Scarr returns to an efficient-causal description, in which the social environment and genetics interact over time.

Efficient cause and material cause are traditionally emphasized by the physical and social sciences, but several authors in this volume incorporate other causal assumptions. As Werner has pointed out, the preferred explanatory principle in transactional approaches is *formal cause,* which concerns the way in which stable or recurring patterns, forms, or configurations are responsible for the occurrence of events. Although perhaps less intuitive than the preceding types of cause, the formal-cause construct is needed to explain how their can be change within an underlying stable structure. For example, our bodies regenerate cells, yet we are essentially the "same" person. Similarly, in Zander's chapter, members enter and exit a group, yet there is still a recognizable overall group.

Cialdini, Kelley, and Konrad and Gutek all assume the operation of formal cause, as well as efficient cause. Cialdini's compliance professional creates a context (e.g., of scarcity) for the target, who recognizes the pattern (i.e., scarcity is present). These formal-cause patterns, rather than specific aspects of the situation, are the critical factors in compliant behavior. For example, the context of reciprocation is generated whether an individual is given a gift, a free meal, or a compliment. In Kelley's chapter, examples of formal-cause concepts include situational structures such as a context of scarce resources or a relationship of symmetric negative interdependence. These are patterns in the social environment to which people respond and that contain the potential for conflict. Konrad and Gutek also embark on formal-cause explanations when they explore the pattern of interrelationships of social distinctions at different systems levels.

According to Aristotle, in order to explain the cause of any phenomenon fully, its purpose or intent must also be specified. These *final-cause* concepts are known as "telic" explanations (from the Greek work "telos," meaning end, goal, or ultimate reason). Zander's framework incorporates final-cause explanations: for example, individuals are motivated to join groups in order to change undesirable situations; the fundamental goal behind the development of group purposes is the anticipation of achieving satisfaction; and a group exists as long as it has utility for the individual members. There is also a purposeful, telic overtone to Scarr's discussion of developmental changes in children as they increasingly select certain activities, thoughts, and behaviors rather than others. Scarr, however, subsumes final-cause constructs under the influence of material cause, since she argues that even active environment-choosing behavior on the part of a child is genetically caused.

The natural sciences, on which the social and behavioral sciences are modeled, adopt efficient- and material-cause explanations and reject formal- and final-cause approaches to explaining phenomena. This is appropriate since natural science has no place for explanations based on teleological reasons (e.g., a stone falls because the person who threw it wanted it to fall). However, rejection of these last two causal constructs by social and behavioral science seems unwise since humans clearly act toward certain ends. A more complete discussion of these issues is found in Rychlak (1981a). Thus a complete answer to the question, "What causes a given social or psychological phenomenon?" is likely to require a response involving several causal perspectives. Accordingly, practitioners and researchers may benefit from considering more than one possible conception of the cause of an event when applying social psychological principles.

Formal Structure

The formal structure of a theory refers to how well its concepts and relational statements are defined and delineated, and this bears on the descriptive, delimiting, and integrative functions of the theory. The framework of a theory consists of essential constructs and relational statements (propositions) that link them. A key characteristic of a theory is the *explicitness* of its theoretical constructs—that is, their description in enough detail to ensure that their meaning is clear. Another important characteristic is the *rigor* or precision of the theory's relational statements, which ensures relatively high agreement among scientists on the predictions made by the theory. For practitioners, explicit constructs help to identify situations where the theory can appropriately be applied, and precise relational statements enable more confident planning of theory-based interventions.

As noted earlier, most of the chapters in this volume do not present formal theories, and so their specification of formal structural concepts is not as systematic as it would be in a purely theoretical presentation. Therefore, our approach in this section has to be mostly confined to a descriptive listing of the major constructs and relationships studied, without definitively assessing their explicitness or rigor of specification. We also offer occasional comments regarding evidence of empirical support, though we recognize that several of the authors were more intent on providing heuristic stimulation than offering empirical substantiation.

From Werner's transactional viewpoint, the three basic constructs are person, place, and time. However, they cannot be explicitly defined, for they are not considered to be separate elements but rather inseparable and mutually defining *aspects* of social situations. The most complete discussion is given to temporal qualities, which are seen as inherent to phenomena and as having both linear and cyclical patterns, which can be subdivided into five subordinate dimensions of salience, scale, pace, rhythm, and sequence. Typical relational statements specify that people are linked to their environment through the psychological processes of appropriation and identity, social rules and relationships, and affordances. Because of its emphasis on formal cause, this approach formulates associative (correlational) relational statements among its constructs rather than antecedent-consequent causal statements. One implication for practitioners is that changes in any one aspect of a situation may affect several other aspects as well.

The two major group-level constructs in Zander's chapter are group purpose (differentiated from a group's goal as being less measurable and less accessible) and group-oriented desire. In addition, environmental conditions and individual motivational constructs based on attainment of satisfaction are included in the discussion. Numerous relational statements are implied throughout the chapter—for example, the more measurable (or accessible, or powerful, etc.) the group's purpose is, the more satisfying the group will be to its members. The constructs and propositions are mainly elaborated through examples, which help to delimit the chapter's scope and suggest possible empirical tests as well as areas of application.

The central construct of Konrad and Gutek's chapter is group composition, defined in terms of the number and size of subgroups. Considerable attention is given to the definitional question of what individual personal characteristics will become important social distinctions that provide the basis for defining subgroups. Though there may be many such social distinctions, most of the relevant empirical research has been done with the dimensions of gender, ethnicity, and socioeconomic status. Through an extensive review of the research literature, the authors demonstrate that each of these dimensions of group composition can have major effects on the evaluation, treatment, and resulting behavior of individual group members, and that when the dimensions are interrelated, the effects are likely to be particularly strong and pervasive.

Since Kelley's chapter aims to develop a taxonomy rather than a theory, it concentrates first on descriptive categories. The central topic of the chapter is interpersonal conflict, explicitly defined as interference by one person with the ongoing chains of thoughts, feelings, or actions of another person. Any interaction sequence involves three crucial constructs—the structure (both situations and persons), the content of the interaction, and the dynamic process of interaction (both interpersonal and intrapersonal). Kelley defines each construct, and he provides concrete examples and empirical evidence of their interaction to form different conflict patterns. These patterns, outlined in his Table 5.4, suggest relational statements distinguishing several types of conflict according to their origins in specific types of persons and situations.

Cialdini's chapter represents a mini-theory of some of the main factors producing compliance with social influence attempts. He discusses three main constructs—reciprocity, scarcity, and authority—each of which strengthens the tendency to comply. The applicability of these constructs is enhanced by Cialdini's explicit definition of each one, together with examples of its operation in various settings and empirical research evidence demonstrating its effects. His relational statements have the following general form: "When conditions of (scarcity, reciprocity, etc.) are present, people feel motivated to (buy, give, etc.), and they will be likely to behave compliantly." As a real-world example, research showed that when grocery chains were informed that future supplies of beef would be limited, their greatly increased orders supported the theoretical notion of a state of desire being created under conditions of scarcity.

Scarr's chapter also ranks high on explicitness because her goal is to present a theoretical statement regarding the development of personality. Her major constructs are genotype and phenotype (already well-defined terms) and the rearing environment of the child. Her major relational statement is that controversial proposition that both the child's phenotype and rearing environment are strongly influenced by the child's genotype. She specifies and defines three separate processes by which the genotype can influence the rearing environment: passive, evocative, and active effects; and she specifies changes in their relative strength from birth to adolescence. For each of these processes she supplies examples, describes the rationale behind the effect, and provides research evidence.

Generativity

There are three sorts of generativity that can stem from a theoretical contribution: stimulation of further research, additional theoretical ideas, or applications to practical problems. However, the generativity of such a contribution can only be adequately assessed in retrospect, perhaps 10 years or longer after its publication. Until enough time has passed for the contribution to become known in its field and to stimulate other related work, its generativity can only be predicted hypothetically, and such predictions often turn out to have been mistaken.

Since the chapters in this volume all present relatively recent research and thinking, they have not had time to generate related research or theorizing. Thus all that can be said about them at present is that they have all grown out of previous empirical findings, some of which are cited in each selection, and they all seem potentially capable of generating additional future research and perhaps also new or revised theoretical positions.

However, concerning these chapters' generativity of practical applications, it may be safer to offer some more definite predictions and conclusions. This is true because many of these selections make explicit suggestions for applications, and other implicit possibilities are clearly evident as well. Thus in the following section we discuss a wide range of possible applications of ideas and findings from the preceding chapters.

Applying Social Psychology

To organize our discussion of the applicability of the preceding substantive chapters in the light of our broad definition of the field of applied social psychology, we have divided the areas of application, somewhat arbitrarily, into five: management of groups, counseling, influence and persuasion, regulatory activity, and other public policy concerns.

Management of Groups

In the practical arena of group management, Zander's long experience with group processes has given him considerable insight into ways that groups can be organized and run to optimize their effectiveness and the satisfaction of their members. He has condensed some of that experience into several lists in his chapter, involving (1) conditions that favor the formation of groups, (2) ways to increase the strength of members' group-orientated desires, and (3) approaches to help a group define its purpose in ways that will satisfy the largest numbers of members. Zander emphasizes the importance of members' satisfaction as a condition that will maintain their motivation and thus may help to make the group more effective. However, at the same time, he points out that in many groups, members' individual motivations need to be amalgamated into a jointly shared desire for the group to reach certain goals; and consequently his suggestions for strengthening group-oriented desires and helping a group define its purpose may be crucial. He stresses the importance to the group of having measurable goals that are accessible through identifiable paths of action, and he suggests the desirability of adopting new group goals in situations where the current goals are unlikely to be reached or are too vague for their attainment to be measured. Finally, he points out that a group's activities may be inappropriate to its intended purpose, and that this often happens when members' individual motives are dominant or when the group's purpose is not measurable and/or accessible.

Zander qualifies most of these suggestions with the admonition that they are plausible hypotheses rather than established findings, and that they should be tested by future research. Certainly, in addition to researchers, group organizers and managers will want to consider and try out these ideas in their continuing work with groups.

Another set of useful suggestions for group management stems from Kelley's proposed taxonomy of conflict structures and processes. Understanding conflict processes requires an awareness of both situational and personal factors, and Kelley's Table 5.4 provides a list of some of the common structures of conflict situations and their associated personal issues and conflict processes. For example, he suggests that situations of symmetric negative interdependence between individuals are associated with personal concerns about esteem or courage and are often resolved through violent processes such as fighting. By contrast, situations of symmetric positive interdependence, but ones where the participants have unequal control over resources, raise personal concerns of fairness or loyalty and are resolved through processes of engagement or avoidance. Other types of conflict situations that Kelley discusses include asymmetric positive interdependence, problems of exchange, and problems of coordination. Group managers could well use such a list as a directory of potential trouble spots and issues in their organization, and when such problems arise, they could use Kelley's analysis in understanding and trying to resolve them.

Kelley's chapter contains a host of potentially helpful insights into group processes. To mention a few examples, reputations for aggressiveness have a self-fulfilling quality in interactions; intrapersonal processes generally accompany and support interpersonal actions;

situational and dispositional factors in conflicts each tend to call forth and sustain the other; personal images, reputations, and self-esteem are particularly important in adult violence.

Though Kelley's taxonomy is not yet complete, one of its strengths is its derivation from a wide variety of social situations, including children's playground disagreements, parent-child interactions, marital partners' conflicts, altercations between police officers and offenders, and incidents of criminal homicide. As Kelley suggests, an understanding of the situational and personal aspects of conflict should have direct applications in training people to defuse conflicts. Among the possible applications are training police officers to handle personal and family disputes, training children in cooperative interaction, and training group leaders and managers to avoid or resolve organizational strife. There may even be a potential for applying Kelley's insights and taxonomy at the level of conflict between large-scale organizations, institutions, and nations.

Werner's chapter also has some lessons for group managers. The transactional worldview that she advocates entails a systems approach to organizations and groups, and this has several resulting implications. First, it emphasizes the importance of the physical environment as an influence on social interaction. Such an approach directs attention to often-overlooked aspects of a situation, such as the shape of a conference table during negotiations or the placement of furniture and barriers in an office setting. Second, the transactional viewpoint stresses the importance of temporal factors as integral aspects of events. As one example, the meaning and the results of an event such as a party or a staff meeting are different at different times, such as at Christmas versus summertime versus performance-review time. Third, transactionalists view all the aspects of a system as inseparably linked, as Werner illustrated in her discussion of the people, equipment, actions, and rules of a tennis match. From this it follows that we should study or try to work with the whole organization and its environment as a total entity rather than with separate elements or parts. One lesson that this approach teaches is to try to envision and then avoid the unintended consequences that may follow from a change in group structure or activities (for example, the undesired changes in group membership that may result from a change in group location, tasks, or meeting times). This emphasis on the inseparability and mutual definition of the persons, objects, places, and times in an organizational system contrasts strongly with bureaucratic approaches to organization and management following principles of hierarchy, separation of person and position, and so on (see Weber, 1947).

Werner's approach suggests that group and organization managers should give more attention to several kinds of psychological processes. These include appropriation and attachment processes, by which people give meaning and importance to their environment and in turn derive a feeling of their own identity (e.g., the posters and signs around my room or workplace display my interests and values); social rules and relationships (often informal and unknown to outsiders or higher-ups) that define appropriate behavior in various settings and circumstances; and affordances and appraisals, which are cognitive-perceptual processes that give meaning to the environment in terms of the functions it can fulfill (e.g., the water-cooler provides a place to socialize, not just to slake one's thirst). All of these processes illustrate the holistic view that all the aspects of a situation—the people, places, objects, and time—are crucial in understanding it. Thus managers who hope to influence organizations successfully need to adopt this multidimensional viewpoint.

Other issues for managers to consider are illustrated in Konrad and Gutek's chapter. The theory and findings that they have reviewed about the effects of group composition (i.e., subgroup proportions within a group) can be crucial in determining the status, treatment, and satisfaction of group members, and in turn the success and satisfaction of the whole group. One of their important conclusions is that group heterogeneity (many small subgroups within the group) is apt to lead to lower social integration of members and increased turnover or dropout of members. They also discuss how stereotyping and unequal treatment of group members will be influenced by prevalent social status categories, but they point out that stereotyping and discrimination should be lower in balanced groups (ones where subgroups are roughly equal in size) than in groups where one category of persons predominates.

In applying Konrad and Gutek's findings, managers need to be keenly attuned to individual members' characteristics that may produce subgroup distinctions. When bringing in new members, managers should try to do so in ways that will enhance the effectiveness of the whole group and also maintain the satisfaction of the old and the new members. These considerations become particularly touchy and difficult when trying to integrate individuals from some low-status minority category (racial, gender, nationality, or religious) into an ongoing group. One approach that has been used successfully to maintain the minority member's self-esteem, satisfaction, and acceptance by the group is first to bring in a potential star, as when Jackie Robinson was the first black to play major league baseball. However, to achieve fuller acceptance for all members of the minority category, not just the star, a more equal balance of subgroup members is required, as was later reached by major league baseball, football, and other sports. Another approach that has facilitated successful minority-group integration entails creation of equal-status contact between subgroups (e.g., the school integration studies of Aronson & Osherow, 1980). These considerations apply equally to introducing women into formerly all-male work groups or occupations, and managers need to keep these points in mind if they hope to retain their new employees as well as keep the loyalty of their previous workers.

Other implications for group management are contained in Cialdini's chapter. All of the basic psychological principles that he analyzes—reciprocation, scarcity, authority—can be used by a manager or a group member to influence other members of the group, as can the other principles that he briefly mentions—consistency, liking, and social validation. Cialdini specifically points out the importance of using reciprocity in organizational management—giving something (such as information, feedback, praise, rewards) to get something from one's employees (such as loyalty, dedication, or information in return). Wise use of the reciprocation norm is also crucial to successful negotiation, for making voluntary concessions can prevent stalemates and stimulate the other side to make concessions in return. The principle of scarcity can also be used effectively by managers, for instance by arranging a competition for valued rewards such as promotions, bonuses, stock options, prizes, or even certificates of recognition; or by setting time deadlines or advertising "limited time offers" for attaining valued goods. The principle of authority, of course, is used constantly by managers who have legitimate or expert power (that is, they have the acknowledged position or the knowledge and expertise that allows them to give directions). Cialdini shows how, even without such a position, one can obtain a reputation for trustworthiness by imparting information that is contrary to one's own self-interest, and then use that acquired authority to influence people toward one's own goals. He also points out that a combination of the principle of authority with reciprocity and/or scarcity, as well as with any of the other triggers of influence, can be even more potent in accomplishing one's aims in group settings.

Though such uses of information or power can be manipulative and unethical, Cialdini has particularly emphasized how they can be performed honestly and ethically for desirable ends. He has also suggested that instead of rewarding unquestioning compliance, managers can create more effective groups by training their employees to think for themselves and to question orders that might be dangerous or damaging to the group enterprise—an approach that would be particularly desirable in situations involving health care or public safety. Cialdini's prescription for the ethical use of knowledge to influence others is to adopt the approach of a *detective* and search for the naturally occurring triggers of influence in a situation, rather than illegitimately smuggling into the situation influence principles that are not inherent there. Such an approach, he suggests, should have long-term benefits for individuals and organizations that use it, since they will come to see themselves and be seen by others as honest, trustworthy, likable, deserving of reciprocation, and so on. This "win-win" approach aimed at benefitting both organizations and their individual members seems very consistent with some of Zander's suggestions for increasing group effectiveness while enhancing members' individual satisfaction.

Counseling

Kelley's chapter will be one of the most helpful ones for counselors and therapists who want to use social psychological principles and findings. As he suggests, one eventual goal for his analysis could be to produce an atlas of interpersonal sequences, in which a counselor or therapist could look up an observed pattern of family interaction and obtain information about its frequency of occurrence, concomitants and implications, and possible ways to modify it.

Kelley's analysis emphasizes that *intra*personal thoughts, feelings, and actions are components of interpersonal conflict, and counselors would normally discuss many of these intrapersonal aspects with their clients as well as analyzing the interpersonal sequences. Conflict structures can be analyzed (in attribution theory terms) as involving both situational and personal causal factors, and each party to the conflict tends to explain their own behavior in terms of external situational factors that they had to respond to, while explaining the other party's behavior in terms of internal dispositions (e.g., "selfish," "hostile," "overly sensitive," "prejudiced"). This pattern is sometimes called the actor-observer bias. Counselors, knowing this pattern, can help each party to see their own personal contributions to a conflict as well as the situational forces that affected the other party's actions.

Kelley's attempt to classify the content of conflicts may also be helpful to counselors by showing the links between recurring conflictual topics and the situational structures and personal issues that predispose toward particular kinds of conflicts. In this regard, Kelley cites research showing differences between couples with distressed relationships and "normal" couples in the types of major episodes in their relationship and in the fine-grain sequences of their actions, such as more cross-complaining sequences, counterproposals, disagreement and interruption, and reciprocation of negative affect for the distressed couples.

Counselors who deal with children and families might also find useful Kelley's discussion of hostile, person-directed aggression versus instrumental, object-directed aggression. As children grow older, their aggression shifts from largely instrumental, physical responses to mostly personal, derogatory verbal attacks. These person-directed, verbal attacks are typically provoked by threats to self-esteem and are linked to attributions about the intentions of the other person. A related finding is that a child's reputation for aggressiveness tends to be a self-fulfilling prophecy, largely because of the attributions made by both the aggressor and the victims. These findings support Kelley's suggestion that attributional training can help to avert conflict situations by teaching children (and adults) to avoid attributions of personal intent to actions of others that interfere with one's own goals.

Scarr's chapter also has helpful information for child and family counselors. Her basic point is that genetic and environmental factors combine in determining the formation and development of personality and social behavior. Though everyone trained in psychology is aware of that principle in the abstract, Scarr presents a number of specific findings and a helpful theory that shows how it applies in individual lives. She points out that parent-child interaction cannot be explained solely in terms of environmental stimuli and their effects, for genetic factors are an inherent part of the parents' behavior as well as of the child's reactions. Furthermore, the child provides a powerful stimulus for the parents (though that is less often realized than the reverse direction), so any causal relationship must be bidirectional. Counselors, whether working with the parent or the child, need to be constantly attuned to these bidirectional relationships, but they are easy to overlook when only one side is heard. Two ways in which conjoint family treatment (as opposed to individual counseling) is often helpful are in identifying the reciprocal stimuli provided by the several family members and in demonstrating concretely the ways in which each member responds to the others.

In emphasizing the often-overlooked genetic influences on personality characteristics, Scarr does not mean to imply that behavioral patterns cannot be modified by environmental stimuli and intervention such as a counselor might use. However, she points out that different people perceive and experience the identical environment in different ways (a point also made in Werner's chapter), and that they tend to seek out different environmental experiences. Scarr identifies three separate ways in which children's genetic makeups contribute to determining their environmental influences: the passive type of influence comes from the rearing environment provided by the parents (linked to their own genotype and hence correlated with the child's); the evocative type is based on the reactions of others to the child; and the active type stems from the child's selective attention and response to various aspects of the environment. In infancy, the passive parental influences on the child are the strongest ones; but as years pass, more non-family members become involved in evoking the child's responses; and by adolescence the child is busily engaged in selecting the environmental elements that he or she prefers to respond to. Counselors, knowing these patterns, can help to prepare parents for such inevitable changes, and they can also relieve parents from possible guilt feelings regarding their responsibility for unfortunate events or behavior patterns in the child.

Werner's chapter also suggests that counselors should pay attention to the importance of patterns. In dealing with families or couples, just as in studying neighborhoods, a systems approach is very helpful. Many elements of a relationship, including the physical environment, the time schedules and patterns of the participants, and their other social contacts, are all interlinked, and the counselor needs to keep all of these aspects in mind. Moreover, trying to change any one of these aspects can have—and probably will have—ramifications on many of the others. Hence the counselor needs to try to view the total pattern and to notice changes on multiple levels and from multiple perspectives. Though counseling using a systems viewpoint is more demanding than similar approaches, its attention to multiple determinants and relationships should make it more effective in the long run.

Konrad and Gutek's chapter offers some information that would be useful in counseling individuals who are involved in work groups, families, or community groups where they are part of a small subgroup (e.g., women breaking into a formerly male company or occupation, or members of one race, religion, or culture marrying into a family having a different background). Such individuals need to realize that they are likely at first to be treated in terms of social stereotypes based on their social category. Also, it is common for individuals outnumbered by a dominant subgroup to experience considerable social isolation rather than integration into the group. However, they can realistically hope for better days ahead, for the initial isolation and negative evaluation often dissipate after the outnumbered individual demonstrates competence in the group's activities. Counselors should help to prepare people for the blows to their pride and self-esteem that usually accompany such subgroup confrontations.

Another contribution to the success of counselors would be a thorough grasp of the principles of social influence elucidated by Cialdini, as discussed in the next section.

Influence and Persuasion

A third area where this volume has applications is in personal influence and persuasion, one of the classical areas of social psychology. Cialdini's chapter is explicitly directed to this topic and contains a host of pointers for influence agents. The fields where it could be applied are numerous, most notably including advertising and marketing, sales, human service occupations, political persuasion, family and social relationships, and (as discussed above) management of groups. Following the inductive or grounded-theory approach, Cialdini has distilled his understanding of the six major principles of influence from real-world observation of influence agents at work—from panhandlers to auto salespersons to evangelists—and thus he knows that they work in applied situations. He has also tested some of the principles in laboratory experiments and thereby helped to spell out why and how and under what circumstances they work.

Though the various triggers of influence can be teased apart and analyzed separately, they are often mixed together to some extent in real-life situations. As Cialdini points out in his example of Roberto the waiter, they can be purposely combined in many ways, and doing so should normally make their overall effect still stronger. A prime example where many influence principles are intentionally combined is in the construction of television commercials and other advertising. For example, a single commercial may contain appeals to authority by citing authoritative-sounding facts and figures, to liking by having an attractive and pleasant narrator, to social validation by stressing that "everybody's doing it," to consistency by seeking a behavioral commitment from the viewer, to reciprocation by offering a rebate or incentive, and to scarcity by setting a deadline for quick action.

With such weapons in the hands of influence agents, what chance does the poor target person have? In his recent book, Cialdini (1985) has suggested that the best answer is to give the same knowledge about influence principles to members of the public and thus to inoculate them against the potential unethical uses of the principles. If such an effort were successful, citizens would then be able to spot unethical uses of the principles when they were being falsely "smuggled" into situations. As a related example, Cialdini points out that some companies have successfully foiled the potential unethical use of the reciprocity principle by not permitting employees to accept gifts from vendor companies.

Scarr's chapter also has some implications for influence agents, which may further dampen their effectiveness. Her emphasis (similar to Werner's) that people choose to respond to only a few of the elements in their complex environment is very relevant to any influence attempt. The principle involved is summarized in the old saying, "You can lead a horse to water, but you can't make it drink." Thus an audience member may pick out of a commercial quite different elements or messages than the advertiser desired—finding unintended humor, reacting to a background stimulus, misunderstanding words or meaning, derogating the source, or counterarguing against the message. So a commercial may be attractive and effective to many people but have no effect or an opposite effect on other individuals.

Regulatory Activity

Another arena of application for social psychological principles is in government regulatory activity, which is typically designed to accomplish such key social goals as providing correct information, fair opportunities, equal competition, or healthful products to the public. Cialdini's discussion of ethical uses of influence is relevant here, for he suggests that a central requirement for ethicality is to present situations truthfully. Though truth in advertising is often hard to define with any consensus, it is a standard that the Federal Trade Commission has tried to enforce over the last several decades in its regulation of false and/or misleading advertising.

Cialdini also touches on an important public issue in his discussion of the reciprocity principle. As mentioned above, many companies have rules against their employees accepting any gifts from suppliers, precisely in order to avoid feelings of obligation that would trigger the operation of reciprocity behavior that could be disadvantageous to the company. In exactly the same way, our elected public officials—such as members of Congress—become indebted to the affluent individuals and political action committees (PACs) that provide the main support for their expensive reelection campaigns, and the frequent result is that they vote on behalf of private commercial interests rather than in the public interest. An excellent way to avoid or diminish such undesirable reciprocity behavior would be to set stringent limits on the amount of money that individuals or PACs could contribute to any candidate's election campaign—a step that public-interest organizations like Common Cause have been advocating for many years.

The other chapter that has direct relevance for government regulatory activity is the one by Konrad and Gutek concerning subgroup proportions within a larger group. There have been many studies showing the creation of in-group favoritism, even based on such trivial characteristics as the supposed ability to estimate the number of dots accurately. However, when in-group favoritism is based on characteristics like sex or race, rather than on ability or experience, it becomes societally detrimental and contrary to U.S. public policy. Konrad and Gutek have summarized many studies that showed stereotyping and unequal treatment of racial and sexual groups in a wide variety of real-world situations. One effect of these factors is for female-dominated occupations to have lower pay and lower status that male-dominated occupations, and the same pattern holds true for female- and male-dominated companies *within* a given occupational category, where the competence requirements would seem to be equal.

Even more pernicious, there is also considerable evidence of *individuals* within groups being evaluated and treated unequally in accordance with common societal status stereotypes. Konrad and Gutek's conclusions show that equality of treatment and of evaluation may be quite likely to be compromised in groups that have very unbalanced proportions of majority and minority subgroups (in terms of race, sex, or possibly other characteristics). Consequently these findings are of great importance for the Equal Employment Opportunity Commission and other agencies that are trying to ensure fair opportunities for all citizens. Such agencies need to pay particular attention to the likelihood of discriminatory practices in previously single-race or single-sex occupations or companies that are now attempting to recruit members of the unrepresented group under affirmative action guidelines. However, it appears that individuals from a high-status social category (e.g., men or whites) normally experience much less discrimination against them when they join a lower-status group than do individuals from a low-status category when they try to join a higher-status group.

Other Public Policy Concerns

Werner's emphasis on a holistic or systems approach to the relationship of variables has an important lesson for public policy officials. Far too often a proposed policy is assessed and chosen with reference only to its expected effect on one or two other variables, and other linkages are unrecognized or ignored. For instance, deinstitutionalization of mental patients in the United States was justified on the basis of saving state mental health funds and getting the former patients back into functioning roles in the community. However, in most states, community mental health clinic and halfway house staff and facilities (intended to help keep the ex-patients in the community) were grossly inadequate for this purpose, so a pattern of repeated acute rehospitalizations was established. Also, board and care homes without any treatment programs proliferated under state reimbursement programs, and in them most ex-patients merely vegetated instead of functioning as competent citizens in the community. As Werner's approach suggests, such complications and problems could have been anticipated and planned for if a less simplistic, more holistic view of all aspects of the social problem had been adopted in the first place.

On a contrasting note, Scarr's chapter provides a salutary warning for social planners. She grants that much of the variance in personality and social behavior is due to individual experiences, and this view might be seen as suggesting that public policymakers should stress the provision of desirable experiences for the social group in question (e.g., jobs or job training for unemployed youth, community therapeutic support for ex-mental patients). However, Scarr also points out the narrow limits of environmental influence on individuals, emphasizing that the main effects of any given environmental treatment are very small in relation to the variability in reactions by different individuals. Thus when potentially beneficial social programs are instituted, many of their expected beneficiaries never hear about them or fail to take advantage of them, while others do enroll but gain a wide variety of lessons from them, many of which are unintended or even counter-productive. This cautionary perspective should not be taken as advice to do nothing, however—merely as a warning to expect varied and conflicting results of any social program and to be alert to evaluate and modify the program to try to minimize any unwanted effects.

The above suggestions and commentary illustrate some of the applications that can be drawn from social psychological work on interpersonal processes. They also demonstrate how applicable research can contribute both theory and findings that, as Lewin (1944/1951) emphasized, are highly practical in understanding and dealing with the world we live in.

References

American Psychological Association. (1981). Ethical principles of psychologists. *American Psychologist, 36,* 633-638.

Aronson, E., & Osherow, N. (1980). Cooperation, prosocial behavior, and academic performance: Experiments in the desegregated classroom. In L. Bickman (Ed.), *Applied social psychology annual* (Vol. 1). Newbury Park, CA: Sage.

Cialdini, R. B. (1985). *Influence: Science and practice.* Chicago: Scott, Foresman.

Deutsch, M., & Krauss, R. M. (1965). *Theories in social psychology.* New York: Basic Books.

Glaser, B., & Strauss, A. (1967). *The discovery of grounded theory.* Chicago: Aldine.

Hall, C. S., & Lindzey, G. (1978). *Theories of personality* (3rd ed.). New York: John Wiley.

Lewin, K. (1951). *Field theory in social science* (D. Cartwright, Ed.). New York: Harper. (Originally published 1944)

Marx, M. H., & Hillix, W. A. (1979). *Systems and theories in psychology* (3rd ed.). New York: McGraw-Hill.

Mayo, C., & La France, M. (1980). Toward an applicable social psychology. In R. F. Kidd & M. J. Saks (Eds.), *Advances in applied social psychology* (Vol. 1). Hillsdale, NJ: Lawrence Erlbaum.

McGrath, J. E., & Brinberg, D. (1984). Alternative paths for research: Another view of the basic versus applied distinction. In S. Oskamp (Ed.), *Applied social psychology annual* (Vol. 5): *Applications in organizational settings*. Newbury Park, CA: Sage.

Oskamp, S. (1984). *Applied social psychology*. Englewood Cliffs, NJ: Prentice-Hall.

Reynolds, P. D. (1971). *A primer in theory construction*. Indianapolis: Bobbs-Merrill.

Russell, B. (1972). *A history of Western philosophy*. New York: Simon & Schuster.

Rychlak, J. F. (1981a). *A philosophy of science for personality theory*. Malabar, FL: Krieger.

Rychlak, J. F. (1981b). *Introduction to personality and psychoanalytic theory* (2nd ed.). Boston: Houghton Mifflin.

Varela, J. A. (1971). *Psychological solutions to social problems: An introduction to social technology*. New York: Academic Press.

Weber, M. (1947). *The theory of social and economic organization* (A. M. Henderson & T. Parsons, Trans.). New York: Free Press.

Author Index

Subject Index

About the Authors

Merry A. Carlson is a National Science Foundation Fellow at the Claremont Graduate School, where she is working toward a master's of public policy degree and a Ph.D. in social psychology. Her undergraduate thesis, conducted at Reed College, was presented at the Second International Conference on Cooperation in Education. Her research interests center on the social psychology of discrimination as it involves gender and the physically challenged, particularly bearing on policy formulation and implementation.

Robert Cialdini, an Arizona State University Distinguished Research Professor, received his Ph.D. in social psychology from the University of North Carolina in 1970. He held a postdoctoral fellowship at Columbia University, and has had visiting appointments at Ohio State University and the University of California at San Diego. His main research interest is in social influence techniques, with special emphasis on persuasion and compliance, and he has recently authored *Influence: Science and Practice.*

Barbara A. Gutek is Professor of Psychology at the Claremont Graduate School. She received her Ph.D. in psychology from the University of Michigan in 1975 and taught at UCLA for five years before moving to Claremont. Her research interests in recent years have focused on the phenomenon of work in two areas: women at work, including sexual harassment, and the impact of computerization on white-collar work. Among her numerous books are *Sex and the Workplace: Impact of Sexual Behavior and Harassment on Women,*

Men, and Organizations; Women and Work: A Psychological Perspective; and *Women and Work: An Annual Review.*

Harold H. Kelley received his Ph.D. in group psychology from the Massachusetts Institute of Technology. He has been Professor of Psychology at UCLA since 1961 and he previously taught at the University of Michigan, Yale, and the University of Minnesota. He has been honored by Distinguished Scientific Contribution Awards from both the APA and the Society of Experimental Social Psychology, and he has been a fellow at the Center for Advanced Study in the Behavioral Sciences. His research interests in the structures and processes of interpersonal relations have resulted in numerous publications including *The Social Psychology of Groups; Interpersonal Relations: A Theory of Interdependence* (both with John Thibaut); *Personal Relationships: Their Structures and Processes,* and the recent *Close Relationships.*

Alison M. Konrad is a postdoctoral fellow at the Graduate School of Business at Stanford University. She received her Ph.D. in applied social psychology in 1986 from the Claremont Graduate School, where her dissertation research studied the impacts of organizational demography on social integration and self-evaluation. Her research interests focus on organizational behavior, with emphasis on the work experience of women, and the impacts of organizational structure on behavior.

Arthur Olguin is currently an American Psychological Association Fellow in organizational behavior and social psychology at the Claremont Graduate School. He holds master's degrees in counseling and psychology, and is a licensed marriage and family therapist. His research interests include program evaluation, job satisfaction, cross-cultural psychology, and organizational iatrogenics.

Stuart Oskamp is Professor of Psychology at the Claremont Graduate School. He received his Ph.D. from Stanford University and has had visiting appointments at the University of Michigan, University of Bristol, London School of Economics and Political Science, and University of New South Wales. His main research interests are in the areas of attitudes and attitude change, behavioral aspects of energy and resource conservation, and social issues and public policy. His books include *Attitudes and Opinions* and *Applied Social Psychology.* He is a Past President of the APA Division of Population and Environmental Psychology and Editor-Elect of the *Journal of Social Issues.*

Sandra Scarr is Commonwealth Professor of Psychology and Chair of the Department of Psychology at the University of Virginia. A Harvard Ph.D. in psychology and social relations, she has held positions at the University of Pennsylvania, the University of Minnesota, and Yale, among others. She is a Past President of both the Behavior and Genetics Association and the APA Divison on Developmental Psychology, and has also been Editor of *Developmental Psychology*. Among her publications are an introductory psychology textbook, *Race, Social Class, and Individual Differences in IQ: New Studies of Old Issues,* and the APA award-winning *Mother Care/Other Care.*

Alexandria Sobolew-Shubin is working toward a Ph.D. in social psychology at the Claremont Graduate School. Her research interests include cognitive factors in coping with health problems, health psychology and women, and sex roles.

Shirlynn Spacapan is Assistant Professor of Psychology at Harvey Mudd College, one of the Claremont Colleges. She received her Ph.D. from the University of Oregon in 1982, where she taught for two years before moving to Claremont. Her research has been on both environmental stressors and organizational turnover. She is currently interested in topics at the interface of environmental psychology and organizational behavior such as perceived control in the workplace and workplace design.

Carol M. Werner received her Ph.D. from Ohio State University in 1973. After a postdoctoral year at the University of North Carolina Chapel Hill, she moved to the University of Utah, where she is currently an Associate Professor of Psychology and head of the social psychology training program. Her research has spanned several areas of applied social psychology (e.g., environmental and forensic psychology), and also examined graduate training issues. She has recently written on temporal qualities of interpersonal relationships, and has edited *Home Environments: Human Behavior and the Environment* (Vol. 8) with Irwin Altman.

Alvin Zander is Professor Emeritus of Psychology and Education at the University of Michigan, where he also held executive positions in the Research Center for Group Dynamics for more than 30 years. He received his Ph.D. from the University of Iowa. His extensive work in group dynamics has resulted in numerous publications, including the classic *Group Dynamics: Research and Theory* with Dorwin Cartwright, *Motives and Goals in Groups, Groups at Work, Making Groups Effective,* and most recently *The Purposes of Groups and Organizations.*

NOTES

NOTES

ABM—7471